Darkness in the Bliss-Out

Darkness in the Bliss-Out

A Reconsideration of the Films of Steven Spielberg

JAMES KENDRICK

BLOOMSBURY
NEW YORK • LONDON • NEW DELHI • SYDNEY

Bloomsbury Academic
An imprint of Bloomsbury Publishing Inc

1385 Broadway	50 Bedford Square
New York	London
NY 10018	WC1B 3DP
USA	UK

www.bloomsbury.com

Bloomsbury is a registered trade mark of Bloomsbury Publishing Plc

First published 2014

© James Kendrick, 2014

All rights reserved. No part of this publication may be reproduced or transmitted in any form or by any means, electronic or mechanical, including photocopying, recording, or any information storage or retrieval system, without prior permission in writing from the publishers.

No responsibility for loss caused to any individual or organization acting on or refraining from action as a result of the material in this publication can be accepted by Bloomsbury or the author.

Library of Congress Cataloging-in-Publication Data
Kendrick, James, 1974-
Darkness in the bliss-out : a reconsideration of the films of Steven Spielberg / James Kendrick.
pages cm
Includes index.
ISBN 978-1-4411-8895-3 (hardback)– ISBN 978-1-4411-4604-5 (pbk.)
1. Spielberg, Steven, 1946—Criticism and interpretation. I. Title.
PN1998.3.S65K36 2014
791.4302'33092–dc23
2013049428

ISBN: HB: 978-1-4411-8895-3
PB: 978-1-4411-4604-5
ePub: 978-1-4411-1250-7
ePDF: 978-1-4411-9307-0

Typeset by Fakenham Prepress Solutions, Fakenham, Norfolk NR21 8NN

for James V

Contents

Preface viii
Acknowledgments xvii

Introduction: Steven Spielberg and the Politics of Bliss 1

1 "I Didn't Want to See This": Weekend America and Its Discontents in *Close Encounters of the Third Kind*, *E.T.* and *Poltergeist* 23
2 "Americans Fighting Americans": Incoherence and Animal Comedy in *1941* 69
3 "What Exactly Are We Applauding?" Indiana Jones and the Ideologies of Heroism and American Exceptionalism 101
4 "Lost and Done For": The Rejection of War Fantasies in *Empire of the Sun* and *War Horse* 139
5 "For the World's More Full of Weeping Than You Can Understand": Humanity and Inhumanity in *A.I. Artificial Intelligence* 171

Works Cited 211
Index 219

Preface

About 15 years ago, a friend of mine made an interesting observation regarding the career of Steven Spielberg. He felt that the experience of making *Schindler's List* (1993), the director's harrowing depiction of a German war profiteer's change of conscience and decision to save as many European Jews as possible from the Holocaust by employing them in his munitions factory, had so scarred Spielberg emotionally that all of his subsequent films bore residual traces of the trauma. He pointed out that, since *Schindler's List*, Spielberg's films—this was 1999 or 2000—were all noticeably darker than his previous works; that is, they seemed more willing to move past comfortable surfaces, acknowledge the inherent complexities of any human endeavor, and engage with the more disturbing and unsettling aspects of life. Spielberg dived right back into the well of historical violence with *Amistad* (1997), which depicted the grotesque inhumanities of the slave trade in telling the real-life story of a mutiny by illegally kidnapped Africans. *The Lost World: Jurassic Park* (1997), the much-anticipated sequel to the blockbuster hit *Jurassic Park* (1993), bore a demonstrably darker and more violent tone than its predecessor. And *Saving Private Ryan* (1998), his World War II combat film, featured what was at the time—and arguably still is—the goriest and most visceral depiction of war carnage ever to be included in a mainstream studio production.

In one sense, my friend's argument felt right. After all, *Schindler's List* was a watershed moment not just in Spielberg's career, but in Hollywood cinema, as it was the first time any filmmaker—much less a popular filmmaker with the kind of massive box office appeal that Spielberg commanded—had dared within the strictures of a studio film to depict with unflinching realism the relentless horrors and violence of Nazi Germany's attempted genocide of European Jews. It was also undeniable that Spielberg's following films bore a demonstrably dark, violent tone, which would seem to suggest that the ghosts of historical genocide were still haunting him. I subsequently read similar arguments in various interviews and accounts of Spielberg's career. For example, in *Citizen Spielberg*, film scholar Lester D. Friedman notes, "Making *Schindler's List* profoundly altered Spielberg as a man and a visual artist."[1]

---

[1] Lester D. Friedman, *Citizen Spielberg* (Champaign: University of Illinois Press, 2006), 43.

PREFACE

Spielberg admitted in an interview with Steven Schiff, "I just was so challenged by *Schindler's List* and so fulfilled by it and so disturbed by it. It so shook up my life, in a good way ..."[2] It became embedded enough in my own thinking that I actually reproduced this exact argument in my initial critical assessment of Spielberg's *War of the Worlds* (2005):

> As a rebuke to his previous alien movies, 1977's *Close Encounters of the Third Kind* and 1982's *E.T.*, *War of the Worlds* is at times shocking, yet it fits well with Spielberg's increasingly dark cinematic worldview, which has been slowly saturating his output ever since he made *Schindler's List* in 1993. In a way, it's like he's never been able to shake the Holocaust, and despite his constant attempts to tack on upbeat endings, his films from the past 10 years have been increasingly preoccupied with loss, trauma, and suffering in ways that even the sunniest of endings can't recuperate.[3]

Yet, the more I thought about it, the more I became convinced that the use of *Schindler's List* as a dividing point in Spielberg's career wasn't quite right. Of course, there is no doubt that Spielberg was changed by his experience making that film and that it had impacted his subsequent filmmaking endeavors—not just the style and approach, but the very projects he chose. Looking over his post-*Schindler* projects, one can detect a strong pull toward obviously darker and more troubling subject matter: both world wars (*Saving Private Ryan*, *War Horse* [2011]); historical dramas set against the backdrop of American slavery (*Amistad*, *Lincoln* [2012]) and terrorism (*Munich* [2005]); and dystopian science fiction (*A.I. Artificial Intelligence* [2001], *Minority Report* [2002], *War of the Worlds* [2005]). He made back-to-back comedies in *Catch Me If You Can* (2002) and *The Terminal* (2004), although they were both structured around severely alienated characters. During this time he also directed two action/adventure films in addition to *The Lost World*—the much belated *Indiana Jones and the Kingdom of the Crystal Skull* (2008) and *The Adventures of Tintin* (2011), a motion-capture computer-animated film based on the Hergé comic book character—which were the only films of this era that were largely free of darker overtones.

However, I couldn't escape the feeling that Spielberg's films hadn't suddenly gotten darker after *Schindler's List*. Rather, the darker elements had always been there, and now they were simply moving closer to the surface.

---

[2] Steven Schiff, "Seriously Spielberg," in *Steven Spielberg: Interviews*, Lester D. Friedman and Brent Notbohm (eds) (Jackson: University of Mississippi Press, 2000), 176.
[3] James Kendrick, Review of *War of the Worlds* (2005), The QNetwork, http://www.qnetwork.com/index.php?page=review&id=1485, accessed April 30, 2013.

They were also more readily recognized now that critics and audiences fully realized that Spielberg was capable of producing some of the most unsettling and powerful imagery ever to be committed to celluloid in a studio picture. As I reflected back on the relentless terrors of *Duel* (1971) and *Jaws* (1975); the broken families of *The Sugarland Express* (1974), *Close Encounters of the Third Kind* (1977), *E.T. The Extra-Terrestrial* (1982), and *The Color Purple* (1985); the conflicted sense of heroism in the Indiana Jones films; the mockery of the military and patriotism in *1941* (1979); and the implacable horrors, both fantastical and real, descended on children in *Poltergeist* (1982)[4] and *Empire of the Sun* (1987), I realized that the darker tendencies that informed *Schindler's List* and Spielberg's subsequent films were not new, but had rather been embedded in virtually all of his films throughout his long career. Darkness wasn't absent from his earlier works; it was there, but had simply been downplayed or ignored in light of the pervasive arguments in both the popular press and in academic film studies that Spielberg's films were supposedly upbeat, paternalistic, and reassuring.

The more I thought about Spielberg's films, particularly the earlier ones with which I had grown up as a child (I was born in 1974, the year *The Sugarland Express*, Spielberg's first studio-produced feature film, was released), the more I started to see them as deeply conflicted, their surface pleasures often cracking open to reveal fissures of darkness, despair, loneliness, and regret that their conclusions, no matter how upbeat on the surface, couldn't fully resolve. I found it ironic that a filmmaker whose best work involves, in *New York Times* critic A. O. Scott's words, "the figure of a lonely boy facing the incomprehension and cruelty of the adult world"[5] could also be dismissed by film scholar Robert Kolker as "the grand modern narrator of simple desires fulfilled, of reality diverted into the imaginary spaces of aspirations realized, where fears of abandonment and impotence are turned into fantasy spectacles of security and joyful action, where even the ultimate threat of annihilation is diverted by a saving male figure."[6]

Academically, I could see the attraction and utility of the argument about Spielberg's supposed conservatism and timidity in the face of literal and

---

[4] While Spielberg is not credited as the director of *Poltergeist*, he was a co-producer, first credited screenwriter, and originator of the story. He was also on-set virtually every day of the production, and his involvement was such that many of those who worked on the film came to think of him as the primary creative intelligence. Despite much debate and analysis, the conflicted authorial status of *Poltergeist* is still largely unsettled, although I argue that, because Spielberg was a powerful creative force in the film's conception, production, and postproduction, it can and should be considered alongside other films on which he is the credited director. For more on this issue, see Chapter 1.

[5] A. O. Scott, "Film Review: Do Androids Long for Mom?," *New York Times*, June 29, 2001.

[6] Robert A. Kolker, *A Cinema of Loneliness*, 4th edn (New York: Oxford University Press, 2011), 305.

PREFACE   xi

existential horrors as a means of explaining his widespread appeal and dismissing him as a major artist, but experientially it didn't add up. I had felt devastated after watching *Schindler's List* for the first time, and given the dead silence in the theater in which I saw it as the credits rolled, I was not alone. Despite Stanley Kubrick's assertion that *Schindler's List* was not, in fact, a film about the Holocaust—"The Holocaust is about six million people who get killed. *Schindler's List* is about six hundred people who don't," he told his *Eyes Wide Shut* (1999) collaborator Frederic Rafael[7]—it felt as close as I could imagine a mainstream narrative feature getting to conveying the magnitude of human evil. I clearly remember the vivid, visceral shock I felt during the opening half hour of *Saving Private Ryan*, particularly the shot inside the Higgins Boat when the door drops open and every soldier inside is immediately and brutally cut down—*eviscerated*—by machine-gun fire. The camera's placement, right in the middle of the carnage, the lens splattered with blood and viscera as the bodies drop, and the sickening mixture of gunfire and bullets thudding into flesh and bone gave me a sense of gut-churning physical proximity I had never felt in a war film, and the soldiers' immediate deaths, literally slaughtered before even raising their rifles, undercut any sense of easy heroism or platitudes about the glories of war. And, while both of those films feature endings that attempt in some sense to assert the perseverance of humanity, they are not nearly enough to recuperate the films' horrible images of humankind turned against itself. I didn't feel reassured or safe, and I certainly didn't feel that the threat of annihilation had been diverted. Rather, that sense of annihilation hung with me, haunting my memories of those films. The same is true of many of Spielberg's pre-*Schindler's List* films, although the darkness is more opaque, scattered, and buried—but not absent.

The goal of this book is to explore the darker recesses and the deeper, sometimes contradictory, layers of some of Spielberg's most well-known films, especially those released before *Schindler's List*. Thus, it is not intended to be a categorical exploration of the entirety of his cinematic output, although one could conceivably approach his career by mining each of his films for their darker themes and internal conflicts, from his made-for-TV haunted house thriller *Something Evil* (1972), to his most recent historical drama *Lincoln*. Rather, I have specifically limited myself to a selection of Spielberg's films, with no particular guiding principle except for the inherent intrigue posited by the films themselves. Thus, the book explores many of Spielberg's most well-known and popular films (*Close Encounters of the Third Kind*, *Raiders*

---

[7] Frederic Rafael, *Eyes Wide Open: A Memoir of Stanley Kubrick* (New York: Ballantine Books, 1999), 107.

of the Lost Ark [1981], *E.T.*), as well as his lesser received works (*Empire of the Sun*, *A.I. Artificial Intelligence*), and even his one outright box-office bomb (*1941*). The goal is to provide a sense of the breadth of Spielberg's films and the manner in which darker themes are woven throughout virtually all of them. The specifically targeted nature of the book's scope means that a host of films that are worthy of entire chapters of analysis—*Jaws*, *Hook* (1991), *Amistad*, *Minority Report*, *Munich*, to name just a few—receive only brief mention. However, any book about an artist as prolific and enduring as Spielberg will, if not designed to cover the entirety of his career, necessarily leave many crucial films for another day.

* * *

Another motivating factor in writing this book was my recognition that Spielberg has been, until recent years, largely ignored by the scholarly community. For a filmmaker of his international stature who has been steadily producing and directing films for four decades and has been widely regarded as a deep influence on modern cinema, there has been surprisingly little serious academic writing about and analysis of his films. There have been scores of glossy, hagiographic popular press books about his career and unauthorized biographies of varying merit, but little of any real substance has been written until recently. Joseph McBride's *Steven Spielberg: A Biography* (originally published in 1997 and updated in a second edition in 2010) was one of the first books to take Spielberg seriously as a major film artist, although close to a decade passed before others joined him.

Since the mid–2000s there has been a steady stream of notable books about Spielberg's films. These include Lester D. Friedman's *Citizen Spielberg* (2006), a comprehensive scholarly study that approaches his body of work from the perspective of genre study and auteur criticism; Warren Buckland's *Directed by Steven Spielberg: Poetics of the Contemporary Hollywood Blockbuster* (2006), which takes the unique approach of studying Spielberg's cinematic practices in detail, "focus[ing] on those slight differences in filmmaking, small details constituting the elusive quality that elevate Spielberg's blockbusters over other blockbusters";[8] Nigel Morris's *The Cinema of Steven Spielberg: Empire of Light* (2007), another comprehensive critical analysis of his entire body of work, whose starting point is the "phenomenal popularity" of Spielberg's films and "what this reveals about commercial cinema and audiences who derive pleasure from it";[9] Dean A. Kowalski's *Steven Spielberg*

---

[8] Buckland, *Directed by Steven Spielberg*, 1.
[9] Morris, *The Cinema of Steven Spielberg*, 3.

and Philosophy: We're Gonna Need a Bigger Book (2008), a collection of new essays in which "thirty years of Spielberg's directorial efforts [are] explored and assessed through the lens of philosophy";[10] Andrew M. Gordon's *Empire of Dreams: The Science Fiction and Fantasy Films of Steven Spielberg* (2008), which offers focused critical evaluation of Spielberg's fantasy, science fiction, and horror films; and Frederick Wasser's *Steven Spielberg's America* (2010), which places Spielberg's cinema within a broad socio-political context, with the goal of analyzing each of his films in order to "elucidate the situation of the audience, the film world, and [the] historical moment."[11] Around the same time these books were being published, the University of Lincoln in the U.K. organized a two-day international conference titled "Spielberg at Sixty," which "brought forth a remarkably wide range of presentations by international scholars, including several authors of books on the filmmaker as well as many younger academics."[12]

There have also been dozens of scholarly articles published over the years about his films, although such articles have rarely if ever appeared in the most prestigious of academic film journals. When Charles L. P. Silet went about collecting "the more significant" of the "serious writing about Spielberg's work from critics and scholars"[13] for his anthology *The Films of Steven Spielberg: Critical Essays* (2002), most of the chapters were reprinted from either nonacademic magazines like the *New York Review of Books* and *Commentary* or non-film-specific academic journals like the *Quarterly Journal of Speech*, *Studies in the Humanities*, and *Arizona Quarterly*. While some of the chapters were reprinted from respected film journals like the *Journal of Popular Film and Television* and *Literature/Film Quarterly*, there are no reprints from the two most revered of film journals: *Film Quarterly* and *Cinema Journal*, the former of which is one of the oldest serious film publications and the latter of which is the official journal of the Society of Cinema and Media Studies (SCMS). This is because very few critical essays that focus exclusively

---

[10] Dean A. Kowalski, "Introduction," in *Steven Spielberg and Philosophy: We're Gonna Need a Bigger Book,* ed. Dean A. Kowalski (Lexington: University Press of Kentucky, 2008), 1.
[11] Wasser, *Steven Spielberg's America,* 16.
[12] Joseph McBride, "A Reputation: Steven Spielberg and the Eyes of the World," *New Review of Film and Television Studies* 7, no. 1 (March 2009): 1. The conference, which was organized by Warren Buckland, Lester D. Friedman, and Nigel Morris, took place on November 20–21, 2007, and featured nearly 30 scholars presenting papers on different facets of Spielberg's films. The fact that the conference took place in the U.K. and featured nearly all British and European scholars (only five of the listed presenters were from the U.S.) suggests that Spielberg, like Alfred Hitchcock before him, has broken through as an object of serious critical study more effectively in Europe than in his home country. See http://www.lincoln.ac.uk/media/spielbergatsixty
[13] Charles L. P. Silet, ed., *The Films of Steven Spielberg: Critical Essays* (Lanham, MD: Scarecrow Press, 2002), xiv.

or even primarily on Spielberg's films have appeared in these publications over the past four decades. Aside from Marsha Kinder's 1974 article "The Return of the Outlaw Couple," which reviewed *The Sugarland Express* alongside Terrence Malick's *Badlands* (1973) and Robert Altman's *Thieves Like Us* (1974), *Film Quarterly* did not publish a single article or essay about Spielberg until Karen Jaehne's review of *Saving Private Ryan* in the Autumn 1999 issue and Tim Kreider's insightful essay on *A.I. Artificial Intelligence* in the Winter 2002 issue. Since then, only two other essays on Spielberg have been published: "Slants of Light," Caetlin Benson-Allott's comparison of the use of light in Spielberg's early films and J. J. Abrams' *Super 8* (2011), published in the Fall 2011 issue, and Jonathan Rosenbaum's "A Matter of Life and Death," a critical re-evaluation of *A.I.*, published in the Spring 2012 issue. Similarly, *Cinema Journal* has only published three articles to date about Spielberg, the first appearing in the Summer 1992 issue and the most recent appearing in 1998.[14]

Thus, it is clear that the academic establishment of film and media studies has downplayed Spielberg as an object of critical study, whether it be through lack of scholars writing about his work or resistance from the editors and review boards of the major journals to publish it. Lester D. Friedman and Brent Notbohm suggest that the "dearth of intellectual work" on Spielberg at the time they published a collection of interviews with the director in 2002 was likely the result of academics "usually prefer[ring] to wield their analytical and rhetorical skills in the service of undervalued creative artists struggling to fund their productions" or, more likely, academics "contemptuously dismiss[ing] Spielberg as little more than a modern P. T. Barnum, a technically gifted and intellectually shallow showman who substitutes spectacle for substance."[15] Either way, there has been a relative dearth of serious academic work on Spielberg, especially from a position that does not take as its starting point the filmmaker's immense popularity or his association with blockbuster cinema. Unfortunately, this critical vacuum, which has only begun to be filled,[16] has intensified the overall perception that Spielberg is a filmmaker of little substance or historical value except as a particularly powerful and instructive marker of popular taste and the insidious appeal of the Hollywood dream factory. This book aims to join the emerging critical voices in taking

---

[14] See Ilsa J. Black, "The Look Back in *E.T.*," *Cinema Journal* 31, no. 4 (1992); Susan Aronstein, "'Not Exactly a Knight': Arthurian Narrative and Recuperative Politics in the Indiana Jones Trilogy," *Cinema Journal* 34, no. 4 (1995); Robert Baird, "Animalizing *Jurassic Park*'s Dinosaurs: Blockbuster Schemata and Cross-Cultural Cognition in the Threat Scene," *Cinema Journal* 37, no. 4 (1998).
[15] Friedman and Notbohm, *Steven Spielberg: Interviews*, viii.
[16] See McBride, "A Reputation."

Spielberg seriously as a major film artist and firmly placing him within the purview of academic film studies.

* * *

In an interview with film critic Gene Siskel, Spielberg said that his "master image"—the one frame from any one of his films that would summarize him as an artist—is the image on the cover of this book four-year-old Barry (Cary Guffey) in *Close Encounters of the Third Kind* opening his front door and facing a blinding, fiery red and yellow light, the source of which is, at that point in the film's narrative, unknown.[17] Yet, as I worked on this project, I kept thinking of another image from that same film, albeit one that the viewer never actually sees because it took place behind the camera.

At one point in *Close Encounters*, Barry, who lives in rural Indiana with his mother, is awakened in the middle of the night by sounds of the film's extra-terrestrials investigating his house. He creeps downstairs, and when he turns the corner into the kitchen he sees the aliens, but all we see is the look on his face, which at first registers fear, then puzzlement, then absolute joy. Spielberg elicited Guffey's astonishing performance, which was captured in a single take, in a unique way:

> I had to the left of the camera a cardboard partition, and to the right of the camera a second cardboard partition. To the left of the camera, I put Bob Westmoreland, our makeup man, in a gorilla suit—the full mask and hands and hairy body. To the right of the camera, I dressed myself up as an Easter Bunny, with the ears and the nose and the whiskers painted on my face. Cary Guffey didn't know what to expect. He didn't know what he was gonna react to. His job was to come into the kitchen, stop at the door, and just have a good time … And just as he came into the kitchen, I had the cardboard partition dropped and Bob Westmoreland was there as the gorilla. Cary froze. Like a deer caught in car headlights … I dropped my partition, and he looked over at me, and there was the Easter Bunny smiling at him. He was torn. He began to smile at me—he was still afraid of that thing. Then I had Bob—I said, "Take off your head." Bob took off his mask, and when Cary saw it was the man that put his makeup on in the morning, Cary began to laugh. Even though it was a trick, the reaction was pure and honest.[18]

---

[17] Roger Ebert and Gene Siskel, *The Future of the Movies: Interviews With Martin Scorsese, Steven Spielberg, and George Lucas* (Kansas City, MO: Andrews and McMeel, 1991), 72.
[18] "Making *Close Encounters*," *Close Encounters of the Third Kind*, directed by Steven Spielberg (1977; Santa Monica, CA: The Voyager Company, 1990), laserdisc.

It is an incredible shot in which a child actor takes us through the entire gamut of emotional responses, which makes it an apt metonym for the experience of Spielberg's varied films, filled as they are with terror, intrigue, and elation—not necessarily in that order or in equal measures. My argument, which is woven throughout the rest of this book, is that Spielberg's films are much more complex than they are typically given credit for, and that much of this complexity emerges from a conflict between the filmmaker's aspirations toward goodness, humanity, and resolution and his unwillingness to let go of the darker elements of the human experience, which are often embodied in his films by intrusions of the horrific, violent and cruel characters, and endings that, while superficially hopeful, are not enough to overcome the anxiety, violence, and despair that has preceded them. Film critic Henry Sheehan said it best when he noted that "Although Spielberg's films are usually described as warm or even exhilarating and euphoric, their most prevalent temper is anxiety."[19] We can see that anxiety in the fear of being alone that often pervades Spielberg's films about children, and we can also see it in the violence of his historical films, the broken families that are frequently the center of his stories, and the fear of the unknown that is sometimes shown to be misguided (as in *Close Encounters*) and at other times is shown to be absolutely deserved (as in *Poltergeist*). All of those anxieties, fears, and trepidations, expressed in myriad ways throughout Spielberg's work, forms what I call "the darkness in the bliss-out."

---

[19] Henry Sheehan, "The Peter Panning of Steven Spielberg: Part 1," *Film Comment* (May–June, 1992).

Acknowledgments

Given that I have been working on this book in some form or fashion for almost four years, numerous people have left their mark on my thinking and writing in various ways. First, I am grateful for the thoughtful criticism and guidance offered by other scholars in the field on whose shoulders I stand. Nigel Morris was exceedingly collegial and generous with his time in helping me shape the initial proposal and Introduction, while Linda Ruth Williams provided invaluable suggestions on later drafts of the chapters and Joseph McBride helped ensure the accuracy of many of the critical and historical details. My good friend Jon Kraszewski not only offered a sympathetic ear at all times, but willingly read virtually all of my initial drafts. Steffen Hantke, Peter Rollins, and Martin Medhurst were on hand to offer advice during the early publication process, and I received useful feedback from Baylor students and faculty in the English Department when I presented an early version of the book's main ideas as part of their 20th Century Studies Research Seminar.

Those same ideas formed the core of a paper I presented at the joint conference of the Popular Culture Association and the American Culture Association in the spring of 2011, which turned out to be a fateful event because it drew the attention of Bloomsbury editor Katie Gallof, who sought me out based on my presentation's title and encouraged me to develop it into a book proposal. I would like to thank Katie, assistant editor Laura Murray, editorial assistant Kaitlin Fontana, and the entire editorial staff at Bloomsbury for their care and attention in seeing this project through to fruition. It has been a challenging and rewarding journey.

I benefited enormously from a semester-long research leave I was granted in the spring of 2012 by the College of Arts and Sciences at Baylor University. I continue to be blessed to work with fantastic faculty and staff in the Department of Communication, who are consistently supportive of my work in all the best ways. I would like to extend special thanks to my department chair, David Schlueter, and Chris Hansen, director of the Film and Digital Media division, for all their support and constant willingness to make sure I have all the resources I need.

My family continues to be a source of encouragement, and I have to offer a special note of thanks to my mother, whose reluctance to allow me to see

Indiana Jones and the Temple of Doom when I was nine years old may very well have planted the seed that sprouted three decades later into this book-length analysis of the darker elements of Spielberg's work.

Finally, I am, as always, forever grateful for my wife Cassie, whose love and encouragement and understanding keeps me both inspired and grounded.

James Kendrick
February 2014

Introduction
Steven Spielberg and the Politics of Bliss

Sometimes in order to see the light you have to risk the dark.
DR. IRIS HINEMAN (LOIS SMITH), *MINORITY REPORT* (2002)

In the first paragraph of her June 14, 1982, review of Steven Spielberg's *E.T. The Extra-terrestrial*, film critic Pauline Kael let loose one of her signature waves of rapturous admiration, calling the film a "dream of a movie" and a "bliss-out."[1] It was likely not the first time the word "bliss" had been used in relation to a Spielberg film, but it turned out to be one of the most significant because, although Kael clearly intended it as the highest form of compliment, it would come to haunt the academic and critical reception of Spielberg's films.

Kael's idea of *E.T.* being a "bliss-out" is intricately connected to her appreciation of Spielberg's mastery of conveying innocence, myth, and emotional resonance, qualities that Kael frequently praised in her reviews. A long-time critic at *The New Yorker* who was probably the most influential American film writer of the 1970s, Kael was never reticent about voicing her disdain for what she saw as the dull artistic pretension and empty ambiguity of fashionable European art films; instead, she celebrated the more primal, emotional pleasures of *movies*, as she insisted on calling them. For Kael, movies were about experience: "At the movies we want a different kind of truth," she wrote in her famous 1969 essay "Trash, Art, and the Movies," "something that surprises us and registers with us as funny or accurate or maybe amazing, maybe even amazingly beautiful."[2]

---

[1] Pauline Kael, "The Current Cinema: The Pure and the Impure," *The New Yorker*, June 14, 1982, 119.
[2] Pauline Kael, "Trash, Art, and the Movies," *Harper's*, February 1969, 102.

It is no surprise, then, that Kael would so generously and seriously use the word "bliss"—which typically conveys joy, delight, and pleasure—to describe *E.T.*, which is funny and accurate and at times amazingly beautiful. However, "bliss" is an intriguingly complex term that carries with it seemingly contradictory positive and negative connotations, making it a more apt description of Spielberg's work than Kael probably realized. The positive is obvious: Spielberg's films, particularly those he made in the 1970s and 1980s, brought and continue to bring great joy and pleasure to audiences in the tradition of the classical Hollywood filmmakers that Spielberg admired and with whom he frequently associated himself in interviews: Frank Capra, Howard Hawks, John Ford, Michael Curtiz, Cecil B. DeMille, and Walt Disney.[3] In fact, for some viewers (Kael included), his films evoke the spiritual dimension of bliss, defined in the *Oxford English Dictionary* as "mental, ethereal, spiritual: perfect joy or felicity, supreme delight; blessedness." At the same time, though, "bliss" is etymologically connected with the word "blithe," which can be defined as "Exhibiting kindly feeling to others; kind, friendly, clement, gentle," but also as "heedless" and "careless."

Whether used positively to suggest pure pleasure or negatively to suggest something oblivious and unmindful, the application of the term "bliss" to Spielberg's films carries with it the implication that they are in some way "safe"—that they are pleasure machines, asking little of the audience but sit in a darkened theater and be moved by easy emotions and strong resolutions that gently chide, yet ultimately reaffirm the comfortable conformity of American middle-class culture. For many critics, Spielberg's films are precisely the kind of bland, mainstream fantasy that the ideological critics of the 1960s—who were influenced primarily by the political and economic writings of Karl Marx, the psychoanalytic theories of Sigmund Freud, and various offshoots of linguistics—sought to unmask as dangerous and mind-numbing in the way they contributed to an apathetic culture of minimal political engagement. The irony is that the rhetoric of Spielberg's strongest admirers, especially mainstream film critics, has often inadvertently supported this claim by focusing on the conventionally "positive" aspects of his work: warmth, familiarity, mythic aspirations, and faith in the possibility of redemption.

It is these qualities that British critic and film scholar Andrew Britton found most objectionable in Spielberg's work, which is precisely why he appropriated (one might say "hijacked") Kael's use of the term "bliss" four years later in the title of his essay "Blissing Out: The Politics of Reaganite

---

[3] See Michael Sragow, "A Conversation With Steven Spielberg," in *Steven Spielberg: Interviews*, Lester D. Friedman and Brent Notbohm (eds) (Jackson: University Press of Mississippi, 2000).

Entertainment." This dense, scathing 42-page indictment of Hollywood in the 1980s offers a wide-ranging formal and ideological criticism of "Reaganite entertainment," which Britton saw as a "general movement of reaction and conservative reassurance" that essentially "rule[d] out the possibility of more interesting, contradictory, and disturbing work."[4] This form of cinema is a self-enclosed, self-referential system that offers only "the ideology of entertainment": "The notion of entertainment corresponds to film's commodity form: to present something as entertainment is to define it as a commodity to be consumed rather than as a text to be read."[5] Thus, "Reaganite entertainment refers to itself in order to persuade us that it doesn't refer outwards at all. It is, purely and simply, 'entertainment'—and we all know what *that* is."[6]

Ironically, Pauline Kael's rhapsodic praise of *E.T.*—which she had also lavished on Spielberg's earlier film, *Close Encounters of the Third Kind* (1977), and, to a lesser extent, *1941* (1979), but withheld from *Raiders of the Lost Ark* (1981)—is essentially the flip side of Britton's indictment of the film. One praises the film, one damns it, but they both see it from the same narrow perspective. Both Kael and Britton focus so intently on *E.T.*'s emotional dynamism—which for Kael is the essence of its effectiveness and purity and for Britton is the chief indicator of its falsity and ideological emptiness—that they are blinded to one of the most compelling and central qualities of not just *E.T.*, but the majority of Spielberg's most well-regarded and popular films: the darkness.

In praising the warmer, mythic qualities of *E.T.*, Kael unwittingly fed into the strongest and most persistent criticism of Spielberg's work, which continues with surprising resilience today despite his stronger overall critical standing in the wake of more "mature" films like *Empire of the Sun* (1987), *Schindler's List* (1993), *Amistad* (1997), *Saving Private Ryan* (1998), *Munich* (2005), and *Lincoln* (2012) and his slowly widening acceptance within the field of academic film studies.[7] Specifically, Kael's euphoria over *E.T.*'s innocence and warmth blinded her to the fact that there is darkness in the bliss-out—darkness, in this respect, being those elements of the film that reflect Spielberg's recognition of the uncomfortable and unsettling aspects of life. The presence of darkness in *E.T.* and other Spielberg films attests to his willingness to look past comfortable surfaces, acknowledge the inherent complexities of any human endeavor, and make those a central element of his work. Spielberg's films are not in any sense shackled to what Ilsa J. Black, paraphrasing Kael,

---

[4] Andrew Britton, "Blissing Out: The Politics of Reaganite Entertainment," *Movie* (Winter 1986): 2.
[5] Ibid., 4.
[6] Ibid., 4.
[7] See Joseph McBride, "A Reputation: Steven Spielberg and the Eyes of the World," *New Review of Film and Television Studies* 7, no. 1 (2009).

called "the politics of bliss": "the sunny, peculiarly Reagan-era attitude of happiness bought with ignorance, magical wish-fulfillment, and historical mutability."[8] Such a characterization of Spielberg's work is all too typical and tends to reflect the critic's desire to utilize Spielberg as an all-encompassing signifier of the shortcomings of Reagan-era neoconservatism rather than the films themselves, which close analysis reveals to be multi-layered and fascinating in their cinematic, intertextual, and ideological complexities. Unearthing and exploring these deeper, sometimes contradictory, layers is the goal of this book.

The darker side of Spielberg's films has certainly been acknowledged by scholars and critics, although it has never been the primary focus of a critical inquiry into his work. For example, in *The Cinema of Steven Spielberg: Empire of Light*, Nigel Morris often draws attention to the darker elements of Spielberg's films, including the "uniformly misanthropic" nature of *The Sugarland Express*,[9] the ominous and sinister introduction of Indiana Jones in *Raiders of the Lost Ark*,[10] and the "dark, obsessively driven, rather than glorious professional soldiering" in *Saving Private Ryan*.[11] Morris suggests that the true interest in *Schindler's List* is the question of "whether [Schindler's] actions teach anything, whether hope is recoverable from the edge of darkness,"[12] and in his discussion of *Munich*, he goes so far as to assert that Spielberg's oeuvre is "so misanthropic that humans are irredeemably flawed."[13] Ryan Gilbey makes a similar assertion about Spielberg's complex view of human nature when he writes that "the most convincing threat [in Spielberg's early films], the force toward which we should feel greatest ambivalence, is human."[14] Frederick Wasser has aptly noted "Spielberg's willingness to represent the dystopia of contemporary American life,"[15] particularly the "barren" nature of the sunbelt neighborhood in *E.T.* and the film's depiction of suburban malaise and government forces as "space invaders," although he asserts that Spielberg ultimately pulls his punches in order to secure a large, mainstream audience—part of his "blockbuster formula of hinting at failure in American life and yet not asking his audience

---

[8] Ilsa J. Black, "The Look Back in *E.T.*," *Cinema Journal* 31, no. 4 (1992): 25.
[9] Nigel Morris, *The Cinema of Steven Spielberg: Empire of Light* (London: Wallflower Press, 2007), 42.
[10] Ibid., 78–9.
[11] Ibid., 284.
[12] Ibid., 220.
[13] Ibid., 372.
[14] Ryan Gilbey, *It Don't Worry Me: Nashville, Jaws, Star Wars, and Beyond* (London: Faber and Faber, 2003), 67.
[15] Frederick Wasser, *Steven Spielberg's America* (London: Polity Press, 2010), 105.

to really look at this failure."[16] Film critics have also picked up on the darker elements of Spielberg's films over the years. For example, in writing about *Jaws* in *The Village Voice* during the film's theatrical release in 1975, Molly Haskell noted the "delight" Spielberg took "in showing us humanity—a kind of lynch mob perennially in the making—at its worst."

Thus, there is no question that Spielberg, despite being regularly cast as a mainstream audience pleaser and chief representative of sunny, ignorant Reaganite entertainment, has a resolutely dark streak throughout his career that creates a fascinating tension with his more optimistic and humanist tendencies. In fact, many of his films play like a reversal of Dwight Macdonald's scathing description of why the producers of *The Sound of Music* (1965) felt the need to include Nazi villains: "the manufacturers were shrewd enough to realize that the milk of human kindness needs to be cut with a little acid."[17] More than a few of Spielberg's films, on the other hand, are like acid cut with a little milk, thereby softening their edges with a palpable and immediately embraceable humanism that is often mistaken for the whole.

Therefore, we need to ask a new set of questions about Spielberg's work, and the darker elements of his films provide a rich starting point. When drawn together and used as a lens through which to view Spielberg's films, how does the persistence of these various darker elements inform his body of work in terms of consistent themes and stylistic devices? How does this perspective reshape our thinking about Spielberg's place in the larger sphere of film history? And what should we make of the dialectic between his films and the various forms of popular and critical taste that have shaped Hollywood cinema over the past four decades?

The uneasy balance between light and dark

One way to think about these issues is to put Spielberg in dialogue with other filmmakers with whom he shares certain characteristics. This is hardly a new project, as Spielberg has been compared to numerous filmmakers over the years, often at his own insistence. His mobility amongst different genres has drawn comparisons to Howard Hawks;[18] the fact that he took Hollywood by

---

[16] Ibid., 109.
[17] Dwight Macdonald, *On Movies* (Englewood Cliffs, NJ: Da Capo, 1969), 41.
[18] Pauline Kael recognized his similarity to Hawks long before he was able to demonstrate his dexterity amongst different genres. In her review of *The Sugarland Express*, she wrote that Spielberg "could be that rarity among directors—a born entertainer—perhaps a new generation's Howard Hawks."

storm at so young an age is reminiscent of the early career of Orson Welles; his dexterity with suspense and thrills has been likened to Alfred Hitchcock; and the emotional effectiveness and general popularity of his films, as well as the recurring figure of the flawed but admirable "everyman," has been compared to the films of Frank Capra.

However, the cinematic figure with whom he is most often compared is Walt Disney, particularly the manner in which many of his films either evoke childhood or convey a childlike sense of wonderment.[19] Disney's films were among the first Spielberg saw as a child, which is telling because, like many of Spielberg's films, they are often unsettling in their mixture of childish whimsy and macabre violence. Spielberg recalled that he came "screaming home from *Snow White* when I was eight years old and tried to hide under the covers," something his parents "did not understand ... because Walt Disney movies are not supposed to scare but to delight and enthrall." Nevertheless, according to Spielberg, his viewing of Disney films like *Snow White*, *Fantasia* (1940), and *Bambi* (1942) helped turn him into "a basket case of neurosis."[20]

The similarities between Spielberg and Disney are particularly interesting because they extend to Spielberg (and, in some ways, amplify) the critical misunderstandings of Disney as a popular filmmaker. As Douglas Brode points out in *From Walt to Woodstock: How Disney Created the Counterculture*, the idea that Disney was a conservative, conventional filmmaker of minimal substance has been repeated so often, particularly within intellectual and academic circles, that "it is no longer considered a subjective opinion [and] has taken on the weight of irrefutable fact."[21] Brode argues with great conviction that Disney, far from being a "provider of pro-Establishment entertainment,"[22] was a socio-politically daring artist whose films are rich with radical ideals involving youth culture, environmentalism, and nonconformity.

---

[19] The frequent comparisons made between Spielberg and Disney in both academic film criticism and in mainstream press articles and film reviews are multitudinous, partially because Spielberg has often noted in interviews the influence and effect Disney had on him as a child. See Joseph McBride, *Steven Spielberg: A Biography*, 2nd edn (Jackson: University Press of Mississippi, 2010), 62–4. In the first sentence of his book *Empire of Dreams*, Andrew M. Gordon describes Spielberg as "director of several of the biggest hits in Hollywood history as well as a producer and entertainment tycoon akin to Walt Disney" (1). In his essay "Laugh, Cry, Believe: Spielbergization and Its Discontents," J. Hoberman suggests that "As a manipulator of the medium, Spielberg ranks with the greatest—king of cute Walt Disney and master of suspense Alfred Hitchcock. In a sense, Spielberg synthesizes Disney and Hitchcock" (121), although the general sentiment about the relation between the two filmmakers is ultimately summarized by the title of Suzanna Andrews's 1992 *New York Times* article: "The Man Who Would Be Walt."
[20] McBride, *Steven Spielberg: A Biography*, 63–4.
[21] Douglas Brode, *From Walt to Woodstock: How Disney Created the Counterculture* (Austin: University of Texas Press, 2004), xi.
[22] Ibid.

And, while his name is often used as shorthand to describe the emptying out and commercialization of art ("Disneyfication"), it is also worth remembering that Disney rubbed shoulders and collaborated with several of the twentieth century's most daring artistic visionaries, including Soviet director Sergei Eisenstein and surrealist painter Salvador Dalí, with whom he collaborated on an animated film called *Destino* in the mid–1940s.[23]

While Spielberg's work, with the exception of his short film *Amblin'* (1968), is not explicitly aligned with the countercultural ideals of the 1960s, the overall arc of almost willful misunderstanding of his films is essentially the same (which is probably why Brode notes in his Introduction that Spielberg is "our current incarnation of Disney").[24] Like Disney, Spielberg has been so frequently and so unproblematically labeled a simplistic, conventional, popular filmmaker that the idea of his works lacking the depth, complexity, and ambiguity associated with critically celebrated art films has passed from "assessment" into "fact." This view is neatly contained in John Simon's review of Spielberg's second theatrically released feature film, *The Sugarland Express* (1974): "Steven Spielberg's film ... has a certain cinematic knack, but is all effect and no real humanity, all manipulation and splash, and no attempt at honest insight."[25] Simon's begrudging respect for Spielberg's technical aptitude ("a certain cinematic knack") and complete dismissal of anything representing honesty or insight was to become a repeated refrain in critical responses to Spielberg's films, even in positive reviews.

Like the greatest works of the classical Hollywood cinema, Spielberg's films tend to operate on multiple, sometimes contradictory, discursive levels. At one far end of the discursive spectrum there is the potentially mindless, conventionally pleasurable level associated with mainstream Hollywood cinema: easily digestible and infinitely comfortable. This is the level that Kael was responding to when she wrote that "*E.T.* is bathed in warmth, and it seems to clear all the bad thoughts out of your head."[26] However, Spielberg's films also operate across a spectrum of multiple, deeper levels that are well worth unearthing for viewers who are able to see past received wisdom and recognize the complex viewing experiences that emanate from the inherent conflicts between light and dark, which his staunchest detractors tend to criticize and his most admiring audiences tend to overlook or ignore. This conflict between light and dark is key to getting beneath the surface and understanding Spielberg's films as difficult and challenging explorations of

---

[23] Due to financial problems at the studio, Disney abandoned *Destino* in 1946, although it was resurrected and completed in 2003, 58 years after it was begun.
[24] Brode, *From Walt to Woodstock*, xxix.
[25] John Simon, *Reverse Angle: A Decade of American Films* (New York: Clarkson N. Potter, 1982), 149.
[26] Kael, "The Pure and the Impure," 119.

human cruelty, insecurity, anxiety, loneliness, and violence. This is not to say that his films are uniformly, or even consistently, dark and despondent. Quite the opposite, in fact: his films are frequently optimistic in their insistence on the intertwined roles of redemption, forgiveness, and familial love as modes of triumph over the darker elements of human existence, which is what makes his films so profoundly humanistic.

However, contrary to what many critics would suggest, such triumph is rarely easy or even complete. The endings of his films, so often savaged for their Herculean efforts to set things right, are not so much artistic failings (although they are frequently the weakest formal element of some of his best films) as they are reflective of Spielberg's own turmoil over the nature of existence and how to represent the perpetually shifting equilibrium between good and evil. Oscar Schindler tearfully noting how many more Jews he might have saved if only he had sold his watch or his car in *Schindler's List* or James Ryan falling to his knees in a Normandy war cemetery and begging his wife to reassure him that he has led a good life in *Saving Private Ryan* are arguably weak scenes dramatically, but they are crucial in demonstrating how Spielberg's desire to leave audiences with a sense of hope and redemption runs headlong into his masterful, sometimes overwhelming, evocation of violence, resulting in films that seem to be pulling in multiple directions. He is, in a sense, *too* good at depicting bloodshed, torment, and chaos to wrap his films up at the end as neatly as he might like. As Spielberg biographer Joseph McBride puts it, the "central trait of Spielberg's artistic personality, which helps explain its richness and complexity, embodies his search for imagined alternatives to the perils he so deeply fears in ordinary existence."[27] In this respect, Spielberg's best films are precisely the kind of "interesting, contradictory, and disturbing work" that Andrew Britton argued was being run out of Hollywood in the 1980s primarily by Spielberg himself.

Understanding Spielberg's complexities and contradictions underscores the fundamental problem with the way in which his career has often been dichotomized in terms of his "commercial" films like *Jaws* (1975), *Raiders of the Lost Ark*, *E.T.*, and *Jurassic Park* (1993), which seek primarily to entertain and are presumably aimed at a younger, less mature audience seeking visceral thrills and temporary escape, and his "serious," usually historical films like *The Color Purple* (1985), *Schindler's List*, *Amistad*, *Saving Private Ryan*, *Munich*, and *Lincoln*, which are aimed at a mature, adult audience and have more obvious social, political, and historical implications. Spielberg himself has contributed to this view of his work. Commenting on the near simultaneous release of *Poltergeist* and *E.T.* in the summer of 1982, he said, "These films

---

[27] McBride, "A Reputation," 6.

are two different animals—one is my dark side and one is my bright side. It's nice that I can release two sides of my personality in 1982 so close to each other."[28] Taking a slightly different, though no less dichotomous, approach, J. Hoberman has suggested that "There is a sense in which Spielberg's oeuvre is divided against itself, characterized by the Good Steven's feel-good movies and the more hostile entertainments devised by his evil twin."[29] Bad Steven "lives to terrorize audiences in the name of fun," while Good Steven "is epitomized by ... movies that, in constructing the audience of kids of all ages, effectively out-Disneyed Disney."[30] Such divisions are largely superficial and function only as a convenient, but potentially misleading, shorthand for summarizing a lengthy and complex career filled with films that are both "feel-good" and "hostile." Spielberg's films consistently fuse entertainment and social relevance (which is why he is able to draw blockbuster-size crowds for movies about the Holocaust and World War II), and variations of the "Good Steven" and the "Bad Steven" personas are often simultaneously present within the same films, sometimes within the same scenes (how else to explain why a movie as "sweet" as *E.T.* has so many elements borrowed from horror movies?). Hoberman notes that aspects of the "Bad Steven" frequently appear in the "Good Steven" movies—for example, the visceral carnage of the opening D-Day sequence in *Saving Private Ryan*—but it goes further than that: each are sides of the same filmmaker that can never fully be separated, and their uneasy coexistence is what makes his films so effective as cinematic experience and so fascinating as objects of analysis.

In short, all of Spielberg's films feature surface joys and primal emotional power, but these are only two facets of an ideologically and aesthetically complex body of work that is defined best by an uneasy balance between light and dark, hope and despair, security and anxiety, intimacy and alienation. Better understanding and appreciation of that balance, with a particular eye toward the darker elements of Spielberg's cinema, is the focus of this book. While other scholars have noted the darker elements of Spielberg's films, the goal here is to use them as a concentrated focal point to assess the aesthetic, emotional, and ideological complexities of Spielberg's films, particularly the mediations that intervene between the opposing poles of light and dark.

However, first it is important that we explore in some depth the ideological role of darkness in art, a crucial element of critical discourse that informs my approach to the complexity of Spielberg's films. Because I am using it as the

---

[28] Dale Pollock, "*Poltergeist*: Whose Film Is It Anyway?," *Los Angeles Times*, May 24, 1982, G2.
[29] J. Hoberman, "Laugh, Cry, Believe: Spielbergization and Its Discontents," *Virginia Quarterly Review* 83, no. 1 (2007): 122.
[30] Ibid.

focal point of my analysis, it is essential that we define with some clarity what is meant by "darkness," how it shapes Spielberg's body of work, and why the lack of attention it has been given by some members of the critical community has been central to Spielberg's long-standing dismissal as a serious film artist.

Darkness, entertainment, and art

As noted earlier, I am defining darkness in art as the expressive result of the artist's recognition of the uncomfortable and unsettling aspects of life—essentially, that which does not reassure. It derives from the artist's willingness to look past comfortable surfaces, acknowledge the inherent complexities of any human endeavor, and make those a central element of the artwork, regardless of form or medium. From a moral perspective, darkness implies that the artist recognizes and integrates into his or her art the potentially disturbing ideas that good does not always prevail, right does not always win out, human suffering is not always understandable, and evil can and often does flourish. It should be noted, however, that what I am calling "darkness" here is distinctly different from nihilism. It does not mean that there is no meaning in life and all is lost, but rather that redemption and victory are never easy and their value and meaning are derived from the difficulty in attaining them. Thus, implicit in the kind of darkness I am writing about is complexity, nuance, and contradiction, caught forever in the middle between bleak nihilism and naïve optimism.

In reference to art, darkness refers to both choice of subject matter and the aesthetic, narrative, and thematic treatment of that subject matter, and the two are not always coexistent. There are certainly films whose dark subject matter is enhanced by the filmmakers' treatment, resulting in a viewing experience that could be described as *despairing*, *harrowing*, or *traumatic*. The range of such films is vast, but it would certainly include films that are built around an aggressive, unrelenting aesthetic of violence (e.g., *The Texas Chain Saw Massacre*, 1974), those that focus on emotional and/or physical suffering with no cathartic release at the end (e.g. *Kes*, 1969; *Requiem for a Dream*, 2000), and those that undermine expectations of redemption or catharsis with a brutal kind of cynicism and irony (e.g. *Chinatown*, 1974; *Taxi Driver*, 1976; *Blow Out*, 1981). On the other hand, the darkness of a film's subject matter can be alleviated, undermined, or otherwise manipulated by its treatment, both purposefully and unconsciously. Witness, for example, Disney's ability to produce a splashy semi-animated musical about slavery in *Song of the South* (1946), the British film industry's long history of depicting colonialism and its associated warfare with a sense of bravado and adventurism, and Stanley Kubrick turning a serious-minded narrative about impending nuclear war into one of the funniest of modern comedies in *Dr. Strangelove, or How I Learned to Stop Worrying and Love the Bomb* (1964).

Spielberg's preoccupation with darker subject matter throughout his career is not in question. He has dealt directly with systematic gendered violence (*The Color Purple*), the Holocaust (*Schindler's List*), the slave trade (*Amistad, Lincoln*), war (*Empire of the Sun, Saving Private Ryan, War Horse*), and terrorism (*Munich*). However, what has not been readily acknowledged is how Spielberg has treated these dark subjects with a brush that is frequently more ambivalent than reassuring, a trait that is more commonly associated with European art cinema and its high-art relatives in other media than the mainstream blockbuster filmmaking with which Spielberg is most frequently linked. The association of European art cinema and other forms of high art with darker themes relating to moral ambivalence, political cynicism, and psychological density should remind us that darkness in the arts is not ideologically neutral nor historically static. In fact, there is an often unacknowledged connection in film criticism between "darkness" and "seriousness," which links the development of film criticism and theory with larger shifts within the established art world during the twentieth century.

As filmmaker and critic Paul Schrader notes in his essay "Canon Fodder," the various assumptions undergirding the concept of the "fine arts" or "beaux arts" for more than 200 years have been increasingly questioned and chipped away during the past century. One of the assumptions that has been crucial in supporting the tradition of fine art is the connection between "art" and "beauty," the latter's definition deriving from medieval religious notions of art being "the expression of God in the universe."[31] The concept of "beauty" is long and much debated, stretching back to the writings of Plato and Aristotle and the ancient Greeks and forming the backbone of the centuries-old philosophy of aesthetics. However, what virtually all definitions of beauty have in common is that its experience brings feelings of pleasure, satisfaction, or delight. For some theorists and philosophers, this pleasure emerges from intrinsic beauty (Plato), while others have suggested that beauty is inherently spiritual (the religious tradition) or that it is based entirely on individual perception (Immanuel Kant, for example, argued that the experience of beauty was a direct result of the human ability to judge and reason). Regardless of the exact definition, the fundamental connection between traditional notions of beauty and art held strong until the modernist

---

[31] Paul Schrader, "Canon Fodder," *Film Comment* (September–October 2006): 39.

movements of the nineteenth and twentieth centuries—surrealism, Cubism, expressionism—permanently separated the two by celebrating art as any form of meaningful expression, which now meant that "the common and the unpleasant had an equal claim to be art."[32]

Modernist thought and its recalibration of aesthetics in the twentieth century heavily influenced the body of film criticism and theory that was growing alongside the development of cinema as a medium and an art. This was at least partly necessary because of the various difficulties the cinema encountered, particularly in the United States, in achieving recognition as an art form and not simply a profit-driven mode of entertainment. Despite the arguments of various writers, philosophers, artists, and critics starting as early as the 1910s, most serious critics and aesthetes dismissed the idea that film could be art. This was especially true for those films produced by the vertically integrated, oligopolistic Hollywood studios, which were fundamentally uninterested in associating their product with the fine arts. The decision by the United States Supreme Court in the 1915 censorship case *Mutual Film Corporation v. Industrial Commission of Ohio* that "the exhibition of moving pictures is a business, pure and simple" denied films protection as free speech under the First Amendment for more than 45 years. But, perhaps more importantly, it gave legal weight to and effectively justified the reluctance of the producers and moguls of the eight Hollywood studios to have film recognized as an art. As David Thomson notes, "[Hollywood] moguls vehemently proclaimed lightness, warmth, an appeal to the heart, and a good show, and fought off any greater gravity in the product."[33] Thus, because the Hollywood studio system effectively and publicly associated "lightness, warmth, and an appeal to the heart" with movies as entertainment and resisted any "greater gravity," it only makes sense that the darker elements of human expression associated with modern art (anomie, despair, loss, war) would have to be privileged as a means of arguing for film's artistic validity while more classical notions of beauty were downplayed, sometimes dismissed, especially if they were associated with simple emotionalism and pleasure.

We can see the connection between darkness and film art in *Sight & Sound*'s "Top Ten Films of All Time" poll, which has been conducted once a decade since 1952 by polling an international array of respected critics and scholars. Even a cursory look at the most recent poll from 2012 gives ample evidence of the pre-eminence of darker themes in the most widely respected films. With the exception of Dziga Vertov's day-in-the-life-of-a-city montage

---

[32] Ibid., 39.
[33] David Thomson, *America in the Dark: Hollywood and the Gift of Unreality* (New York: William Morrow, 1977), 226.

documentary *Man With a Movie Camera* (*Chelovek s kino-apparatom*, 1929), every film on the critics' list deals to some degree with dark themes, and many of them end in either downbeat or ambiguous fashion: *Vertigo* (1958), Alfred Hitchcock's complex meditation on sexual obsession and his most distinctly audience-unfriendly film; *Citizen Kane* (1941), Orson Welles's monumental depiction of the corruption of idealism and the inability to truly know anyone; *Tokyo Story* (*Tôkyô monogatari*, 1950), Yasujiro Ozu's emotionally devastating portrait of the breakdown of the traditional Japanese family; *The Rules of the Game* (*La règle du jeu*, 1937), Jean Renoir's satire of the French bourgeoisie that was deemed so corrosive at the time of its release that it was banned by the French government; *Sunrise* (1927), F. W. Murnau's expressionistic romantic tragedy; *2001: A Space Odyssey* (1968), Stanley Kubrick's aesthetically rigorous, epic depiction of the end of humankind and its possible evolution; *The Searchers* (1956), John Ford's complex depiction of frontier racism that cast John Wayne as a vicious anti-hero; *The Passion of Joan of Arc* (*La passion de Jeanne d'Arc*, 1929), Carl Theodor Dreyer's harrowing film about the trial and execution of Joan of Arc; and *8½* (1963), Federico Fellini's blackly comic depiction of artistic malaise.

In some way or another all of these "great" films are direct products of the modernist movement in film, which tended to be inherently dark and often pessimistic. This movement arguably started in the 1920s with German expressionism and its emphasis on lack of order, diminished human subjectivity, and a sense of history as loss. In the post-World War II years, the modernist strain of cinema continued with Italian neorealism, which developed as a reaction against the country's "white telephone" films (studio-produced American-style romantic comedies) by focusing on the hard realities of everyday existence and avoiding any aesthetic and narrative tropes that might artificially soften those realities. The critical success of neorealist films like Roberto Rossellini's *Rome, Open City* (*Roma, città aperta*, 1945) and Vittorio de Sica's *Bicycle Thieves* (*Ladri di biciclette*, 1948) helped set off a flurry of "new waves" throughout international cinema of the 1950s and 1960s, all of which rejected the idea of art in the literary tradition, as well as classical notions of beauty as pleasure and satisfaction. These included the British New Wave of the 1950s, which was rooted in the earlier Free Cinema movement and was built around adaptations of "angry young men" novels and plays and an embrace of the working-class realism of so-called "kitchen sink dramas" set in the industrial north of England, and the French New Wave, which merged independent and documentary production strategies with radical reworkings of Hollywood genres to produce politically cynical films that featured young, alienated protagonists living on the margins of a politically and morally corrupt world.

These various film movements, all of which were directly influential on the filmmakers of the New American Cinema of the 1960s and 1970s, including Steven Spielberg, were essential to raising awareness of film from the realm of entertainment into art by exploring the darker elements of human existence and intertwining them into both their aesthetics (gritty black and white cinematography, location work, discontinuous editing, increasingly graphic depictions of sex and violence) and their narrative strategies (looser modes of storytelling that are more reflective of lived existence, ambiguous character psychology, open or deliberately downbeat endings). Even before the New American Cinema, some classical Hollywood directors in the post-war era had begun to explore similarly darker elements in their films, and although they were not always celebrated at the time, in retrospect they have been taken more seriously by critics and academics than the majority of studio-era genre work. One might think of Warner Brothers' budget-conscious Depression-era films like Mervyn LeRoy's *I Am a Fugitive From a Chain Gang* (1932), which are now applauded as serious social statements; John Ford's *The Searchers*, which has been elevated to canonic status (as its placement on the aforementioned *Sight & Sound* poll testifies), based largely on the director's willingness to subvert the John Wayne mythos he helped create by exploring the character's underlying viciousness and racism; or Douglas Sirk's Technicolor melodramas like *All That Heaven Allows* (1955) and *Written on the Wind* (1956), which are now seen as subversive masterpieces of social and ideological critique.

The correlation of darker themes and a more mature, fully artistic form of cinema is made clear in writer and filmmaker Lewis Jacobs' elated commentary on the state of European art cinema in 1969 (what he called "The Creative Present"), which he saw as being stripped of overt censorship and oppressive corporate oversight and reinvigorated with young, self-aware artists who "demand from movies the same intellectual and esthetic level which is expected from artists in other media":[34]

> For this group of film makers, there are no "forbidden" topics and no proscribed themes. Part of the broad cultural upheaval of an era that has recognized the changed condition of man in contemporary society, these men are exploring arresting new areas of subject matter. The celebration of man as the idealized hero-figure of an earlier, more stable society has been swept away and replaced by an image of man as the anxiety-ridden victim, confronting a life that seems to have lost its coherence in a world both confusing and uncertain. The assumptions and conventions

---

[34] Lewis Jacobs, *The Emergence of Film Art* (New York: Hopkinson and Blake, 1969), 286.

of codified dramatic problems, and the surface exploration of political and social issues, with their clear-cut answers, no longer seem valid in a world threatened by the big bomb, the cold war, and other factors which help break down humanistic values and impose a sense of crisis in modern life.[35]

Thus, while Jacobs draws indelible links between the cinema of the new generation of filmmakers and true art, one cannot help but notice the delight he takes in noting how they address issues of anxiety, victimhood, crisis, and the breakdown of humanism without any suggestion of redemption or reaffirmation of traditional values. Rather, the turn to darker material is itself a criterion value of film as art, bringing the current cinema in line with the great predecessors of film history such as Soviet montage, German expressionism, Italian neorealism, and the French New Wave, all of which made themselves heard by attacking what at the time was the cinematic status quo.

We can see the same operation at work in film historian Peter Biskind's discussion of the effect Steven Spielberg and George Lucas had on American cinema in the late 1970s and throughout the 1980s. Picking up on critic Robin Wood's derisive description of how 1980s cinema was afflicted by the "Lucas–Spielberg Syndrome"—"films catering to the desire for regression to infantilism, the doublethink phenomenon of pure fantasy"[36]—Biskind writes, "To infantilize the audience of the sixties and empower the audience of the seventies, to reconstitute the spectator as child, Lucas and Spielberg had to obliterate years of sophisticated, adult moviegoing habits. *Star Wars* came on the heels of nearly a decade of wise-ass, cynical, self-conscious moviemaking."[37] Thus, Biskind makes it clear that "sophisticated, adult moviegoing habits" revolve around "wise-ass, cynical, self-conscious" cinema, and because Spielberg and Lucas's films were perceived as embracing myth, innocence, and redemption, they couldn't possibly be taken seriously except as symptoms of a declining cinematic and political culture. Similarly, essayist Tim Kreider, in his discussion of Spielberg's *A.I. Artificial Intelligence* (2001), defines "adult films" as "complex, ambiguous, brutal, and cold,"[38] thus collapsing the experiential and intellectual difficulty of the artistic experience ("complex, ambiguous") with its philosophical outlook and tone ("brutal, and cold").

---

[35] Ibid., 287.
[36] Robin Wood, *Hollywood From Vietnam to Reagan* (New York: Columbia University Press, 1986), 175.
[37] Peter Biskind, "Blockbuster: The Last Crusade," in *Seeing Through Movies*, ed. Mark Crispin Miller (New York: Pantheon, 1990), 121–2.
[38] Tim Kreider, "Review: *A.I. Artificial Intelligence*," *Film Quarterly* 56, no. 2 (Winter 2002): 33.

Thus, there tends to be critical suspicion, especially within the academic community, of films that are thought to be comforting, reassuring, and enjoyable to a mass audience because such emotional appeals are supportive of the status quo and the status quo is always to be questioned. As film scholar Robert Kolker notes, "The nature of conventional fiction is to present a clean and concentrated view of life,"[39] a tendency that is particularly true of American art. According to David Thomson,

> Americans do not admire or readily tolerate a kind of reserve or difficulty of personality that is honored in Europe. Despite the legend of violence and disruption bristling from America, it is an orderly country. It makes great efforts to be understandable and believes in clarity ... it sometimes seems that Americans do not explore their own nature but proffer a visible, communicable personality—one that is easy-going and tidy.[40]

The incursion of darkness into American cinema, particularly in the New American Cinema of the 1960s and 1970s, clearly conflicts with these longstanding tendencies, although it has been successfully marginalized in most mainstream Hollywood productions since the 1980s. Nevertheless, those darker elements still persist, although what is interesting about them is not the darkness itself—that quickly devolves into simple nihilism—but rather the uneasy, but ultimately invigorating dialectic it develops with the ideals of hope and redemption, which we can see clearly in many of Spielberg's films.

Thomas Hibbs notes this dialectic in his book *Arts of Darkness: American Noir and the Quest for Redemption*, which looks at the generally unexamined overlap between film noir and the religious film. The complex moral, political, and emotional underpinnings of both classic noir and neo-noir that Hibbs discusses provide a useful structure for examining what is so complex and fascinating about Spielberg's films, albeit inverted in terms of general expectations. While noir is popularly thought of as being a genre of despair, alienation, social decay, and violence, Hibbs argues that many of these films contain "glimpses of redemption" that "are always partial rather than revolutionary, and personal rather than political."[41] Similarly, while Spielberg's films are often popularly conceived as upbeat, reassuring, and heartening, they also tend to feature only "glimpses of redemption" that are more "personal

---

[39] Robert Kolker, *A Cinema of Loneliness*, 4th edn (New York: Oxford University Press, 2011), 14.
[40] Thomson, *America in the Dark*, 225.
[41] Thomas Hibbs, *Arts of Darkness: American Noir and the Quest for Redemption* (Dallas, TX: Spence Publishing, 2008), xvi.

than political" and are invariably limited by the violence, tragedy, and trauma that preceded them.

The fact that the darker elements of Spielberg's body of work have not been as readily or systematically acknowledged as other typically Spielbergian characteristics is arguably responsible for his persistent dismissal as a film artist and therefore need to be assessed in a concentrated form. The correlation between darkness and serious, important cinema is inescapable at this point, and while I do not believe that a film's artistic validity necessarily requires darker elements in either subject matter or treatment, it is true that many of the "great films"— Spielberg's included—tend to gravitate toward more serious, complex, and unsettling subjects. This book's focus on these darker elements in Spielberg's films and exploration of how they work in concert with his other, more conventionally appealing characteristics will demonstrate how Spielberg successfully straddles a rarely crossed line between the pleasures of mainstream Hollywood cinema and the challenges associated with European art film.

Approaching Spielberg: Ideology, genre, auteur

Previous books on Spielberg have drawn from auteur and genre criticism,[42] biography,[43] specific analysis of filmmaking practices,[44] and psychoanalytically driven examination of text and process,[45] all with fruitful results that have helped expand and deepen the critical appreciation of his body of work. Because this book focuses particularly on the underlying contradictions of specific films within Spielberg's larger body of work—the battle between light and dark—the theoretical framework adopted here comes, ironically, from Robin Wood, whose oft-reprinted 1977 *Film Comment* article "Ideology, Genre, Auteur" provides a useful roadmap for tracing the source of and better understanding these contradictions.

Wood's goal was to demonstrate how the auteur theory, genre theory, and theories of ideology can be combined to produce what he called "synthetic criticism."[46] Each approach has played an important role in elevating film

---

[42] See Lester D. Friedman, *Citizen Spielberg* (Champaign: University of Illinois Press, 2006).
[43] See McBride, *Steven Spielberg: A Biography*; John Baxter, *Steven Spielberg: The Unauthorized Biography* (New York: HarperCollins, 1998); Frank Sanello, *Spielberg: The Man, the Movies, the Mythology* (Dallas, TX: Taylor Publishing, 1996).
[44] See Warren Buckland, *Directed by Steven Spielberg: Poetics of the Contemporary Hollywood Blockbuster* (New York: Continuum, 2006).
[45] Morris, *The Cinema of Steven Spielberg*.
[46] Robin Wood, "Ideology, Genre, Auteur," in *Film Genre Reader I*, ed. Barry Keith Grant (Austin: University of Texas Press, 1995), 60.

studies as a serious academic discipline, yet each also has limitations, especially when used in isolation. Auteurism, first proposed in the 1950s by French critics like François Truffaut as a means of critically elevating previously marginalized directors by privileging them as the "authors" of their respective films, was historically distorted to argue for the director and his or her personality as the locus of all meaning. Genre theory has sought to understand how the organization of different cinematic narratives and recurring tropes affects both our understanding of certain films and how films of a similar nature are continuously produced, but has also run into theoretical problems involving either overly deterministic arguments that suggest the spectator is manipulated by the ideological agendas inherent to particular genres or exceedingly vague ritualistic theories in which audience desires are proffered as the primary factor determining which genres prevail and which genres fade away. Ideological criticism came to prominence in the late 1960s as a means of situating cinema within the larger socio-political context by reading filmic representations primarily through the lenses of gender, race, and socio-economic status, although it has frequently fallen prey to overly deterministic arguments that rely heavily on speculative Marxist and psychoanalytic discourse to advance a political agenda.

Nevertheless, understanding the role of ideology in Spielberg's films is particularly crucial because it has been in this arena that Spielberg has been most frequently and harshly criticized, largely because critics and scholars have failed to appreciate the ideological complexities inherent in his films. In its broadest sense, ideology is the system of meaning individuals and groups use both consciously and unconsciously to make sense of their world. Cultural theorist Stuart Hall defines it as "the mental frameworks—the languages, the concepts, categories, imagery of thought, and the systems of representation—which different classes and social groups deploy in order to make sense of, define, figure out and render intelligible the way society works."[47] Ideology is frequently internalized in such a way that it feels completely natural and is therefore unquestioned, which is why ideological criticism is frequently so intense in its tone and tenor: it must confront and deconstruct what is viewed as natural and inherent. When applied to film, ideological criticism looks at both a broad spectrum of representation—how, for example, certain assumptions regarding the connection between the Protestant work ethic and financial reward are embodied in Hollywood cinema—and individuals films that are either particularly representative of

---

[47] Stuart Hall, "The Problem of Ideology: Marxism Without Guarantees," in *Stuart Hall: Critical Dialogues in Cultural Studies*, David Morley and Kuan-Hsing Chen (eds) (London: Routledge, 1996), 26.

a dominant ideology or undercut it in interesting ways. This does not mean, however, that there is a single, dominant ideology; rather, there are multiple, intersecting ideologies that are frequently contradictory, even in a relatively homogeneous culture with a stable set of shared values. In this regard, movies are most interesting ideologically not as blunt tools of oppression, but rather as sites in which ideological contradiction is played out.

Andrew Britton's aforementioned essay, "Blissing Out," is clearly indebted to the method of ideological criticism laid out by *Cahiers du cinéma* editors Jean-Luc Comolli and Jean Narboni in their oft-reprinted essay "Cinema/Ideology/Criticism," which was first published in 1969. Comolli and Narboni argue that, because film is "a material product of the [capitalist] system, it is also an ideological part of the system."[48] Using that as their base, they constructed a catalog of cinematic categories based on film's relation to ideology, with the largest category, (a), consisting of "those films which are imbued through and through with the dominant ideology in a pure and unadulterated form, and give no indication that their makers were even aware of the fact."[49] While Britton saw "the ideology of entertainment," which corresponds roughly with Comolli and Narboni's (a) category, embodied in virtually every film produced by Hollywood during the 1980s, he singled out Spielberg's films as particularly endemic of this trend, which, "if persisted in, would make a valuable popular cinema in American impossible."[50]

In fact, many of Spielberg's films, especially the ones discussed in this book, would be best categorized in Comolli and Narboni's system not as films "imbued through and through with the dominant ideology in pure and unadulterated form," but rather in the fifth category, (e), which is worth quoting at some length:

> ... films which seem at first sight to belong firmly within the ideology and to be completely under its sway, but which turn out to be so only in an ambiguous manner. For though they start from a nonprogressive standpoint, ranging from the frankly reactionary through the conciliatory to the mildly critical, they have been worked upon, and work, in such a real way that there is a noticeable gap, a dislocation, between the starting point and the finished product ... The films we are talking about throw up obstacles in the way of the ideology, causing it to swerve and get off course ... If one reads the film obliquely, looking for symptoms; if one looks beyond

---

[48] Jean-Luc Comolli and Jean Narboni, "Cinema/Ideology/Criticism," in *Film Theory and Criticism: Introductory Readings*, 5th edn, Leo Braudy and Marshall Cohen (eds) (New York: Oxford University Press, 1999), 754.
[49] Ibid., 755.
[50] Britton, "Blissing Out," 34.

its apparent formal coherence, one can see that it is riddled with cracks: it is splitting under an internal tension which is subordinate to the text.[51]

Although Comolli and Narboni were writing two years before the made-for-television movie *Duel* (1971), which was Spielberg's first professionally produced feature film to receive a theatrical release, and five years before *The Sugarland Express*, their description of commercial films riddled with internal contradictions and fissures, their surface pleasures constantly challenged by their internal cracks and tensions, is an almost perfect description of Spielberg's films. William Brown (2009) recognizes this in his "playful" analysis of the relations between Spielberg's films and "the processes of capitalism itself."[52] In order to illustrate the ambiguous nature of Spielberg's politics, Brown argues that Spielberg can be seen as a conservative director whose films either advocate the hostile destruction of "the other" or reinforce the dominance of white males by presenting them as saviors of sympathetic others; at the same time, though, Brown shows that he can be seen as a potentially radical filmmaker who presents youthful protagonists and outsiders capable of transcending boundaries and challenging capitalism's hegemony—sometimes within the same film.

These productive contradictions in Spielberg's body of work are thus best explored via a focus on how the ideology of his films is informed by the imbrications of his role as an auteur and his use of popular genres. In combining these previously disparate theoretical approaches to cinema, Robin Wood not only created a robust means of looking at a film from multiple perspectives simultaneously, but also demonstrated how these different approaches were not only *not* discreet, but were deeply intertwined. Thus, Wood argues that the development of genres is rooted in ideological contradictions and that this ideological conflict is most clearly understood when viewed through the work of an individual auteur.[53] As he puts it, "It is only through the medium of the individual that ideological tensions come into particular focus, hence become of aesthetic as well as sociological interest."[54]

The key, then, is the importance of structural oppositions within the same film, which Wood notes are central to the American ideals of capitalism, happy endings, brave heroes, and so forth, all of which are riddled with contradictions. This approach emphasizes the interconnected nature of different genres via their shared oppositions; Wood's primary example is the "home/wandering" opposition that exists in both westerns and small-town comedies,

---

[51] Comolli and Narboni, "Cinema/Ideology/Criticism," 757.
[52] William Brown, "It's a Shark Eat Shark World: Spielberg's Ambiguous Politics," *New Review of Film and Television Studies* 7, no. 1 (March 2009): 13.
[53] Wood, "Ideology, Genre, Auteur," 61–3.
[54] Ibid., 63.

two genres that otherwise would seem to have little in common. Similarly, individual directors, who at least since Andrew Sarris's Americanization of the *politiques des auteurs* in his 1968 book *The American Cinema* have been understood primarily in terms of their narrative, aesthetic, and ideological consistencies, are also best understood in terms of conflict and tension. "It can perhaps be argued," Wood writes, "that works are of especial interest when the defined particularities of an auteur interact with specific ideological tensions and when the film is fed from more than one generic source."[55]

It is not surprising that Wood, when demonstrating the utility of this synthetic criticism, chose as his examples two films, one by Alfred Hitchcock and one by Frank Capra, filmmakers who, as previously noted, bear many striking similarities to Steven Spielberg formally, ideologically, and critically. And, just as Wood demonstrated that *Shadow of a Doubt* (1943) and *It's a Wonderful Life* (1946) are both deeply conflicted films that offer numerous subversive elements that are variously "contained" with differing levels of success, this book will critically examine a number of Spielberg's films with an eye toward their ideological contradictions and tensions as evidenced in their narrative and formal structures. It is not in any way intended to be a comprehensive overview of Spielberg's entire output as a filmmaker to date, but rather a concentrated study of a select group of films that best demonstrate the productive tensions within his work.

In the end, Pauline Kael was right: *E.T.* is a bliss-out. But, it is the darkness contained within that bliss and the struggle between them that keeps that film, along with most of Spielberg's work, firmly lodged in our cultural consciousness when so many other feel-good blockbusters have faded from memory.

---

[55] Ibid., 63.

1

"I Didn't Want to See This"

Weekend America and Its Discontents in *Close Encounters of the Third Kind*, *E.T.* and *Poltergeist*

Released within a four-year span, *Close Encounters of the Third Kind* (1977), *E.T. The Extra-Terrestrial* (1982), and *Poltergeist* (1982) form what film scholar Andrew M. Gordon has called Spielberg's "suburban trilogy."[1] These three films, which more than any others helped to solidify in the popular imagination what a "Steven Spielberg film" is (albeit for mostly the wrong reasons), have a great deal in common, so much so that they feel like different riffs on the same themes and could be easily combined into a single master narrative. As Gordon points out, *Close Encounters*, *E.T.*, and *Poltergeist* are "closely linked" in four important ways: subject matter ("contemporary American suburban families under stress, kidnapped children, and paranormal phenomenon"), emotional tone ("a mix of mystery, suspense, fear, comedy, warmth, breathless anticipation, and wonder"), technique ("awing the viewer by the power of light, sound, spectacle, and special effects"), and underlying psychological concerns ("separation anxiety, the fear of death, and the return of repressed material in the fantastic form of aliens or ghosts").[2] They are also among the most directly autobiographical of Spielberg's career, as many

---

[1] Andrew M. Gordon, *Empire of Dreams: The Science Fiction and Fantasy Films of Steven Spielberg* (Lanham, MD: Rowman & Littlefield, 2008), 55.
[2] Ibid., 55–6.

of their images, storylines, and characters derive directly from his childhood experiences, fantasies, and nightmares. Thus, this chapter will employ a more biographical approach than other chapters, linking elements of the films with Spielberg's life, much of which he has willingly recounted in numerous interviews over the years.

Critics at the time of the films' theatrical releases also noted the interconnections among them and how they reflected on Spielberg's cohering sensibilities as a filmmaker. Writing about *E.T.* in *The New Yorker*, Pauline Kael compared it favorably to *Close Encounters* twice in the first two paragraphs, writing, "If the film seems a continuation of 'Close Encounters,' that's partly because it has the sensibility we came to know in that picture, and partly because E.T. himself is like a more corporeal version of the celestial visitors at the end of it."[3] She took a dismal view of *Poltergeist*, arguing that it lacked precisely what made *E.T.* such a great film: "the emotional roots of the fantasy, and what it means to children."[4] *New York Times* film critic Vincent Canby, on the other hand, saw *E.T.* and *Poltergeist*, which were released within weeks of each other during the summer of 1982 and often played in multiplexes side-by-side, as so interconnected that they "fuse[d] … into a single artistic achievement about the world as imagined by children."[5] Canby recognized, however, that despite their similarities, the two films were paradoxically opposites, to the point that "anyone who is charmed by one will probably be disappointed by the other,"[6] a point that perfectly presages Kael's criticism, which was published the following day. In trying to distinguish between the two films, Canby wrote, "'E.T.' is Mr. Spielberg's sweet, graceful, wish-fulfilling dream in which small children lead us toward the light of universal understanding as they munch Reese's Pieces. 'Poltergeist' is a delicious nightmare in which children are subjected to all sorts of indescribable terrors and emerge triumphantly, their egos intact."[7]

On both counts, Canby is only partially right. While there is plenty of sweetness and grace and light in *E.T.*, there is also a great deal of darkness and fear and terror and disappointment, while the children and adults in *Poltergeist*, after being subjected to terror and violence, do not emerge triumphant or intact, but rather shattered and broken and barely alive, a

---

[3] Pauline Kael, "The Current Cinema: The Pure and the Impure," *The New Yorker*, June 14, 1982, 119.
[4] Ibid., 124.
[5] Vincent Canby, "Amid Gloom, Good Comedy Staged an Exhilarating Comeback," *New York Times*, December 26, 1982, H17.
[6] Vincent Canby, "Exploring Inner and Outer Space With Steven Spielberg," *New York Times*, June 13, 1982, H29.
[7] Canby, "Amid Gloom," H17.

foreshadowing of what awaits the child protagonists of *Empire of the Sun* (1987) and *War of the Worlds* (2005) and, in a more complicated sense, the mecha child in *A.I. Artificial Intelligence* (2001). Similarly, while *Close Encounters* is often described in terms of cinematic religious spectacle,[8] with the arrival of the alien spacecraft at Wyoming's Devil's Tower playing the role of God descending on Mount Sinai, there is a much darker agenda at play beneath the surface. The powerful light show that brings the film to a close is a distraction from, but hardly a solution to, the film's myriad social and interpersonal issues, none of which are resolved. While on a surface level *Close Encounters* does play, at least on first viewing, as "a psychological phenomenon, the expression of urgent unconscious desires, wish-fulfillment which reassures the audience,"[9] closer inspection reveals that its "wish fulfillment" is perilously fragmented; for one character to achieve blissful harmony with the cosmos, he must leave behind not only his family, but the entirety of humankind, which, with few exceptions, is left unchanged and untouched by the extraterrestrial encounter. In fact, if there is a binding tie among these three films beyond their shared suburban setting, it is the manner in which their effects-laden conclusions—exhilarating and emotionally rapturous in *Close Encounters* and *E.T.*, and terrifying in *Poltergeist*—create barely sustainable resolutions that easily crack apart beneath the strain of what has happened throughout each film and what has been left unresolved. In one form or another, the supernatural phenomena in each of the films dazzles and excites, but ultimately leaves behind broken families and homes, both figuratively and literally.

"Weekend America" on screen

Spielberg's early cinematic fascination with suburbia and the culture of what he called "weekend America"[10] may be partially explained by the fact that he was a child of the suburbs, unlike many of his urban-born-and-raised contemporaries who also rose to prominence in the "New Hollywood" of the 1960s and 1970s. Martin Scorsese, for example, grew up in the Little Italy neighborhood

---

[8] Pauline Kael, "The Current Cinema: The Greening of the Solar System," *The New Yorker*, November 28, 1977; Stanley Kauffmann, "Epiphany," *New Republic*, December 10, 1977; Tony Williams, "Close Encounters of the Authoritarian Kind," *Wide Angle* 4, no. 5 (1983).
[9] Andrew M. Gordon, "*Close Encounters*: The Gospel According to Spielberg," *Literature/Film Quarterly*, no. 3 (1980): 158.
[10] Dave Pirie, "A Prodigy Zooms In: A Child Cineaste Who Now Makes Movies and Money With Equal Facility," in *Time Out Interviews 1968–1998*, ed. Frank Broughton (London: Penguin Books), 105.

of Manhattan; Francis Ford Coppola spent most of his childhood in Woodside, Queens; and Brian De Palma grew up in Philadelphia.[11] Not surprisingly, many of their early films reflect the urban environments of their childhood and adolescence: Scorsese's *Who's That Knocking at My Door* (1967), *Mean Streets* (1973), and *Taxi Driver* (1976) are all indelibly New York-centered films, as are Coppola's *You're a Big Boy Now* (1966) and *The Godfather* (1972) and De Palma's *Greetings* (1968), *Hi, Mom!* (1970), and *Sisters* (1973). Virtually the entirety of Spielberg's childhood and adolescence, on the other hand, was spent in various suburban areas, starting on the East Coast and then moving west, first to the Sun Belt and finally to the West Coast. Each of his family's moves marked a step up the socio-economic ladder and took them further away from densely populated, ethnically defined urban areas and into increasingly sprawling, affluent, white suburban neighborhoods.

Although there is some debate as to what exactly constitutes a "suburb," there is general agreement that the term is used primarily to refer to "any kind of settlement on the periphery of a large city,"[12] as well as the outlying areas around small towns and the "population blips at the intersection of major highways."[13] Arguments over definitions are largely academic, though, as the terms "suburban," "suburbs," and "suburbia" are immediately familiar to the vast majority of Americans and conjure up a shared network of images, feelings, and meanings. Suburbia has been "the dominant American cultural landscape" at least since the mid-twentieth century when housing developers started building record numbers of affordable single-family dwellings around the edges of major cities, drawing young families to the promises of open spaces, safety for their children, and convenient access to the benefits of nearby urban centers without their congestion and crime. In other words, the suburbs merged the benefits of rural and city living, and as a result suburbia quickly became "the site of promises, dreams, and fantasies ... a landscape of the imagination where Americans situate ambitions for upward mobility and economic security, ideals about freedom and private property, and longings for social harmony and spiritual uplift."[14] More Americans now

---

[11] In a 1991 interview with film critic Gene Siskel, Spielberg noted, "I was raised in suburbia; it's all I know. I wasn't raised in a big city. I wasn't raised under the shadows of skyscrapers. I lived under the sky all through those formative years, from third grade right through high school. That's my knowledge of a kind of lifestyle." See Roger Ebert and Gene Siskel, *The Future of the Movies: Interviews With Martin Scorsese, Steven Spielberg, and George Lucas* (Kansas City, MO: Andrews and McMeel, 1991), 70.
[12] Robert Fishman, *Bourgeois Utopias: The Rise and Fall of Suburbia* (New York: Basic Books, 1987).
[13] Douglas Muzzio and Thomas Halper, "Pleasantville?: The Suburb and Its Representation in American Movies," *Urban Affairs Review* 37, no. 4 (2002): 547.
[14] Dolores Hayden, *Building Suburbia: Green Fields and Urban Growth, 1820–2000* (New York: Random House, 2004), 3.

live in the suburbs than in rural areas and urban centers combined; thus, the suburbs, "in all their variety and in their shifting visual cultural, political, and economic forms, are now central to everyday American life."[15]

Yet, the suburbs are rarely depicted in a positive light in American cinema, as filmmakers have seemingly internalized the harsh critiques of post-war intellectuals and artists who saw them as inauthentic consumption centers, conformity factories, and a refuge from racial and socio-economic "undesirables."[16] While films that depicted the suburbs during the earliest years of the silent era tended to be light-hearted social comedies, the 1950s saw increasingly satirical films that eventually turned to "outright scorn, ridicule, and condemnation" in the 1960s and 1970s.[17] The gentle satire of *Mr. Blandings Builds His Dream House* (1948) and *Father of the Bride* (1950) gave way to the vitriol of *The Graduate* (1967), *Bob & Carol & Ted & Alice* (1969), and *The Stepford Wives* (1975). The criticisms of suburbia and what it represented could also be found in nonfiction books, including William H. Whyte's *The Organization Man* (1956) and A. C. Spectorsky's *The Exurbanites* (1958), while novelists attacked it in fictional form in books like Sloan Wilson's *The Man in the Gray Flannel Suit* (1956), John Keats's *The Crack in the Picture Window* (1957), and Richard Yates's *Revolutionary Road* (1961). For post-war intellectuals, the inauthenticity and conformity of the suburbs was most clearly embodied in Levittown, the first and then-largest mass-produced planned community, which was constructed on Long Island by the building firm Levitt & Sons between 1947 and 1951. With its literally interchangeable Cape Code and ranch style houses, which were constructed on assembly lines and organized into geometric rows across a flat, treeless space that had formerly served as a potato farm, Levittown was a ready-made symbol of both the efficiencies of post-war manufacturing and the bland homogeneity of the new suburban lifestyle.[18]

Although it was artistically and intellectually fashionable in the 1950s and 1960s to deride the conformity and materialism represented by suburbia, some sociologists and cultural critics began to realize that, despite the surface homogeneity, suburbia and its denizens were widely varied in numerous ways. Researchers in the 1950s had declared suburbanites a "new breed" of Americans who were fundamentally different from their forebears

---

[15] Greg Dickson, "The *Pleasantville* Effect: Nostalgia and the Visual Framing of (White) Suburbia," *Western Journal of Communication* 70, no. 3 (July 2006): 215.
[16] Muzzio and Halper, "Pleasantville?," 556; see also Lee Siegel, "Why Does Hollywood Hate the Suburbs?," *Wall Street Journal*, December 27, 2008, http://online.wsj.com/article/SB123033369595836301.html (accessed March 25, 2012).
[17] Muzzio and Halper, "Pleasantville?," 559.
[18] "Up From the Potato Fields," *Time*, July 3, 1950.

in the city and country. In "Up From the Potato Fields, "a 1950 article in *Time* magazine about the construction of Levittown, the author describes it as "an entirely new kind of community" and makes special note of the residents' limited age range ("Few of its more than 40,000 residents are past 35"), the rules imposed on them to ensure a consistent appearance from the street (fences were not allowed, yards must be mowed once a week, and laundry could not be hung out on traditional laundry lines), and especially the sense of isolation and estrangement ("Said one housewife last week: 'It's not a community that thinks much about what's going on outside'"). However, the "suburbanites as new breed" view was soon challenged. Sociologist Bennett Berger's *Working-Class Suburbs* (1960) demonstrated that there was a great deal of variety in the suburbs, while *The Changing Face of the Suburbs* (1976), a compilation of studies edited by sociologist Barry Schwartz, indicated a wide range of views regarding race, religion, and politics, thus supporting the argument that there is no coherent or dominant "suburban attitude." Suburbanites, as it turned out, weren't so much a new breed as they were the same breed of Americans who had, for the previous three centuries, sought a better life for themselves and their children and were simply following the spatial, economic, and cultural developments of their generation—which included Spielberg's family.

A child of the "Baby Boom," Spielberg was born on December 18, 1946, in Cincinnati, Ohio, to a Jewish family whose history biographer Joseph McBride describes as "reflect[ing] the archetypal Jewish-American journey of the last hundred years, from persecution in Russian cities and *schtetlach* (small towns) to religious freedom in the New World, and in succeeding generations from the comforts and limitations of a traditional mid-western Jewish-American community to the hazardous opportunities offered by the largely WASPish suburbs."[19] Spielberg's first three years of life were spent in the Cincinnati suburb of Avondale, which since the 1920s had become the city's largest Jewish enclave and at the time was a lower middle-class neighborhood comprised primarily of large, older homes that had been subdivided into duplexes and apartments.[20] Avondale provided a safe, comfortable environment; Peggie Hibbert Singerman, one of the Spielberg family's neighbors, described it as "a lovely neighborhood. [The houses had] big backyards, huge porches on the front, swings."[21] In 1949, Spielberg's father, Arnold, a World War II veteran who had recently finished his degree in electronic engineering at the University of Cincinnati and secured a

---

[19] Joseph McBride, *Steven Spielberg: A Biography*, 2nd edn (Jackson: University Press of Mississippi, 2010), 20.
[20] Ibid., 28–9.
[21] Ibid., 29.

job with RCA, moved the family, which included his wife Leah and Spielberg's three younger sisters, to New Jersey. They spent three years living in a large apartment complex in Camden before moving to Haddon Township, a relatively affluent commuter suburb in proximity to both Camden and Philadelphia, where they lived in a white, two-story colonial-style house in the Haddonleigh section, a tree-lined neighborhood recently built on land formerly occupied by an eighteenth-century potato farm known as Hinchman homestead and later the Haddon Country Club.[22] In 1957, when Spielberg was ten, the family moved again, this time all the way to Arizona, where they took up residence in a newly constructed ranch house on a large lot in Phoenix's Arcadia neighborhood, which had recently sprung up on a former citrus farm near the foot of Camelback Mountain. Spielberg came to identify Phoenix as his "true boyhood home," and it was the place where he first developed his love of cinema and had numerous experiences that fed into his later films, from his father taking him out into the desert in the middle of the night to watch a meteor shower, to the growing acrimony and estrangement between his parents that would later lead to their divorce.[23] In the spring of 1964, near the end of Spielberg's junior year in high school, the family moved yet again, this time to Saratoga, California, an upper middle-class bedroom community of 25,000 near Silicon Valley in the foothills of the Santa Cruz Mountains.[24]

Spielberg's suburban upbringing has consequently shaded his work as a filmmaker, in that many of his films prominently feature, if not take place entirely within, a suburban environment, oftentimes one that looks like either the Arcadia neighborhood in Phoenix or the hilly streets of Saratoga. The association of suburban neighborhoods and Spielberg is so strong, in fact, that he has been referred to as "the poet of suburbia," especially during the early 1980s.[25] *Close Encounters of the Third Kind*, *E.T.*, and *Poltergeist* are what

---

[22] William B. Brahms and Sandra White-Grear with the Haddon Township Historical Society, *Haddon Township* (Charleston, SC: Arcadia Publishing, 2011), 31.
[23] Frederick Wasser, *Steven Spielberg's America* (London: Polity Press, 2010), 20.
[24] McBride, *Steven Spielberg: A Biography*, 115.
[25] In his biography of Spielberg, Joseph McBride cites the label "poet of suburbia" as coming from *New York Times* film critic Vincent Canby (*Steven Spielberg: A Biography*, 19), who Gene Siskel quotes in an interview with Spielberg (Ebert and Siskel, *The Future of Movies*, 70). However, Canby never actually used that term in any of his writings to describe Spielberg (although it is possible that he used it in private conversation with Siskel). More likely, the "poet of suburbia" moniker is a misquote of something Canby wrote in his 1982 year-end article "Amid Gloom, Good Comedy Staged an Exhilarating Comeback": "Mr. Spielberg, who takes life in housing developments seriously, may be the closest thing we now have to a Middle American poet and, next to François Truffaut, he is the best director of children making movies today" (H17). There is also the possibility that Siskel was citing the wrong critic, as Chris Auty used the phrase "poet of suburbia" in his article "The Complete Spielberg?," which appeared in the autumn 1982 issue of *Sight & Sound*.

Douglas Muzzio and Thomas Halper call "suburban-centered films," defined as films in which "suburbia is so essential to a film's nature that it could not take place elsewhere without being fundamentally altered."[26] Suburbia also features prominently in other Spielberg films as either a place the protagonist leaves before facing danger in the wilderness, as in *Duel* (1971) and *Jaws* (1975), or a place that the protagonist feels compelled to escape, as in *Hook* (1991) and *Catch Me If You Can* (2002). It is also crucial that both of Spielberg's futuristic science fiction films, *A.I. Artificial Intelligence* and *Minority Report* (2002), have sequences set in the suburbs, thus suggesting that their familiar environs will persist into the future with only minimal change.

Spielberg's cinematic fascination with suburbia arguably began with *Duel*. *Duel* was originally produced as a made-for-TV movie that aired on ABC's *Movie of the Weekend* series on November 13, 1971, but it proved so successful with critics and audiences that Spielberg was commissioned to expand it by 16 minutes with newly shot footage so that it could be released theatrically in Europe the following year. Much of the additional material for the theatrical version is arguably unnecessary in terms of the film's primal plot about an ordinary businessman named David Mann (Dennis Weaver) who is terrorized on the desert mountain highways of central California by a menacing truck whose driver remains largely unseen. However, new footage added to the beginning expands on the film's subtext regarding the protagonist's status as a suburbanite whose comfortable, complacent existence is challenged by a faceless menace. This is particularly true of the opening credits sequence. While the television version of the film begins with David already on the open highway, the theatrical version begins with a fixed, low-angle point-of-view shot from the bumper of the car as it pulls out of the garage of a middle-class home and, through a series of dissolves, drives through a suburban neighborhood, into downtown Los Angeles, and eventually out to the highway, thus visually reinforcing the character's departing the safety of suburbia and entering the wilderness, which is characterized by the isolation of David's car on the highway and the barrenness of the mountain landscape.

In an interview with Dave Pirie that was originally published in *Time Out* in 1978, Spielberg elaborated on his view of *Duel*'s protagonist:

---

[26] Interestingly, Muzzio and Halper categorize *E.T.* and *Poltergeist* as "suburban-set" films, which they define as "movies [that] could have been set elsewhere, usually in a conventional small town, without much difficulty" (547). While one could imagine both *E.T.* and *Poltergeist* being set in small towns, their setting in the suburbs is so crucial to their overall effect that they would have turned into much different films had they been set elsewhere, hence my contention that that they are "suburban-centered."

The hero of "Duel" is typical of that lower middle-class American who's insulated by suburban modernisation. It begins on Sunday: you take your car to be washed. You have to drive it but it's only a block away. And, as the car's being washed, you go next door with the kids and you buy them ice-cream at the Dairy Queen and then you have lunch at the plastic McDonald's with seven zillion hamburgers sold. And then you go off to the games room and you play the quarter games: the Tank and the Pong and Flim-Flam. And by that time you go back and your car's all dry and ready to go and you get into the car and you drive to the Magic Mountain plastic amusement park and you spend the day there eating junk food. Afterwards you drive home, stopping at all the red lights, and the wife is waiting with dinner on. And you have instant potatoes and eggs without cholesterol, because they're artificial—and you sit down and you turn on the television set, which has become the reality as opposed to the fantasy this man has lived with that entire day. And you watch the primetime, which is pabulum and nothing more than watching a night-light. And you see the news at the end of that, which you don't want to listen to because it doesn't conform to the reality you've just been through primetime with. And at the end of all that you go to sleep and you dream about making enough money to support weekend America.

This is the kind of man portrayed in "Duel." And a man like that never expects to be challenged by anything more than his television set breaking down and having to call the repair man.[27]

There are several notable elements in this passage, particularly Spielberg's use of the second person, which collapses the reader and David Mann, implicating both in his view of suburban life. The description is littered with allusions to the primary criticisms of suburbia, namely its inauthenticity (reflected in the McDonald's and Magic Mountain being "plastic" and the instant potatoes and eggs being "artificial") and conformity (the perceived need to keep the car clean and be a good citizen by stopping at all the red lights). His description of prime time television as "pabulum" that works together with the "fantasy" of suburban existence to insulate us from the harsh realities of the world and the explicit statement regarding the man being "insulated by suburban modernization" connects with Spielberg's comments in a later interview from June 1982,[28] in which he refers to the "anesthetic of suburbia," implying that suburban existence is, in some way,

---

[27] Dave Pirie, "A Prodigy Zooms In," 105.
[28] Michael Sragow, "A Conversation With Steven Spielberg," in *Steven Spielberg Interviews*, Lester D. Friedman and Brent Notbohn (eds) (Jackson: University Press of Mississippi, 2000).

not "real life." Everything Spielberg describes in "weekend America" is a mass-produced commodity of consumer culture, from the car that needs to be washed, to the Dairy Queen, to the junk food at Magic Mountain, to the "seven zillion" McDonald's hamburgers and the instant dinner at home. And, most importantly, Spielberg ends his description on the bittersweet notion that such a life is both within reach and yet constantly in danger of being lost, hence the dreams of "making enough money to support weekend America." Suburbia is thus both dream and nightmare, freedom and imprisonment.

This passage from Pirie's interview, which the author describes as displaying "unexpected penetration about the film's implications,"[29] has been reprinted in several essays and books about Spielberg. In his book *Spielberg's America*, Frederick Wasser uses it as evidence of Spielberg's increased political sensibility in the late 1970s. When *Duel* played in Italy, Spielberg refused to agree with Italian critics that the film was a metaphorical depiction of the conflict between the American upper class and working class, instead arguing that "he intended the film as an 'indictment of machines' and a fight for survival between man and machine-made danger."[30] While Wasser contends that Spielberg was "not overtly political as the term was understood at the time," his views changed over the years, and by 1978 "he was fully capable of his own bitter class-oriented interpretation of *Duel*."[31] However, Wasser also notes that Spielberg's view of suburbia was still conflicted: "Was he describing a man trapped or a man who has embraced his limited fate?"[32] Similarly, Chris Auty reprinted the "weekend America" passage in his essay "The Complete Spielberg?" as evidence of his argument that "the theme of his work is not primarily the story of Everyman's escape into the never-never. It is suburban life in all its contradictions, as a kind of mysterious lake of social and libidinal possibilities which have no direction *in themselves*."[33]

For Andrew Britton, on the other hand, Spielberg's remarks about David Mann, regardless of their apparent critical intention, are indicative of his collusion with the suburban ideal and subsequent inability to escape its hegemonic allure. He chastises Spielberg for his failure to demonstrate in his depictions of modern suburbia the complex interweaving of astringency and compassion seen in Douglas Sirk's melodramas, instead falling prey to a shallow gesturing toward suburbia's limitations and flaws, a position that is undermined in his films by plots revolving around either the need to defend

---

[29] Pirie, "A Prodigy Zooms In," 105.
[30] "Spielberg Ducks Politics," *Variety*, September 12, 1973; see also Wasser, *Steven Spielberg's America*, 52.
[31] Wasser, *Steven Spielberg's America*, 52–3.
[32] Ibid., 53.
[33] Chris Auty, "The Complete Spielberg?," *Sight & Sound*, Autumn 1982, 277.

"weekend America" against the intrusion of something abjectly evil, as in *Duel*, *Jaws*, and *Poltergeist*, or the arrival of a redeemer, as in *E.T* and "Kick the Can," Spielberg's segment in the omnibus film *Twilight Zone: The Movie* (1983). As Britton puts it, the intervention of either the "Power of Evil" or the "Power of Good ... demonstrate[s] that the banality and oppressiveness of weekend America are really something else, and that the world in which one feels trapped and from which one wishes to escape are worth having and fighting for after all."[34]

While Britton accurately captures the paradox of Spielberg's depiction of suburbia, his reading is limited by his own political perspective, which does not allow for any sense of contradiction or complexity, despite his allusion to Sirk's "complex poise."[35] Rather, in line with the progressive post-war intellectuals of the 1950s and 1960s, Britton sees no value in suburbia whatsoever and simply wants to see it torn down, literally and figuratively, and replaced with something else—an alternative that he argues Spielberg is incapable of envisioning.[36] There is no room for contradiction when Britton writes that "there is something *appallingly wrong* with 'weekend America' and ... life lived in this way is *banal and deforming*" and later describes it as "monstrous."[37] Therefore, in Britton's view, Spielberg's films are doomed to fail by virtue of the simple fact that they recognize and attempt to deal with both the good and the bad, the virtues and failings of suburban life. Or, as Chris Auty puts it, "This is Eden on the eve of the Fall. To the child it is a paradise of play, the largest Amusement Park ever built. To the adult it is a treadmill of prosperity, an endlessly incomplete dream of 'freedom'. Spielberg's films track back and forth across this divide between the two views, in a place without a name that is, subjectively, either heaven or hell."[38]

The suburban trilogy

Each film in Spielberg's suburban trilogy tells the story of ordinary characters whose lives in "weekend America" are rocked by some kind of fantastical or supernatural intrusion. In *Close Encounters*, Roy Neary (Richard Dreyfuss),

---

[34] Andrew Britton, "Blissing Out: The Politics of Reaganite Entertainment," *Movie* (Winter 1986): 35.
[35] Ibid.
[36] See also Robert Kolker, *A Cinema of Loneliness*, 4th edn (New York: Oxford University Press, 2011); Robin Wood, *Hollywood From Vietnam to Reagan* (New York: Columbia University Press, 1986).
[37] Britton, "Blissing Out," 35–6 (my emphasis).
[38] Auty, "The Complete Spielberg?," 277.

a 30-something husband and father in Muncie, Indiana, who works as a technician for the local power company, becomes obsessed with strange visions and five musical notes after he sees several UFOs one night, as do Jillian Guiler (Melinda Dillon), a young mother, and her three-year-old son Barry (Cary Guffey). In *E.T.*, ten-year-old Elliott (Henry Thomas), the middle child of a broken suburban family in California, befriends a gentle alien creature who has been stranded on Earth. And in *Poltergeist*, the Freelings, a suburban California family headed by father Steve (Craig T. Nelson) and mother Diane (JoBeth Williams), endure a violent haunting by poltergeists who are intent on kidnapping their youngest child. Both separately and together, these three films are particularly illuminating because Spielberg was more deeply involved in their initial creation than he had been on his previous films (*Duel*, *The Sugarland Express*, and *Jaws*), all of which were pre-existing projects he was hired to direct, leaving him with only minimal input on the screenplay.

Close Encounters of the Third Kind[39] was the first studio film Spielberg directed from his own script, and the film's ideas stretch all the way back to his high school days in Phoenix, where he wrote, directed, and shot *Firelight* (1964), a feature-length 8mm film about scientists investigating UFO abductions around the fictional town of Freeport, Arizona. *Close Encounters* is, in many ways, a big-budget, studio-produced reimagining of his adolescent sci-fi epic, something that he had hoped would happen since 1964 when he envisioned *Firelight* as a calling card that would provide him entrance to the world of professional filmmaking.[40] Spielberg was 17 years old when he made

---

[39] There are three separate versions of *Close Encounters of the Third Kind*: the original 1977 theatrical version; the 1980 theatrical Special Edition, which both deleted footage from the original theatrical version and added new footage (including a missing battleship discovered in the Gobi Desert and shots inside the alien mother ship at the end); and the 2001 Director's Cut, which was released on DVD and later on Blu-ray and kept all of the new footage added to the Special Edition except the interior of the mother ship (which Spielberg had never wanted to show and only shot as a concession to Columbia Pictures so they would fund the "Special Edition") while also restoring some of the footage and edits from the original theatrical version. Until 1990, the Special Edition was the only version available on home video. That year, the Criterion Collection released a laser disc that offered viewers the option of programming their player to play either the original theatrical version or the Special Edition. When the Director's Cut was released on DVD in 2001, the two-disc set contained neither the 1977 nor the 1980 versions. Finally, when the film was re-released on DVD for its 30th anniversary in 2007 and subsequently on Blu-ray, all three versions were made readily available in a single package for the first time. While the differences among the three versions have been laid out in detail elsewhere (including a convenient fold-out guide in the 30th anniversary Blu-ray), for my argument the changes of significance lie in Spielberg's alterations to the film's depiction of the Neary family and Roy's obsession with the alien-implanted images in his head. These differences will be noted in the text as needed.

[40] McBride, *Steven Spielberg: A Biography*, 14. In a 1978 interview at the American Film Institute, Spielberg said, "I even made *Close Encounters* when I was sixteen [referring to *Firelight*]. It was almost the exact same story." See George Stevens Jr., *Conversations at the American Film Institute With the Great Moviemakers: The Next Generation* (New York: Alfred A. Knopf, 2012), 631.

Firelight, which cost roughly $600 to produce and was shot on a Bolex-H8 Deluxe with synchronized sound recorded with a Bolex Sonerizer, the first consumer-grade sound system. The film features numerous ingenious home-made special effects, many of which were executed in Spielberg's garage in collaboration with his father, including various optical effects, double exposures, miniatures, lap dissolves, and stop-motion animation.[41] Running 135 minutes in length, it played one night at the Little Theatre in downtown Phoenix, selling enough tickets at 75 cents a piece to turn a small profit. As Joseph McBride notes, *Firelight* plays like a primer for Spielberg's recurring thematics, especially as embodied in his suburban trilogy. It "introduces the themes of supernatural intruders, suburban alienation and escape, broken families and abducted children, scientific adventure, and spiritual renewal."[42]

Spielberg has often said that *E.T.* is his most personal film, especially in 1982 after he had completed *1941* (1979) and *Raiders of the Lost Ark* (1981), both of which he felt less connected to personally, even though they reveal quite a bit about his sensibilities. *E.T.*, on the other hand, came directly from his personal feelings and memories. In interviews at the time of the film's release, he described it as "a film that was inside me for many years"[43] and noted, "*E.T.* is a personal film because it's about people and personalities and relationships that I have some experience in."[44]

Spielberg claims that the actual idea for *E.T.* came to him during production on *Raiders of the Lost Ark*, when he was feeling particularly lonely:

> I remember wishing one night that I had a friend. It was like when you were a kid and had grown out of dolls or teddy bears or Winnie the Pooh, you just wanted a little voice in your mind to talk to. I began concocting this imaginary creature, partially from the guys who stepped out of the mother ship for ninety seconds in *Close Encounters* and then went back in, never to be seen again.
>
> Then I thought, what if were ten years old again—where I've sort of been for thirty-four years, anyway—and what if he needed me as much as I needed him? Wouldn't that be a great love story? So I put together the story of boy meets creature, boy loses creature, creature saves boy, boy saves creature—with the hope that they will somehow always be together, that their friendship isn't limited by nautical miles.[45]

---

[41] McBride, *Steven Spielberg: A Biography*, 102–4.
[42] Ibid., 105.
[43] Sragow, "A Conversation With Steven Spielberg," 108.
[44] Susan Royal, "Steven Spielberg in His Adventures on Earth," in *Steven Spielberg Interviews*, Lester F. Friedman and Brent Notbohm (eds) (Jackson: University Press of Mississippi, 2000), 87.
[45] Sragow, "A Conversation With Steven Spielberg," 110.

Thus, *E.T.* emerged primarily from the intersection of Spielberg's imagination and his painful emotional memories of isolation, loneliness, and childhood confusion, particularly regarding his parents' divorce when he was in high school and the overall sense of alienation he felt as a Jewish child in a largely WASPish suburban world: "*E.T.* was about the divorce of my parents, how I felt when my parents broke up."[46] However, unlike *Close Encounters*, Spielberg's name does not appear on the screenwriting credits, even for story origination. Rather, sole screenwriting credit was given to Melissa Mathison, with whom he discussed his ideas on the set of *Raiders of the Lost Ark* (Mathison, who had previously written *The Black Stallion* [1979], was dating *Raiders* star Harrison Ford at the time). She was able to take Spielberg's general ideas and work them into a feature-length screenplay. In her review of the film, Pauline Kael even suggested that "Mathison could see what [Spielberg] needed more deeply than he could himself, and could devise a complete structure that would hold his feelings in balance."[47]

E.T. also had roots in another film project tentatively titled *Night Skies*,[48] on which Spielberg had been collaborating with writer/director John Sayles. Spielberg's impetus for developing the story came primarily from his desire to keep Columbia Pictures from making a sequel to *Close Encounters* without his involvement, as Universal had done with *Jaws 2* (1978). Spielberg derived the plot of *Night Skies* from the infamous "Kelly–Hopkinsville encounter," a 1955 incident in which members of a rural Kentucky farm family reported contact with three-and-a-half-foot aliens around their house. From Spielberg's original treatment, Sayles wrote a single 100-page draft, which featured five aliens terrorizing a farm family that included an autistic son. The leader of the aliens, named Scar in homage to the Comanche warrior in John Ford's *The Searchers* (1956), is contrasted with Buddy, one of the more benign aliens who is left behind at the end of the film after he befriends the autistic son. The idea of a gentle alien stranded on Earth befriending a human child was the only element of *Night Skies* that survived once the project was shelved, although one of the film's ideas, in which the malevolent aliens could kill something by simply touching it with one of their long, bony fingers, was inverted in *E.T.* into a healing touch.

While *E.T.* sprang from a complex well of both conflicted emotional memories about childhood pain and wishful desires for healing and

---

[46] Wayne Maser, "The Long Voyage Home: Steven Spielberg's Film, *Schindler's List*," *Harper's Bazaar*, February 1994.
[47] Kael, "The Pure and the Impure," 119.
[48] The original title of *Night Skies* had been *Watch the Skies*, an homage to both the final line of dialogue in *The Thing From Another World* (1951) and Spielberg's appropriation of that dialogue in *Close Encounters*.

companionship, *Poltergeist* emerged entirely out of Spielberg's darker sensibilities. While he described *E.T.* as coming "directly from my childhood fantasies,"[49] *Poltergeist* sprang directly from his childhood nightmares. There are several specific moments in the film that derive explicitly from Spielberg's personal childhood fears, and it is not incidental that they are all directed at Robbie (Oliver Robbins), the Freelings' preteen son and only boy. The scene in which an ominous tree outside Robbie's window comes to life and tries to devour him was inspired by a tall, spindly maple tree illuminated by a streetlight that stood just outside Spielberg's home in Haddonfield Township and "haunted" him at night.[50] Similarly, the scene in which Robbie is disturbed by the presence of a leering clown doll that sits at the end of his bed and eventually comes to life and attempts to strangle him has roots in Spielberg's childhood fear of clowns.[51] Clowns were only one part of an extensive list of fears and phobias that gripped the filmmaker as a child, which included the fear of monsters living under his bed and in his closet and concerns that the stress fractures in the plaster above his closet door were caused by something lurking in the ceiling.[52] As a child, Spielberg began exorcising his fears by spinning them into elaborate horror stories that he told his younger sisters, friends, and neighbors, and *Poltergeist* can be seen as the most elaborate of them all.

The exact nature of Spielberg's involvement in *Poltergeist* and how much of the film can be attributed to him has long been in dispute and will likely never be fully resolved. Spielberg is credited as co-producer along with Frank Marshall; first screenwriter, followed by Michael Grais and Mark Victor; and story originator. However, Spielberg hired Tobe Hooper, best known for helming the cult hit *The Texas Chain Saw Massacre* (1974), to direct the film, even though Spielberg was on set virtually every day of the production and, to many of the crew members, seemed to be as involved with the film's direction, if not more so, than Hooper. Rumors flew throughout the film's production that Spielberg was functionally acting as the film's director, culminating in a lengthy article by Dale Pollock in the May 24, 1982, issue of the *Los Angeles Times*, a full two weeks before the film's June 4 theatrical release. Pollock's interviews with several people involved in the production seemed to verify the rumor that Spielberg was effectively in charge of the film. Marshall confirmed that Spielberg "did the design for every story board,"[53] which correlates with the creative process Spielberg favored as a director when

---

[49] Royal, "Steven Spielberg in His Adventures on Earth," 87.
[50] McBride, *Steven Spielberg: A Biography*, 51.
[51] Ibid., 53.
[52] Ibid., 51–2.
[53] Dale Pollock, "*Poltergeist*: Whose Film Is It?," *Los Angeles Times*, May 24, 1982, G1.

designing his films prior to *E.T.*, although Hooper is quoted as claiming credit for half of them. In addition to designing the storyboards, Spielberg also noted that "he was involved in all the camera setups and the designing of specific shots."[54] In the same article, Willie Hunt, a production executive who supervised *Poltergeist* for MGM, is quoted as saying that, while Hooper directed the film, "Steven was *the* creative force in my opinion; his stamp is on the film, even though there was a good, solid, competent director there." At the time, Spielberg readily took credit for much of the film, saying, "[*Poltergeist*] derived from *my* imagination and *my* experiences, and it came out of *my* typewriter."[55]

The advertising campaign by MGM, the film's distributor, added to the confusion by overtly stressing Spielberg's name value and contributions in both print ads and theatrical trailers while downplaying Hooper's.[56] Thus, the reception of *Poltergeist* by both audiences and critics was shaped to emphasize the view that it was "a Spielberg film." In his review in the *Washington Post*, Gary Arnold noted that "The premise and the technique of systematically juxtaposing comic and scary touches may be easily recognized as Spielberg's trademarks. The suburban setting in 'Poltergeist' and the upcoming 'E.T.,' an acknowledged Spielberg credit, are obviously similar and

---

[54] Ibid.

[55] Ibid.

[56] The film's teaser poster is telling. A stark, monochromatic design that is dominated primarily by text above a black-and-white image of the suburban neighborhood depicted in the film, it blatantly pushes the idea that Spielberg is the film's true author with the following paragraphs, which take up the top third of the poster and are designed to catch the eye with a large drop cap:

> Steven Spielberg has been called the American screen's master story-teller. From the thrashing terror of "Jaws" to the awesome spectacle of "Close Encounters of the Third Kind" to the globe-trotting adventure of "Raiders of the Lost Ark," he has delighted, mystified and scared more audiences ... more imaginatively ... than any filmmaker of our time.
>
> As producer and co-author of "Poltergeist," Spielberg is joined by co-producer Frank Marshall, with whom he made "Raiders of the Lost Ark," co-authors Michael Grais and Mark Victor, director Tobe Hooper, and the special effects wizardry of Oscar winner Richard Edlund ("Star Wars") and Industrial Light and Magic.

Not only is Spielberg and his previous films made the primary emphasis of the text, but Hooper, the film's director, is reduced to one of several collaborators who "joined" him on the film, ranked fourth behind the co-producer and two co-writers. The minimizing of Hooper's contribution to the film reached its nadir with the film's theatrical trailer, which opens with a title card reading "A Steven Spielberg Production" and ends with Spielberg's production credit in font twice the size of Hooper's director credit, which violated a section of the 1981 Director's Guild of America Basic Agreement regarding the size of a director's credit in the trailer, resulting in a $15,000 fine for MGM. See "MGM Is Ordered to Pay $15,000 to the Directors Guild of America and to Director Tobe Hooper for Violating Guild Credit Size Requirements in Trailer Advertising for 'Poltergeist,'" Entertainment Law Reporter, August 1, 1982.

identifiable as his characteristic social terrain."⁵⁷ Pauline Kael was even more direct in her review, asserting Spielberg's dominance of the film and noting that he wrote the initial story, shared screenwriting credit, produced the film, storyboarded it, supervised the final edit, and "took over [direction] in considerable part," thus leading her to conclude that, "Whatever the credits say, [Spielberg] was certainly the guiding intelligence of 'Poltergeist.'"⁵⁸

As a result, the idea that Spielberg was largely responsible for the look and feel of *Poltergeist* has long calcified in most people's minds. Film scholar Warren Buckland, however, took a different approach to the issue by examining the film using a version of the statistical style analysis popularized by Shakespeare scholar Donald Foster to attribute the anonymous novel *Primary Colors* to journalist Joe Klein and the "Unabomber Manifesto" to Theodore Kaczynski. Using shot-by-shot analysis, Buckland compared compositional factors and editing patterns in *Poltergeist* to a selection of films unproblematically attributed to Spielberg (*E.T.* and *Jurassic Park*) and Hooper (*'Salem's Lot* and *The Funhouse*). While Buckland concedes that such an analysis is speculative and can never be absolutely certain,⁵⁹ he concludes that the film is more reflective of Hooper's work in terms of camera movement, shot scale, and shot duration, while it is more reflective of Spielberg's work in terms of camera position (particularly the prevalence of low camera angle shots) and duration of large-scale shots. Buckland argues, contrary to prevailing wisdom, that "Hooper *did* demonstrate a sufficient amount of control over the style of *Poltergeist*, at least in the preproduction and production stages" and, as a result, it should be considered a film directed by Hooper, not Spielberg.⁶⁰

Nevertheless, even if the question of who truly directed *Poltergeist* is never fully answered, Spielberg was clearly an important creative force in shaping the film out of ideas that originated with him, which more than justifies its inclusion alongside *Close Encounters* and *E.T.* as one of his most important and revealing films.

Themes in the suburban trilogy

As noted earlier, it is readily apparent that *Close Encounters of the Third Kind*, *E.T.*, and *Poltergeist* have a great deal in common, particularly with

---

⁵⁷Gary Arnold, "Horror With the Spielberg Touch," *Washington Post*, June 4, 1982, D1.
⁵⁸Kael, "The Pure and the Impure," 122.
⁵⁹Warren Buckland, *Directed by Steven Spielberg: Poetics of the Contemporary Hollywood Blockbuster* (New York: Continuum, 2006), 157–8.
⁶⁰Ibid., 167.

regard to their suburban settings, and looking at them together offers a useful way of examining the conflicts and contradictions in Spielberg's view of contemporary suburban existence. Despite belonging to the fantastical genres of science fiction and horror, the films in the suburban trilogy are most intriguing in the way they reflect and comment on the lived realities of American suburban family life in the late 1970s and early 1980s. While it may be that the fantastical elements of the films—the first appearance of the mother ship in *Close Encounters*, the soaring bike ride through the sky in *E.T.*, the ghostly apparitions drifting down the staircase in *Poltergeist*, all brought to life with then-state-of-the-art visual and sound effects—are what first grab the viewer, repeated viewings of the films increasingly draw our attention to Spielberg's preoccupation with the importance of the ordinary world and the terrors involved when it is invaded by outside forces.

For Spielberg, the suburbs represent an ordinary "norm," a kind of fundamental benchmark of middle-American existence that is then threatened or challenged by an otherworldly force, whether it be aliens or ghosts. This is one of the primary reasons why his films appeal so broadly to the mainstream moviegoing public. Yet, there is a surprising perversity to Spielberg's focus on middle America because, if there is an overriding theme in his depictions of suburbia, it is that the environment's sense of safety, its most prized aspect, is largely illusory. Roy Neary cannot escape his alien-implanted obsession over a mountain within the confines of his home, and Jillian Guiler is unable to save Barry from alien abduction in her kitchen; Elliott and his family cannot stop an intrusion by federal agents into their home to forcibly take E.T. away from them; and the Freeling family has their house literally taken from them by malevolent spirits and turned into a prison for their youngest daughter. The suburban life, as it turns out, is immensely vulnerable, and the films leave us with an incomplete sense of closure that resolves in some way the supernatural element, but leaves questions about family and ordinary life curiously open-ended. Thus, far from "re-creat[ing] Spielberg's boyhood home in suburbia and attempt[ing] to overcome the destruction of that idyllic experience,"[61] *Close Encounters*, *E.T.*, and *Poltergeist* are constantly torn between recognizing and celebrating the everyday comforts of middle-American existence and the sadness, loneliness, isolation, and sense of failure that often hides behind the otherwise serene façade of ranch houses, well-manicured yards, and white picket fences.

---

[61] Gordon, *Empire of Dreams*, 56.

Portraits of suburbia

The specific manner in which Spielberg visually presents the suburban world in his films is crucial for understanding their complex dialectic between the everyday and the otherworldly. Unlike many of the suburban-set films of the 1950s and 1960s, as well as the vast majority of television sitcoms from that era, *Close Encounters of the Third Kind*, *E.T.*, and *Poltergeist* were all shot on location in actual neighborhoods, rather than on studio back lots, which lends the films a palpable sense of realism in their depictions of the suburban milieu.

Although *Close Encounters* was actually shot in Mobile, Alabama, a location chosen because it offered an airplane hangar large enough for the massive indoor set needed for the film's climax, much of the story ostensibly takes place in Muncie, Indiana, which was famously used under the telling pseudonym "Middletown" as the site of a series of sociological studies on the typical small American city in the 1920s and 1930s and then again in the early 1980s.[62] Both *E.T.* and *Poltergeist* take place in unnamed southern California suburban communities that look similar enough that the two films could very well be taking place on different streets in the same neighborhood.[63] The locations of all three films roughly correspond with Spielberg's own suburban upbringing, with the flat, one-story ranch-house-dominated neighborhood in *Close Encounters* visually reminiscent of the neighborhood in Phoenix where he lived from age 10 to 16, while the *E.T.* and *Poltergeist* neighborhoods, with their winding streets, modern-design two-story homes, and hilly geography, look similar to the Saratoga neighborhood where he spent his senior year in high school.

These suburban settings are established at some point in each film with a high-angle wide shot[64] that emphasizes the Levittown-esque geometrical

---

[62] The first study, published in 1929 as *Middletown: A Study in Contemporary American Culture*, was the result of work by a team of sociologists led by Robert and Helen Lynd. In 1937 the same team published *Middletown in Transition: A Study in Cultural Conflicts*, which studied the community during the Depression. More than 40 years later, the National Science Foundation conducted another major study resulting in the publication of two books, *Middletown Families* (1982) and *All Faithful People* (1983), both authored by Theodore Caplow.

[63] The exterior work on *E.T.* was shot in a new housing development in Tujunga, a small, semi-rural community north-east of Burbank at the foot of the San Gabriel Mountains. Exterior work in *Poltergeist* was done at two locations: The house itself is located in a neighborhood in Simi Valley, a bedroom community nestled beneath the Santa Susana Mountain range, while establishing shots of the neighborhood were done in Agoura Hills, a small, affluent community about 20 miles south-east in the eastern Conejo Valley between the Simi Hills and the Santa Monica Mountains.

[64] This was not initially the case with *Close Encounters of the Third Kind*. In the original theatrical version, Spielberg established the Neary household with an interior scene, although when he re-edited the film for the 1980 Special Edition, he added a preliminary aerial shot of the neighborhood.

conformity of the streets and the arrangement of the houses, all of which are of similar shapes and sizes. They are also largely devoid of color. The establishing shot in *Close Encounters* takes place at night, so the houses are all reduced to a grid of grayish rectangles punctuated with lighted windows, while the neighborhoods in *E.T.* and *Poltergeist* are dominated by stucco façades of various shades of white, brown, and tan. The resulting effect is one of conformity and bland homogenization, the very essence of the post-war intellectual critiques of suburbia and its overly planned spaces and lack of heterogeneity and spontaneous cultural production. However, the blandness also produces a sense of safety, as if the precision of the street layout and conformity of the housing designs will ward off anything dangerous, criminal, or otherwise threatening.

Yet, Spielberg's establishment of the suburban milieu is also tinged with conflicting elements of menace and threat that, in foreshadowing the horrific invasions yet to come, suggest that suburban safety is just a constructed illusion. Given that it is a horror film, it is not surprising that we see this most clearly in the establishing shots of the neighborhood in *Poltergeist*, which follows a brief opening sequence that takes place inside the Freeling house. In the opening sequence, the camera follows the family dog, a big, shaggy Golden Retriever, as he makes his way around the house scavenging for food, eventually waking five-year-old Carol Anne (Heather O'Rourke) in the process. As if in a trance, she is drawn downstairs to the flickering light of the static-filled television screen (an anachronism in the post-broadcast world of 24-hour cable and satellite TV). She kneels down in front of the TV and begins loudly replying to voices she hears emanating from it. A simple sequence that functions to both introduce us to the Freeling family and establish the presence of something otherworldly, the sequence's overall effect is one of creepy defamiliarization of the ordinary suburban home, as the bluish strobe-like effect of the TV static renders the otherwise mundane environment of the living room both ghostly and disorienting. The family dog's search for food throughout the house has a similar effect, as it undercuts the blissful serenity of the suburban family slumbering away by emphasizing their vulnerability while asleep in bed, a location in which family members will be attacked again and again by the poltergeists throughout the film.[65]

We then cut to the next morning with a wide shot of a sloping hill crested by two gnarled, skeletal trees standing in stark contrast to the open blue sky behind them—a metonymic image that is simultaneously gothic and pastoral. The visual conflict in the image is then compounded with the

---

[65] Three years earlier, *The Amityville Horror* (1979) had begun with a deranged young man shooting and killing his entire family while they slept.

FIGURE 1.1 Weekend in America. *The high-angle establishing shots of the neighborhoods in* Close Encounters of the Third Kind *(top),* E.T. *(middle), and* Poltergeist *(bottom) create a sense of conformity, bland homogenization, and safety. (Digital Frame Enlargement)*

opening strains of Jerry Goldsmith's theme music, whose soft, almost lullaby-like quality underscores the camera movement as it pans to the right, revealing the suburban neighborhood at the base of the hill as the "A STEVEN SPIELBERG PRODUCTION" credit fills the middle of the screen. The camera continues panning right, revealing the extensiveness of the neighborhood, and is followed by several more shots of the environment, some static, some panning, while the rest of the credits fade in and out. The use of a telephoto lens flattens the space and exaggerates the tightness of the neighborhood layout, giving the impression of similar-looking houses stacked on top of each other. The homogeneity of the houses themselves is visually re-emphasized later in the film when a shot inside the Freelings's kitchen dissolves into a perfectly aligned shot of the exact same kitchen in a model home that Steve is showing to potential buyers. Steve's salesmanship further cements the appeal of suburbia's comforting sense of similarity, as he tells the buyers how they soon won't be able to distinguish among the neighborhood's different "phases" and how they have a saying "The grass grows greener on every side." The buyer confirms Steve's comments by saying to his wife, "Honey, I can't tell one house from the other."

Returning to the opening shots of the neighborhood, the seemingly benign homogeneity of the area is interrupted only by the repeated and seemingly out-of-place presence of large skeletal trees, one of which almost completely fills the frame at one point as the camera pans past it and another of which stands ominously in the middle of a street, towering dramatically over all of the houses and the tiny figures of neighborhood kids riding their bikes. The trees demand attention graphically because their enormous size, almost blackish color, and twisted shapes contrast sharply against the light colors and straight lines of the angular houses, yards, light poles, and sidewalks. The *Poltergeist* neighborhood, like many new suburban developments, was built on an open, largely treeless space that the viewer later learns used to be a cemetery (rather than coming up from a potato field, as Levittown and Spielberg's neighborhood in Haddon Township did, it has come up from the grave). Thus, the trees are relics, leftover bits of nature in the raw that could be said to persist defiantly amid the human construction around them except that they were purposefully left to stand by the construction company, perhaps in a bid to make the environment seem more "natural."

Like both *Close Encounters* and *Poltergeist*, *E.T.* begins at night, and the first glimpse we get of its suburban environs is from the top of a surrounding mountain looking down at an abstract geometrical grid of lights that signify civilization, in contrast to the primeval forest where E.T. is accidentally abandoned. The first time we see Elliott's house is that same night, in a long shot that captures the house in its entirety sitting against the black of night,

FIGURE 1.2 The gothic and the pastoral. *The out-of-place presence of large, skeletal trees interrupt the seemingly benign nature of the neighborhood in* Poltergeist *and foreshadow the revelation that it has been constructed on top of a cemetery. (Digital Frame Enlargement)*

looking forlorn and isolated, the security light above the garage illuminating nothing but the empty concrete of the large, steep driveway leading up from the street. We see the neighborhood as a whole the following morning as Elliott rides his bike out of the garage and down a sloping, unpaved street that winds along the side of a barren hillside.[66] The juxtaposition of the hill on the right-hand side of the screen and the developed houses below on the left-hand side establishes the rural–urban nature of the newly built neighborhood, just recently carved out of the hilly terrain, while also re-emphasizing the isolation of Elliott's house, which underscores the film's depiction of Elliott's family as broken and hurting.

Interior domestic spaces in the suburban trilogy are just as charged with meaning, especially since it is in these spaces that the family dynamics

---

[66]The hillside in this shot is clearly a matte painting, although the neighborhood around it is real.

play out. In a word, the homes in *Close Encounters*, *E.T.*, and *Poltergeist* are *messy*. They are truly lived-in spaces whose clutter and chaos reflect the busy schedules, hectic activities, and frequent disconnect among the family members living there. Television sets are always turned on, day or night; clothes haven't been put away; toys are strewn about; dishes haven't been washed; and the decorative knick-knacks, picture frames, and lamps that adorn various shelves and tabletops are in constant competition for space with the detritus of daily living (empty soda cans, opened magazines and newspapers, board games, and so forth). This is particularly true of the Neary house in *Close Encounters*, which is clearly lower middle class with its odd assortment of mismatched furniture and wallpaper and reappropriation of non-domestic objects, such as Roy's use of plastic crates hung on the living room walls to create makeshift shelving. The Neary home is extremely cluttered, partially because Roy has taken over much of the living room with his model train set, which pushes everything else to the margins. Thus, even though the houses are relatively large with spacious rooms, particularly in *E.T.* and *Poltergeist*, there is still a sense of claustrophobia, as if the rooms are closing in with the plastic junk of "weekend America."

Fractured, shattered, and threatened families

In addition to providing the *mise-en-scène* with a sense of lived-in realism, the cluttered interior spaces also visually reinforce the fractured, fragmented, and stressed nature of the traditional nuclear families at the heart of all three films. While the Neary family in *Close Encounters* is fully intact at the beginning of the film, it is immediately clear that there is a great deal of tension among the family members—not just between Roy and his wife Ronnie (Terri Garr), but also between Roy and his three children. The family in *E.T.*, on the other hand, has already been broken, with the unseen absent father having deserted them for another woman, leaving behind his wife, Mary (Dee Wallace), and three children. The family in *Poltergeist* is the strongest in terms of stability, yet they are summarily torn apart, rather than drawn together, by the ghostly invasion of their home. In all three films, the supernatural visitation serves primarily to separate family members: Roy is drawn away from his family by the aliens, who also abduct Barry; friendship with E.T. draws Elliott and his siblings, older brother Michael (Robert MacNaughton) and younger sister Gertie (Drew Barrymore), together while further isolating their lonely and newly single mother who is too consumed with "holding it together" to even realize that her children are hiding an alien right under her nose; and the Freelings suffer both abduction and general torment by the ghosts, leaving them visibly defeated at the end of the film as they stumble into an uncertain future.

The familial portraits can be usefully summarized by comparing and contrasting scenes that take place in the home during the opening 20 minutes of each film. The first family scene in *Close Encounters*, though scripted and shot during the initial production, was not part of the 1977 theatrical release, but was added to the 1980 Special Edition. Its inclusion makes a substantial difference to the film's tone, as it clearly establishes from the outset that the Neary family is wracked with tensions, which are then exacerbated by Roy's growing obsession with his UFO sighting and subsequent visions of a mountain, whereas in the original version his obsession feels like an intrusion into an otherwise normal family. The scene in question, which first introduces us to the Neary family, takes place largely in the living room and adjoining breakfast nook. Spielberg composes the scene in depth as a means of keeping multiple family members simultaneously in frame to emphasize their emotional disconnection despite their physical proximity. The overall tone of the scene is reflected in its dim, yet harsh lighting, which creates pools of light and dark and casts multiple shadows throughout the space, making it feel even more cluttered and claustrophobic.

The scene opens with Roy's eight-year-old son Brad (Shawn Bishop) asking him for help with his math homework while Roy works on his elaborate model train set, which covers a huge table in the middle of the living room and effectively dominates the space. Rather than playing the role of the helpful father, Roy is reluctant to assist his son, responding sarcastically, "That's why I graduated. So I don't have to do problems." When he does finally agree to help him, he uses his train set to create a fractional math problem, but offers Brad no explanation for how to solve it and creates unneeded time pressure that renders his efforts completely useless.

Roy also demonstrates an unconscious aggression toward his children, which is revealed in the repeated use of threats of violence against them. Even though it is clear that he doesn't mean to follow through with the threats, their repetition suggests an underlying hostility that he is unable to recognize and therefore deal with. When Brad rebukes Roy's suggestion that the family go see the re-release of Disney's *Pinocchio* at the local theater, he asks him how old he is, and when Brad says he is eight, Roy replies, "You wanna be nine? Then you're going to see *Pinocchio* tomorrow night." Ronnie calls him out on his inappropriate parenting tactics, the second time in this scene that she criticizes him in some way, following her complaint that his "stuff" has "taken over" her breakfast table. Roy brushes her off by saying he wasn't serious. However, less than a minute later he viscerally explodes at Toby (Justin Dreyfuss), his younger son, who has been standing in a playpen in the background repeatedly smashing a plastic doll against the railing: "Toby! You are close to death! Come out here!" His verbal explosion interrupts his capitulation to Ronnie about his behavior toward Brad—"I'm wrong. I'm wrong Roy"—thus connecting Roy's tensions with his children and tensions with his wife and emphasizing his sense of domestic entrapment. It is clear, in just these few minutes, that Roy is not a particularly happy or satisfied family man and that his emotional connection with his family is already deeply fractured.

The family dinner sequence in *E.T.*, which follows Elliott's first sighting of the eponymous extra-terrestrial behind the house, is similar visually and tonally to the scene in *Close Encounters* in the way it focuses on the various tensions among family members, although now we are seeing a family that is not in the process of fracturing, but is rather already broken. It opens with a wide shot from the corner of the living room looking into the kitchen where the family is eating dinner. Although the architectural design of the interior space is "open concept," meaning the rooms are not separated by walls, the space is still clearly divided and broken up by the placement of heavy furniture (particularly an enormous L-shaped couch), a built-in booth that separates the kitchen from the dining room and the living room, and the pools of light and dark created by two hanging lights and a table lamp. While the family is together at the dinner table—the epitome of middle-American familial "quality time"—this initial shot immediately creates a sense of loneliness and isolation. The characters are minimized in the frame by the camera distance, isolated under a pool of light, and visually dwarfed by their environment. They look small and sad.

The conversation at the table is already tense because it revolves around the rest of the family's not believing Elliott's claim that he saw a "goblin" in the field behind their house the previous night. Elliott is sulking and feeling frustrated, and when Michael ribs him by suggesting that he dress as a goblin for Halloween and proposing that maybe he saw an elf or a leprechaun, Elliott stands up and yells, "It wasn't anything like that, penis breath!" Elliott's awkwardly vulgar name-calling has a comical effect, one that his mother can't help but recognize as she laughs in surprise before regaining her composure and telling him to sit down. Yet, Elliott's name-calling is laced with real anger and resentment, which also comes out in his follow-up remark aimed at Mary: "Dad would believe me." It is a mean jab at his mother that he turns into an even sharper barb when he replies to her suggestion that maybe he should call his father by saying, "I can't. He's in Mexico with Sally." The manner in which Elliott delivers this news makes it clear that he intends for it to hurt. When he first starts speaking, he is slumped in his seat with his head down, but with each word he raises his head up a little, cocking it almost defiantly

FIGURE 1.3 Family tensions. *The dinner sequence in* E.T., *which should be the epitome of middle-American family togetherness, instead creates a sense of loneliness and isolation, with the characters minimized in the frame by camera distance and visually dwarfed by the environment. (Digital Frame Enlargement)*

as he says "with Sally." It is a stark emotional moment, crammed with all manner of complex familial tensions that Spielberg allows to play out in the characters' faces: the pain of a newly single mother being reminded that she has been left for another woman and disempowered by her young son knowing their whereabouts while she does not; the defensive cruelty of an emotionally angry child lashing out in ways he doesn't entirely understand; and the subsequent divisiveness between siblings as Michael, old enough to recognize the emotional damage of Elliott's thoughtless remark, angrily chastises him.

The scene is also impressive for the manner in which it balances the emotional experiences of the adult in the room and the children, which belies the criticisms that Spielberg sees the world only from a child's perspective and seeks to infantilize the audience. Rather, he expresses with remarkable dramatic economy and clarity how everyone in the room is feeling and how and why those feelings are often at odds with each other: Mary's need to hold the family together and maintain some sense of composure and authority amidst her own pain (which we already saw compromised in an earlier scene where she is unable to stop Michael and his friends from going outside to investigate Elliott's claims of having encountered something in the garden shed) is at odds with Elliott's need to be taken seriously, which is at odds with Michael's need, as the eldest sibling, to play some kind of surrogate father role in the absence of their real father, even though he is emotionally ill-equipped to do so. At the end of the age spectrum, Gertie is there primarily to react to those around her, whether it be her wide-eyed surprise at Elliott's "penis breath" insult or her sadness in sensing the abrupt shift in tone after Elliott informs Mary about Dad being in Mexico with Sally.

The breakfast scene in *Poltergeist* is entirely different and plays as a kind of inverse of the scenes in both *Close Encounters* and *E.T.* Rather than emphasizing familial tensions and visual darkness, the scene is bright and lively, a poignant depiction of a generally happy family going about their morning routine. Like the *Close Encounters* scene, there is a certain amount of chaos, as is typical in a suburban kitchen on a weekday morning as Steve, the father, is tying his tie and talking on the phone while Diane feeds both the dog and the kids, who are sitting around the breakfast table spending more time talking and playing with their food than eating. In the background outside the windows, a construction crew is beginning to dig a new swimming pool. Like the *E.T.* dinner scene, the kids are giving each other a hard time and throwing insults around: Dana (Dominique Dunne), the family's 16-year-old daughter, repeatedly tells Robbie that he's "obnoxious," while Robbie tells Carol Anne that she's a "barf bag," to which she replies that he's a "doggie bag." Unlike Elliott's high-pitched "penis breath" insult, though, the name-calling in *Poltergeist* is light-hearted, little more than kids trying to one-up each other without actually hurting anyone's feelings. The only moment of tension in the scene is when an unseen force causes Robbie's milk glass to shatter, splashing milk on the table and Dana's clothes, which upsets her because she has to be at school in 20 minutes. But even this small instance of conflict is over almost as soon as it begins, suggesting that the family members are capable of dealing with each other and the little stresses of everyday life.

While these three scenes do not comprise the entirety or even the majority of family life in the three films, they are generally reflective of each film's depiction of their respective suburban families, creating a kind of spectrum. At one end we have *Poltergeist* and its representation of an ideal, happy, secure suburban family. *E.T.* stands at the other end of the spectrum, representing a family that has been fractured by divorce and is deeply stressed by divisiveness among family members and repressed emotions. In the middle we have *Close Encounters*, with its portrait of a family that is strained by internal tensions, but not yet broken. Taken out of the context of the films' larger narrative trajectories, these cinematic families are certainly interesting insofar as how they represent a cross-section of middle-American familial life in the late 1970s and early 1980s, neither confirming absolutely the ideals of the nuclear family nor giving in to the despair regarding escalating divorce rates and single parenthood that helped fuel the rise of the Moral Majority during the Reagan years. However, the state of the individual families, whether intact, broken, or in the process of breaking, is ultimately crucial to each film's fundamental meaning and emotional impact as it relates to the subsequent invasion narratives.

Physical, spiritual, and psychological invasions

In one way or another, the suburban homes in *Close Encounters*, *E.T.*, and *Poltergeist* are all invaded by external forces, which is a particularly potent and disturbing thread that binds the films together, especially given their frequent misreading as films of reassurance and wish fulfillment. The prevalence of these invasion narratives has a social corollary in that, during the years these films were being written and produced, there was significant fear among the general population that crime was rising and spreading throughout the country. No longer contained in the dangerous cities, crime was now spilling over into the suburbs.

Since the initial development of modern suburbs in the 1940s, one of their primary draws has been the sense of safety they engender, especially in comparison to the older city centers, which had substantially higher crime rates and a generally seedy reputation. And, while the suburbs maintained overall lower crime rates in comparison to urban areas over the years, the mid–1970s saw a substantial rise in suburban crime. According to the FBI's annual Uniform Crime Report, there was a continual escalation in violent crime throughout the 1960s and 1970s, peaking in 1980 before declining for the next five years.[67] In 1976, *Time* magazine reported that the suburbs were "gaining on the cities," with a 10 per cent rise in crime in 1975 over the previous year.[68] The years 1973 to 1977 saw the suburban crime rate rise 42 per cent, the rural crime rate rise 51 per cent, while the urban crime rate rose only 13 per cent. There was speculation that the increase in crime in suburban and rural areas was due to increased mobility via highways, which allowed criminals to come into suburban areas, commit crimes, and then quickly leave. In other words, the increased suburban crime was a form of invasion, an external threat descending upon what had previously been seen as a safe space.

Of course, none of the films in Spielberg's suburban trilogy have anything directly to do with crime, at least consciously. Rather, the fear of violent crime is transformed via the films' fantastical genres into supernatural invasion stories whose details, whether considered speculative or completely

---

[67] In 1960 the violent crime rate in the U.S. was 160.9; by 1970 it was 363.5; and by 1980 it was 596.6, an increase of 270 per cent (see Uniform Crime Reporting Statistics: http://www.ucrdatatool.gov (accessed March 15, 2012).
[68] "Gaining on the Cities," *Time*, September 6, 1976.

outlandish, still strike the same emotional chords that are jarred by reading about rising crime statistics in the morning newspaper. That is, the films in different ways tap into generalized human fears about the sanctity of their home being compromised, the last refuge being not a place of safety, but rather of intense vulnerability, with a particular focus on the breakdown of the perception of safety in the suburbs.

In *Close Encounters*, the invasion by aliens is both physical and psychological. Unlike the Cold War-era UFO invasion movies like *Invaders From Mars* (1953), *War of the Worlds* (1953), and *Earth vs. the Flying Saucers* (1956), the aliens in *Close Encounters* are not overtly destructive and intent on wiping out the human race. Their lack of laser cannons and other methods of mass destruction have led many commentators to describe them as "benign" and "friendly," but like the rest of the film, the aliens in *Close Encounters* are paradoxical and their actions are often inexplicable, suggesting that Spielberg has conflicted emotions regarding the prospect of intelligent alien life. After all, unlike the aliens in Robert Wise's *The Day the Earth Stood Still* (1951) or James Cameron's *The Abyss* (1989), the aliens in *Close Encounters* ultimately offer nothing to the human race outside of confirmation of their existence. The fact that *Firelight*, the 8mm teenage epic on which he based *Close Encounters*, featured more traditionally fearsome alien invaders, as did his post–9/11 version of H. G. Wells's *War of the Worlds* (2005), is further evidence that Spielberg, an admitted believer in UFOs,[69] hopes for the best, but fears the worst.

A crucial part of the alien invasion in *Close Encounters* is psychological, that is, the aliens implant images and sounds into the minds of several major characters, including Roy Neary and Jillian and Barry Guiler, without their knowledge. The purpose of this psychological invasion is to draw these characters to Devil's Tower in Wyoming, the place the aliens have chosen to land and officially communicate with the human race, although why they were selected is left unexplained. While this would seem to make Roy and the others "chosen ones," this psychological invasion is emotionally torturous (not to mention arguably unnecessary given the aliens' almost godlike capabilities), turning the characters inside out as they grapple with unfamiliar, yet obsessively compelling images and sounds that they can't get out of their heads and feel forced to replicate.

We see the effects of this psychological invasion most clearly on Roy, who becomes so obsessed with the implanted image of Devil's Tower that

---

[69] See Richard Combs, "Primal Scream: An Interview With Steven Spielberg," in *Steven Spielberg Interviews*, Lester D. Friedman and Brent Notbohm (eds) (Jackson: University Press of Mississippi, 2000).

he begins seeing it everywhere—in a handful of shaving cream, in his plate of mashed potatoes—and eventually tries to recreate it, culminating in the literal destruction of his living room as he throws uprooted plants from the yard, chicken wire, a wheelbarrow full of dirt, and a plastic garbage can through the kitchen window in order to construct a massive model of the image from his mind. The destruction of the suburban home is a potent strand throughout the suburban trilogy, visualizing in no uncertain terms the vulnerability of hearth and home. (In *E.T.*, Elliott's home is eventually encased in plastic by the government, turning it into a scientific laboratory fully cut off from the rest of the world, while the Freelings' home in *Poltergeist* is progressively damaged by the ghostly intruders before also being turned temporarily into a scientific lab for paranormal researchers and eventually destroyed altogether, sucked into oblivion by the forces that invaded it.) To exorcise his fixation, Roy must destroy his suburban existence, both literally in terms of his purposefully trashing his house to recreate the mountain in his mind, but also in terms of his relationship with Ronnie, who doesn't understand what he is going through and can't help him, no matter how hard she tries. Her ideas about going to family therapy are well meaning, but hopelessly mundane in the face of a paranormal invasion that she can't fathom.

Roy's obsession drives him further and further away from his family, essentially breaking apart what was already cracked, as demonstrated in the opening domestic scene in the Neary living room. When Roy catches himself compulsively sculpting his mashed potatoes at the dinner table and sees the frightened looks on the faces of his wife and children, he begins to cry and says in a bit of pathetically failed self-deprecation, "Well, I guess you've

FIGURE 1.4 "Something's a little strange with Dad." *In* Close Encounters of the Third Kind, *the aliens' psychological invasion of Roy Neary's (Richard Dreyfuss) mind drives him to literally destroy his suburban existence. (Digital Frame Enlargement)*

noticed something's a little strange with Dad. It's okay, though. I'm still Dad." It's a sad moment, particularly in the way Spielberg frames the shot with Roy in close-up profile on the right-hand side of the screen while the left-hand side shows Brad trying unsuccessfully to hold back tears as he watches his father losing his mind, thus inverting both spatially and tonally the scene in *Jaws* (1975) in which Martin Brody's young son quietly mimics his stressed father's every move at the dinner table, culminating in a scene of poignant bonding between father and son. The scene is also somewhat ironic, as Roy's strained assertion that he's "still Dad" is small comfort given that he had not proved to be a particularly good father prior to his alien encounter. Self-absorbed, unwilling to help Brad with his homework, impatient, and unconsciously aggressive toward his children, he was already the "bad father," albeit in a way that is aligned just enough with conventional male prerogative to not stand out unduly and therefore remain largely unrecognized, especially to Roy himself.

It is in this regard that numerous critics and scholars fatally misread the family dynamic in *Close Encounters*. Roger Neustadter suggests that the characters in the film comprise a two-tier system of the "childlike" and the "nonchildlike," with the former being idealized as "the bearers of eternal verities and immutable values,"[70] while Andrew M. Gordon argues that the characters "divide along questions of *belief*: grownups like Ronnie who treat the saucers as childishness, nonsense, or insanity, versus those who are children at heart, like Roy, and believe in magic."[71] According to Gordon, then, Roy's family, headed by "grownup" Ronnie, the symbol of "dreary domesticity," is "negatively characterized," which lets Roy off the hook when he abandons them to chase his rendezvous with the aliens and "ascend totally into the realm of the fantastic";[72] Neustadter makes a similar argument when he suggests that "All adults [in Spielberg's films] not informed by love and innocence are by implication unauthentic and sterile."[73] When Gordon describes Ronnie as "conventional and close-minded," at best, and a "bad mother" and "the evil wife-mother," at worst,[74] it dismisses her desperation as churlishness, forging all sympathy with Roy and none with Ronnie, who in reality should be the character for whom we feel. After all, she is the one who is left behind at the end of the film, deserted by her husband to raise three

---

[70] Roger Neustadter, "Phone Home: From Childhood Amnesia to the Catcher in Sci-Fi—The Transformation of Childhood in Contemporary Science Fiction Films," *Youth and Society* 20, no. 3 (1989): 234.
[71] Gordon, *Empire of Dreams*, 64.
[72] Ibid.
[73] Neustadter, "Phone Home," 234.
[74] Gordon, *Empire of Dreams*, 64.

children on her own. Ronnie is not the "bad mother," but rather a reasonable, sensible person; Roy is the "bad father," as he threatens violence against his own children, ignores them, and feeds his own narcissism, which culminates with his entering the mother ship at the end. Ronnie, in this sense, is Mary from *E.T.* before that film begins, and Mary's life is what Ronnie has to look forward to.

Readings of the film play into the idea that Roy is a screen surrogate for Spielberg himself, thus providing ample evidence of the filmmaker's simplistic celebration of childishness as a virtue—in his characters, in himself, and in his audience. Yet, such a reading rests on Roy's childishness being a virtue, and the film offers no evidence in that regard. While Dreyfuss is an appealing actor who generates the necessary sympathy for Roy's plight (otherwise the film would be completely unacceptable to mainstream audiences), his childishness is ultimately based largely in narcissism and lack of self-awareness. We see this lack in his misremembering and therefore misunderstanding of Disney's *Pinocchio*, which he describes as being about fuzzy animals and magic, conveniently ignoring the story's darker and more frightening imagery and narrative implications.[75] After all, *Pinocchio* tells the story of a wooden puppet who gets his dream to become human while all the other "bad children," who have been turned into donkeys by a slave trader and sent to work in the salt mines, are left behind and conveniently forgotten—just as Roy's family will be. In order to follow the self-centered protagonist to his dream, both *Pinocchio* and *Close Encounters* leave enormous plotlines unresolved at the end, dangling in the background and reminding us that one person's wish fulfillment does not right all wrongs or heal all wounds and may even require the sacrifice of others. And, lest we forget, Roy is not magical for being obsessed about the aliens; rather, the ideas were implanted in his head against his will. Like Pinocchio, he is a puppet.

More problematic, however, is the misuse of the term *belief* in relation to Roy and his family. The word itself tends to carry with it a special charge that endows Roy with an extraordinary quality: he believes where others are skeptical. He keeps the faith. He is strong. Like a saint, he perseveres despite all the naysaying and cynicism around him. From this perspective, trashing his house and driving his family away is a mark of nobility—his willingness to follow through on his fervent belief that is then rewarded in the climax when he alone is chosen to enter the mother ship and fly off into the cosmos.

---

[75] Spielberg was traumatized as a child by Disney films, reporting that he "came home screaming from *Snow White*" when he was eight years old and "tried to hide under the covers," which baffled his parents, who thought that "Walt Disney movies are not supposed to scare but to delight and enthrall." As Spielberg put it, "Between *Snow White*, *Fantasia*, and *Bambi*, I was a basket case of neuroses." See McBride, *Steven Spielberg: A Biography*, 63–4.

It's no wonder that the film has sustained so many religious and spiritual interpretations.

The problem, though, is that this reading fundamentally ignores what is actually happening inside Roy's mind. He does not *believe* anything, at least not of his own choice; rather, he has images and sounds forcibly implanted into his head that he never asked for and never sought. The key line of dialogue, in this regard, is spoken by Roy at a staged meeting between government officials, the news media, and all the people who have encountered the UFOs: "I didn't want to see this," he says. Roy is a reluctant protagonist, forced into a psychological connection with the aliens that quickly devolves from initial excitement and exhilaration into frustration, anger, and madness. Roy's reluctance is contrasted with the fervent desire of Claude Lacombe (François Truffaut), a French scientist who has been actively seeking the aliens, and yet, in an ironic twist, is not fully rewarded at the end. It is Roy who is taken into the mother ship, not him, as he is left behind with all the others, perhaps touched by this encounter of the third kind, but nothing more (his last words to Roy are, "Monsieur Neary, I envy you").

Roy, who asked for and sought nothing, recognizes that something is "happening to him," as he puts it, but he doesn't understand it and, more importantly, is frightened and angered by it, turning him into a boiling cauldron of compulsiveness and self-loathing. As he tells his family at the dinner table, he knows that what he's thinking and feeling is "important" and "means something," but he doesn't know what, and in the next scene he becomes so enraged after being unable to recreate the image in his mind with modeling clay that he storms into the backyard, looks up at the sky, and screams, "What is it? What is it?" then says quietly, almost to himself, "It's not fair. Tell me." In the following scene,[76] Ronnie finds Roy in the shower fully clothed at four o'clock in the morning, as if he is desperately trying to wash his madness away, which leads to the film's most painfully emotional conflict, with Roy asking Ronnie to comfort him while she, pushed beyond her limits, rejects him and his "bullshit." The fact that this heated clash transpires in front of their children, leading Brad into an emotional meltdown in which he repeatedly slams the bathroom door and screams that his father is a "crybaby" is one of the more painful moments of childhood emotional trauma in Spielberg's films. The suburban trilogy, in particular, is awash in childhood trauma, whether it be Elliott's anger at his father's absence in *E.T.* or Carol Anne being tormented and abducted by ghosts in *Poltergeist*. Like the invasions in *Close Encounters*,

---

[76]This scene, while shot during the original production, was not included in the 1977 theatrical version of the film, but was added to the 1980 Special Edition and retained in the 2001 Director's Cut.

trauma in the suburban trilogy is both internal and external, psychological and physical.

The physical invasion in *Close Encounters* is most memorably rendered in two sequences at Jillian and Barry's house in rural Muncie. The family is fatherless, a situation that is left unexplained, although the presence of moving boxes and the general disarray of the house suggests the possibility of divorce with Jillian having recently moved to the isolated farmhouse to "start over" (like Mary in *E.T.* and Ronnie at the end of *Close Encounters*, she is a single mother trying to hold it together). In the first scene, Barry is awoken from his slumber by the sound of the wind blowing through his open window. In a visual and tonal foreshadowing of the opening sequence of *Poltergeist*, which also involves a young child awoken by a strange feeling, we first see Barry in extreme close-up, his face and the pillow next to him lit by an uncanny play of light and shadow produced not by television static, but rather by the moonlight, fluttering curtains, and swaying tree limbs outside. A toy monkey sitting on his book shelf suddenly comes to life, making a strange screeching noise before banging its cymbals together, which then seems to awaken the rest of the room. A record player starts playing an educational children's song, a Frankenstein's monster toy begins moving its elongated arms up and down while its face lights up red, and toy cars and airplanes begin moving across the floor, all of which is made indelibly creepy by the constantly shifting interplay of bluish light and dark shadow. Barry is drawn downstairs by a flashing light where he discovers that something has been rummaging through the refrigerator, leaving a trail of spilled and smashed food across the kitchen floor. In one of the film's most indelible moments, Barry sees one of the off-screen aliens, and our impression of it is gleaned entirely from the register of his face, which goes from surprise, to bafflement, to fear, to giddy wonder—a kind of summation of the mixed emotions the film engenders as a whole.

Barry's house is invaded again later in the film, except this time in more spectacular and directly horrifying fashion. Prefaced by howling dogs and a massive, undulating storm cloud that emits a series of bright, floating lights (an image that will be repeated almost verbatim inside the Freeling house in *Poltergeist*), this invasion is visceral and violent, shaking the house to its core. Jillian tries to protect Barry, closing and locking the windows and putting a chair against the door, but it is to no avail. Just as Carol Anne is drawn to the "TV people" in *Poltergeist*, Barry is drawn to the aliens, telling them with a child's innocence that they can "come in and play now" as his mother frantically tries to close down all entrances to the house, including the fireplace flue. The alien presence is embodied in intense light, which constantly breaks into the house, whether through the keyhole in the front door, the windows whose blinds seem to fly open on their own, or a floor heating grate that unscrews and opens itself. As in Barry's room in the earlier scene, domestic objects take on a life of their own: the vacuum cleaner revs up and begins moving briskly about the living room, lamps flicker on and off, and the television set switches on. The scene climaxes with the kitchen going into chaos, as all the appliances begin shaking and turning on, the refrigerator lurches forward with its door swinging open like a hungry beast, the oven opens and emits a hellish red glow, and the top-loading dishwasher flies open and disgorges its contents. Barry is finally abducted by the aliens as he crawls out the doggy-door, momentarily torn between his mother, who is holding onto his legs, and the alien force that is gripping the rest of his body and pulling him upward. This primal scene of a mother trying and failing to protect her child from an invasive force inside her own home is repeated in both *E.T.* and *Poltergeist*, suggesting that all of these films function as parental nightmares in which parents are unable to guard their children.

Although *Close Encounters* is a science fiction film, these scenes in the Guiler house are more aesthetically and tonally in line with horror films, particularly in the way their main effect is fear, rather than wonder, and it comes as little surprise that numerous elements in these scenes are replayed with only minimal variation in *Poltergeist*. The aliens themselves often act similarly to the ghosts in *Poltergeist*, as will the titular mayhem-makers in *Gremlins* (1984), which Spielberg executive produced. Although their ultimate goal appears to be communication with humankind, the aliens also abduct people for reasons that are never explained and terrorize them for no apparent reason. Throughout the film it is made clear that energy sources are depleted whenever the aliens are nearby, so Barry's toys coming to life when they are inside the house and the kitchen turning into chaos as Jillian tries to protect Barry make no sense except as deliberate, possibly even cruel, attempts by the aliens to inflict trauma. However benign and friendly they appear at the end of the film, their presence is tainted by their earlier behaviors.

Aesthetically, the scenes in the Guiler house embody virtually every feature of horror cinema: "point-of-view camera shots, dark or chiaroscuro lighting, jump cuts and variations in pacing, visual (and often violent) spectacles that employ make-up, prosthetic, animatronic, digital, and other special effects, and discordant or otherwise unsettling musical cues and other sound effects."[77] Comparisons to *Poltergeist* and other haunted house films are plentiful, especially in the way ordinary objects take on a life of their own, but the aesthetic features of the invasion sequences also bring to mind other horror movies as varied as *The Evil Dead* (1981), whose over-the-top

---

[77] Brigid Cherry, *Horror* (London: Routledge, 2009), 53.

use of a subjective camera crashing through the forest with a screeching growl is predated by a similar shot and sound effect in *Close Encounters* as the aliens come down the chimney, and *The Shining* (1980), whose unsettling modernist mix of human vocals, rising strings, and discordant horns is also characteristic of Jerry Goldsmith's score for Spielberg's film, particularly the moment when Jillian first sees the UFOs descending out of the storm cloud. Interestingly, one of the driving images in Spielberg's cinema memory that helped inspire *Close Encounters* was the "Night on Bald Mountain" sequence from Disney's *Fantasia* (1940), which matches Russian composer Modest Mussorgsky's formidable score with horrific, demonic magery of such calculated power that it could only be balanced by ending the film with Schubert's "Ave Maria."

Thus, in addition to the diegetic alien invasion portrayed, the film itself is the victim of an invasion by the horror genre. Just as Robin Wood noted how the conflicted relationship between different genres and auteurs is often embodied in one genre invading the other, as in the "disturbing influx of film noir into the world of small-town domestic comedy" in *It's a Wonderful Life* (1946),[78] *Close Encounters* demonstrates how the wonders of science fiction and the terrors of the horror genre are emotional opposites that paradoxically tend to bleed over into each other. As noted earlier in the Introduction, when asked by film critic Gene Siskel about his "master image"—one frame from a film that would summarize his artistic career—Spielberg replied, "I think it's the little boy in *Close Encounters* opening the door and standing in that beautiful yet awful light, just like fire coming through the doorway. And he's very small, and it's a very large door."[79] His recognition of the light as both awe-inspiring and terrifying, as well as the manner in which the image conveys vulnerability in the presence of great power, is key to most of Spielberg's films, but particularly the suburban trilogy, with their interplay of the ordinary and the supernatural, the fantastic and the terrifying. This idea is also reflected in the film's dialogue when a Mexican peasant who witnessed the aliens describes what he saw as "Una luz muy bonita pero muy espantosa"—"A very beautiful but very frightening light."

We see this invasion of science fiction by the horror genre in *E.T.*, as well, perhaps even more overtly and disturbingly given that *E.T.* is usually thought of as a children's film. As in *Close Encounters*, Spielberg deploys many of the visual aesthetics of the horror film throughout *E.T.*, especially in the opening scenes, which present Elliott's house as strangely isolated atop its hill, barely

---

[78] Robin Wood, "Ideology, Genre, Auteur," in *Film Genre Reader II*, ed. Barry Keith Grant (Austin: University of Texas Press, 1995), 63.
[79] Ebert and Siskel, *The Future of Movies*, 72.

FIGURE 1.5 *"A very beautiful but very frightening light." Spielberg's self-described "master image" from* Close Encounters of the Third Kind *of Barry opening the front door "and standing in that beautiful, yet awful light, just like fire coming through the doorway" is key to the interplay of the ordinary and the supernatural in the suburban trilogy. (Digital Frame Enlargement)*

lit and enshrouded in an almost supernatural mist (not incidentally, it looks extremely similar to night-time shots of the Freeling house in *Poltergeist*, which also emphasize mist, exterior lights, and a sense of isolation via framing that cuts out the surrounding houses). The backyard is a notably evocative and frightening realm, especially for a small child, as its borders disappear into mist-enshrouded wheat fields that could hide anything, and the garden shed at the rear of the yard radiates a ghostly light from within, which makes it both visually compelling and sinister—an archetypal "bad place" where something evil might be lurking. There are comical touches, such as Elliott's surprised reaction when he tosses a baseball into the shed only to have it summarily tossed back to him, but if one were to watch only the first 20 minutes of *E.T.*, it would be reasonable to assume it were a horror film; even the opening credits, despite the purple color of the font, unfold slowly over a black screen and a mournful score, setting a tone that, like Roy Neary's misremembering of *Pinocchio*, is quite contradictory to most people's warm memories of the film. Spielberg even noted how his son, who was two and a half the first time he saw *E.T.*, was "frightened in the first twenty minutes … He was terrified. He didn't know what an E.T. was. He didn't know whether E.T. was to be trusted. He didn't know whether E.T. was going to bring some sort of shadows of harm to the child in the bedroom."[80] In one way or another, virtually *everything* in *E.T.*'s opening minutes is threatening: the forest is dark and primal; government agents are faceless entities with a potentially

---

[80] Ebert and Siskel, *The Future of Movies*, 43.

sinister agenda; Elliott's house and backyard are dimly lit and isolated; and E.T. himself, although chased by the agents, is an unknown entity, possibly benign, but possibly dangerous.

However, unlike *Close Encounters* and *Poltergeist*, where the paranormal elements are the source of potential danger, in *E.T.* it is humankind itself that turns out to be dangerous. E.T., although initially presented in brief fragments that suggest something potentially threatening, is ultimately a gentle, wizened creature endowed with supernatural healing powers. His presence in Elliott's house is not an invasion like the aliens' assault on the Guilers' home in *Close Encounters* because Elliott draws him there and invites him in. Although initially frightened by E.T.'s appearance, Elliott senses that he means him no harm, and one imagines that E.T. feels the same way, as his initial reaction to seeing Elliott is to scream just as Elliott does. One must also remember that E.T.'s initial encounter with Elliott followed his being tracked and pursued by government agents in the forest, who Spielberg depicts entirely with low cameras that capture them from the chest down, thus dehumanizing them and emphasizing their threatening, faceless nature.

That threat is fully realized later in the film when government agents descend on Elliott's house and invade it in ways that are abjectly horrific, not just in the way it terrorizes Elliott and his family, but also in the way it seems to confirm Elliott's concern at the beginning of the film that, if the authorities were called, they would lobotomize E.T. and make him the subject of horrible experimentation. The invasion is foreshadowed with the unnaturally elongated shadow of the lead government agent known only as Keys (Peter Coyote) cast on the driveway, which confirms his presence while also keeping him mysteriously off-screen. Following is a sequence in which Michael finally lets Mary in on the secret that he and Elliott and Gertie have been hiding E.T. in the house. At this point, E.T. and Elliott, who are psychically linked, are deathly ill, Elliott barely able to speak and E.T. having turned a sickly white color. Mary's immediate response to get her children away from this unfamiliar, moaning creature seems imminently rational, albeit not to Elliott and his siblings. Despite their protestations that it is "okay" and that E.T. is not going to hurt her, she instructs Michael to grab Gertie and take her downstairs while she gathers Elliott in her arms.

What follows is one of the most surreal and compelling sequences in all of Spielberg's films, mixing familiar aesthetic motifs from expressionistic horror films and *Night of the Living Dead* (1968) into a singular presentation of suburban horror. In an unbroken shot, Michael opens the front door and, bathed in an unnaturally reddish light, is confronted with something that confounds him. As he steps back in frightened awe, Mary runs down the stairs behind him and steps into the frame in close-up, her shocked look confirming what Michael has seen. Spielberg then cuts to the reverse angle as a government agent in a bulky astronaut suit walks slowly through the door, his raspy breath taking over the suddenly vacant soundtrack. The sight of the astronaut is profoundly strange in its simultaneous familiarity and extreme out-of-placeness, not to mention the manner in which it turns an image that had previously been a source of American pride into something invasive and terrifying and weird.

After the initial shot of the invader coming through the front door, we cut back to Mary, who clutches Elliott tighter to her as she backs up, her face eventually consumed by the astronaut's shadow. In a long shot we see the invader slowly stepping toward them, arms outstretched in the manner of Frankenstein's monster or a zombie. Mary finally turns and runs the other way, only to collide with another astronaut-suited agent who has already entered the house from another location. They run away again, heading for another door, only to be met by yet another invader who comes in through the living room curtains, arms outstretched in menacing fashion. The camera tracks with them as they back away to the other side of the living room, and we see behind them as a light begins to flood through a large window that another invader is beginning to enter, forcing his arms through the blinds as Mary screams in desperation, "*This is my home!*"

Like both Jillian's panicked scream for the aliens to "*Go away!*" as they surround her house, and Diane Freeling shrieking "*Don't touch my baby!*" as she is forcibly thwarted by the angry spirits in *Poltergeist* from saving her children from their torment, Mary's desperate cry is indicative of the suburban trilogy's frequent focus on violence toward children and their parents' failed attempts to protect them. As the only overt horror film in the trilogy, *Poltergeist* is particularly resonant in this theme. From the outset, the Freeling home is surrounded by small indicators of death: the hulking dead tree by Robbie's window; the death of Carol Anne's canary, which she ritualistically entombs in a cigar box and buries in the back garden, where it stays only briefly before being casually disinterred by a bulldozer digging the pool (a foreshadowing of the greater desecration of the human graves below by the neighborhood's construction company); and even the broadcast of *A Guy Named Joe* (1943), a sentimental Spencer Tracy movie about a deceased World War II bomber-pilot-turned-guardian-angel that Spielberg remade as *Always* in 1989.

These little insinuations of death haunting the fringes of weekend America set the stage for the manner in which *Poltergeist* turns specific places of safety into entry points for the malevolent ghosts. Their first entry point is the television set, which, as previously noted, is a constant presence in Spielberg's suburban milieu. Always turned on, ostensibly for comfort and

FIGURE 1.6 "This is my home!" *The primal image of a mother clinging desperately to her child in an attempt to protect him or her from a violent invasion of the home is a recurring image in all three films of the suburban trilogy, suggesting that they function as parental nightmares about parents' inability to protect their children. (Digital Frame Enlargement)*

familiarity, it now plays as a constantly open portal for evil to sneak in and wreak havoc, which it does literally as a spectral, skeletal hand that suddenly emerges from the static. The swimming pool being dug in the backyard, perhaps the epitome of the suburban ideal of materialist attainment, is later filled with rotting corpses, and the ghosts also possess the tree outside Robbie's window, thus betraying his father's assertion that he purposely had the house built next to the "wise old tree" to "protect" them. When the poltergeists possess Robbie's clown doll and makes it attack him, the film moves past the creepy, yet ultimately harmless nature of the possessed toys in *Close Encounters* and makes them directly murderous. And finally, there is particular perversity in the closet in Robbie and Carol Anne's room becoming the entry point into the poltergeists' realm when it had previously been viewed by Carol Anne as a source of comfort in the dark of night ("Closet light! Closet light!" she cries when Diane puts her to bed).

Thus, the film also works primarily as a film about childhood victimization (which carries over from *The Sugarland Express* and *Jaws*). This is particularly true of Carol Anne, who is literally taken prisoner by the house and reduced to little more than a terrified, disembodied voice coming from everywhere and nowhere. As with the rising crime rate in the late 1970s and early 1980s, this metaphysical abduction resonated strongly with real-life child abductions, which were a significant concern at the time,[81] particularly with the extensive media coverage of the kidnapping and murder of six-year-old Adam Walsh in 1981 and his parents' subsequent campaign that led to the passage of the Missing Children's Assistance Act and the creation of the National Center for Missing and Exploited Children by Congress in 1984.[82] The horror in *Poltergeist* derives precisely from the way in which it invites the audience to identify with both the children and parents as victims of the suburban invasion. In one of the film's most harrowing scenes, Steve and Diane are forced to listen to Carol Anne's terrified voice crying out that she's scared of the presence of another entity with her and she needs help, pleas to which her parents cannot respond, even with the help of a trio of paranormal investigators. Steve and Diane's inability to do anything about the violence being inflicted on their children is frightening for parents because it reminds them that they are not always in control and are not always able to protect their children in a world filled with danger and threat, and for children it is frightening because they

---

[81] "Child Abductions a Rising Concern: With 150,000 Incidents Each Year, Units Are Forming to Aid Victims' Families," *New York Times*, December 5, 1982.

[82] Interestingly, JoBeth Williams also starred as the mother of the abducted boy in the based-on-a-true-story TV movie *Adam* (1983) and its sequel *Adam: His Song Continues* (1986), the latter of which was released the same year she reprised her role as Diane Freeling in *Poltergeist II: The Other Side*, a film with which Spielberg was not involved, nor were any of his regular collaborators.

are reminded of their own vulnerability. Yet, it is also important to remember that none of the films present children as idealized innocents. Rather, like the messy interior spaces of the suburban homes, the children and adolescents in *Close Encounters*, *E.T.*, and *Poltergeist* are complex characters whose imaginative nature, resourcefulness, and emotional candor are tempered by some uglier tendencies, which we see, for example, in Toby smashing the doll against the playpen in *Close Encounters*, the kids at the bus stop in *E.T.* making fun of each other, and Michael wanting to dress up as a terrorist for Halloween ("But all the guys are!" he protests when his mother says "no").

Unlike the seemingly random "choosing" of Roy Neary in *Close Encounters* and the happenstance of E.T. being deserted near Elliott's house, the ghostly invasion of the Freeling home and subsequent abduction of Carol Anne are rooted in a specific occurrence, namely the construction of their neighborhood on top of a cemetery whose bodies were never removed. Thus, the seemingly placid opening shots of the neighborhood are undermined at the end of the film when it is revealed that the comfortable homes and wide streets have been literally built on the bones of others, desecrating their remains and their memories. In this regard, the skeletal trees that provided an uncanny counterpoint to the familiar suburban milieu suddenly take on new meaning, standing in for that which modern suburban progress would like to forget in the name of profit and convenience.

Lack of comfort and reassurance in the end

Given that the endings of Spielberg's films are often accused of compromising the works as a whole by offering pat conclusions and neat wrap-ups that contain whatever trauma was previously inflicted, it is worth spending some time at the end of this chapter interrogating the nature in which each of the films in the suburban trilogy concludes. On the one hand, each film appears on the surface to offer some form of reassurance and comfort, even outright wish fulfillment, thus confirming the notion that Spielberg is desperate in his attempts to make everything right and assure that his audience leaves the theater feeling good. Yet, upon closer inspection, it becomes readily apparent that the endings of these films are not as simple or neat as they might first appear and in fact barely disguise a great deal of loss, pain, and open-ended questions that have no easy resolution—all things that none of the film's characters wanted or asked to "see."

I have already noted several times throughout this chapter that the ending of *Close Encounters of Third Kind*, which finds Roy Neary chosen by the aliens as the only human to enter the mother ship and ascend into the cosmos, is predicated on Roy fulfilling his role as the "bad father" by deserting his family and leaving them with an uncertain future. While Neary's ascent with the aliens functions on one level as an obvious kind of wish fulfillment, in which a distinctly unhappy man who felt discontented with his conventional suburban existence is able to transcend the mundane by entering into a fantastical, paranormal world, it also functions as the ultimate confirmation of his narcissism. However grand and spellbinding the final images of *Close Encounters* may be, their visual brightness tries, but fails, to hide the dark underside of Roy's journey, which leaves in its wake a broken home and fatherless children whose last memory of their dad is him running around the yard in his bathrobe, manically shoveling dirt through the kitchen window.

The ending of *E.T.* is similar, in that the film concludes on a visually majestic image of a massive spaceship rising up from the earth and shooting off into outer space, leaving behind a rainbow-colored trail in the night sky, except this time the protagonist, Elliott, is left behind. *E.T.* ends on an unavoidably bittersweet note, as the goal of Elliott, Michael, and Gertie has been to help E.T. communicate with his people and have them return for him, which necessarily entails losing him. Spielberg has suggested his own hope that the bond forged between E.T. and Elliott will somehow transcend the physical realities of space and time, and the final image of Elliott's upturned face, bathed in the light of E.T.'s ship, suggests that he has been somehow transformed by his experience; he is no longer the angry, lonely child we first met. Yet, as with Roy's transformative experience in entering the mother ship at the end of *Close Encounters*, the end of *E.T.* resolves the film's paranormal elements while leaving the issues of middle-American existence untouched. However much Elliott may have been transformed, he will still be the child of a broken home whose absent father was only temporarily replaced by E.T., a void that will once again be felt. Some critics have argued that the placement of Keys, the sympathetic federal agent, in the film's final moments standing next to Mary suggests the recreation of the nuclear family and evidence that Spielberg is incapable of imagining anything outside of the healing of familial wounds. And, while the image itself does present the appearance of a complete family, there is no reason to assume it is anything other than a brief, shared moment because the film never suggests that there is any romantic connection between Keys and Mary, much less the idea that he could or would fill the father void in Elliott's life. Rather, Keys is presented as a grown-up version of Elliott, telling him that E.T.'s arrival was a "miracle" that he's been waiting for since he was a "ten-year-old boy." The ending of *E.T.*, with its soaring music and bittersweet dramatics, is one of the film's most appealing elements, reducing many viewers to tears, yet like the ending of *Close Encounters*, there is a darkness at the edges reminding us that the film's paranormal intervention is only temporary and has not healed all wounds.

The ending of *Poltergeist* is the most overtly downbeat of the three films, in that it does not attempt to offer any sense of reassurance or victory, which keeps the film in line with the modern (post–1960s) horror genre, whose generally open-ended narratives suggest that the struggle between good and evil is rarely if ever fully resolved. Nevertheless, Robin Wood downplays the horror in *Poltergeist*, arguing that it "enlists the genre's radicalism and perverts it into 80s conservatism,"[83] primarily because the family is not held directly responsible for the invasion of their home due to their being unaware that it was built on top of a cemetery (while Steve is a highly valued sales representative with the construction company that built the neighborhood, his boss failed to inform him that only the headstones had been moved, not the bodies).

As I have argued elsewhere,[84] what Wood fails to recognize is that the horror in *Poltergeist* isn't radical because of its source (i.e. something external, rather than within the family itself, as in much 1970s horror), but rather because it is victorious in the end. After tormenting the family for weeks and successfully driving them away, the poltergeists fold the house in on itself, leaving only a gaping scar in the suburban neighborhood that was once a source of comfort and security. *Washington Post* critic Gary Arnold took particular note of this ending, writing that "Even if no harm comes to the characters in the long run, there's something peculiarly insidious and threatening about the destruction of their home."[85] Spielberg also recognized this, joking in an interview, "After most movies, you can return to the safety of your house. For this movie, I would have liked to steal the ad line from *Jaws II*: 'Just when you thought it was safe to go home … *Poltergeist*.'"[86]

On the surface, *Poltergeist* seems to adhere to the worldview often attributed to Spielberg in that the family survives in the end and remains intact, thus seemingly confirming Wood's assertion that "the suburban bourgeois nuclear family remains the best of all possible worlds" in Spielberg cinema.[87] However, it must be noted that the Freelings' survival is only in the most basic physical meaning of the word. That is, they are still alive. The final shot of the film shows us the exhausted, tattered family shuffling silently into a Holiday Inn motel room where they will spend the night. This final shot

---

[83] Wood, *From Hollywood to Reagan*, 180.
[84] James Kendrick, *Hollywood Bloodshed: Violence in 1980s American Cinema* (Carbondale: Southern Illinois University Press, 2009), 179.
[85] Arnold, "Horror With the Spielberg Touch," D1.
[86] Sragow, "A Conversation With Steven Spielberg," 114.
[87] Wood, *Hollywood From Vietnam to Reagan*, 182.

ends the film on a dreary note of defeat, despite being punctuated by the visual joke of Steve rolling the TV—the entry point for the poltergeists in their home—out the door. The suburban ideal and its associated dreams of safety, comfort, and the good life, have been torn from the Freelings, leaving the same uncertain future facing the families at the end of *Close Encounters* and *E.T.*

2

"Americans Fighting Americans"

Incoherence and Animal Comedy in 1941

The building no longer stands, having been torn down in 2005 and replaced by a Kohl's department store, but from 1969 to 2001, Spielberg's "good luck theater," the Medallion, operated at the corner of Northwest Highway and Skillman in north-central Dallas, Texas. Spielberg considered the Medallion "good luck" after having held there successful preview screenings of *The Sugarland Express* (1974), *Jaws* (1975), and *Close Encounters of the Third Kind* (1977). Thus, when it came time to preview his big-budget war comedy *1941* in October 1979, it only made sense that Spielberg would choose the Medallion. However, as Spielberg put it, the preview for *1941* "wasn't like the first three previews." Instead, it was a decidedly "unhappy experience" in which "people laughed and tittered at the beginning of the film, and as the film got noisier and more confusing and more riotous, the laughter became wonderment and the wonderment became amazement."[1] One could substitute for "wonderment" and "amazement" the words "shock" and "bewilderment," as the preview audience, which consisted entirely of "specially picked movie buffs" chosen by a research firm,[2] had no idea what to make of Spielberg's 146-minute descent into lunacy.

---

[1] Laurent Bouzereau. "The Making of *1941*." *1941*, directed by Steven Spielberg (1979; Universal City, CA: Universal Home Video, 1996), Collector's Edition DVD.
[2] John Anders, "No Sneaks, No Squeaks at Preview," *Dallas Morning News*, October 26, 1979, 29.

One thing they could agree on: it was loud. The film's profusion of ear-rattling sounds—echoing gunshots, exploding bombs, rumbling tanks, collapsing buildings, panicked crowds screaming, big band music blaring, and characters constantly yelling at each other—accumulate in such a way that the film's sound design could be justifiably described as "assaultive." Halfway through the screening Spielberg looked over the audience and estimated that at least 20 per cent of the viewers were holding their hands over their ears, a spectacle he had never witnessed. "I knew we were in trouble at that point," he said, an assessment duly confirmed by the post-screening "hangdog huddle" of executives from Columbia Pictures and Universal Pictures, the two studios that had co-financed the film.[3] Despite a moderately better second preview in Denver, a Los Angeles premiere scheduled for November 15 was quickly cancelled so that Spielberg and editor Michael Kahn could whittle the film down. After a month and a half they produced a more manageable, if less coherent, 118-minute version that was given a splashy "Old Hollywood"-style premiere at the Cinerama Dome in Los Angeles.[4] But, the negative response at the premiere by both the audience and the press only confirmed everyone's worst fears: Spielberg had made his first "flop."

With more than three decades of hindsight, there is still no easy way to discuss *1941* because there is nothing easy about the film. An expensive, sprawling, self-described "comedy spectacular" set against the backdrop of invasion fears following the Japanese attacks on Pearl Harbor, it is a film of grand ambitions, scattered brilliance, classical film allusions, and immense self-indulgence, the product of what Spielberg called his "Little General period" when he wanted "the bigness, the power, hundreds of people at my beck and call, millions of dollars at my disposal, and everybody saying, Yes, yes, yes."[5] The film was critically scorned at the time and is now marginalized, if not outright ignored, in many accounts of Spielberg's career because it seems so wantonly out of step with the rest of his films.

However, it is for that very reason that we should look at *1941* more closely and consider the ways in which its vulgar comedy and subversive spirit taps into the darker recesses of Spielberg's cinematic imagination. *1941* is routinely castigated for not being "funny," which is surprising given how effectively Spielberg has incorporated humor throughout his films, albeit

---

[3] Bouzereau, "The Making of *1941*."
[4] Discussion of *1941* in this chapter refers exclusively to the original 146-minute version of the film. Although this is not the version that played theatrically in late 1979 and early 1980, it reflects Spielberg's preferred cut of the film, evidenced by the fact that it is the only version that has been available on home video since 1996.
[5] Joseph McBride, *Steven Spielberg: A Biography*, 2nd edn (Jackson: University Press of Mississippi, 2010), 306.

typically in small, ironic doses—Roy Scheider's immortal "We're gonna need a bigger boat" line after his startling first encounters with the shark in *Jaws*, Harrison Ford's casual one-liners in the Indiana Jones movies, Tom Hanks' aborted knock-knock joke in *Catch Me If You Can* (2002), or even the parade of grisly ironies sprinkled throughout the gut-punching violence of *Saving Private Ryan* (1998). Critics at the time of its theatrical release blamed *1941*'s dearth of laughter on its overemphasis on special effects, its huge budget, and the deafening nature of its soundtrack. Writing in the *New York Times*, film critic Vincent Canby effectively summarized the major gripes against the film in writing, "No wonder, then, that audiences watching '1941' do not laugh with the abandon they exhibited when they watched 'Animal House.' They are, instead, stunned by technology, overwhelmed by scale and numbed by what may be the loudest sound effects since World War II itself."[6]

However, we might consider another reason that audiences weren't laughing in the way they were expected: the film's surface mania functions as an overemphatic attempt to corral the film's much darker comedic impulses. Spielberg has repeatedly maintained that *1941* was a film out control—"Comedy is not my forte," he told a *Time* reporter eight months before the film premiered. "I don't know how this movie will come out. And yes, I'm scared"[7]—which presents the tantalizing suggestion that, more so than his other films, *1941* taps into Spielberg's darker recesses, an absurdist form of auto-writing writ large as a big-budget comedy spectacular that executive producer John Milius liked to describe as "socially irresponsible."

While Spielberg's previous films had poked critically at various social and political institutions, nothing could prepare audiences and critics for the manner in which *1941* cast such aspersion on both the American populace and the American military, both of which are depicted as inept and unable to maintain any semblance of control or dignity when faced with a threat. *1941* is, in every sense, the complete opposite of a jingoistic war film in that it focuses almost intently on "Americans fighting Americans," a sight that Dan Aykroyd's verbose Sgt. Frank Tree regularly reminds the viewer is a sight he "won't stand for," although he (along with everyone else) proves incapable of stopping it. The film systematically derides the traditionally patriotic, gung-ho mentality of combat films while embracing the same anarchic, animalist spirit that had turned John Landis's *Animal House* (1978) into one of the previous year's biggest hits while taking it to a scale so enormous that it becomes almost abstract in its ambitions.

---

[6] Vincent Canby, "'1941' and a Mirthless Future," *New York Times*, December 23, 1979, D19.
[7] "*Animal House* Goes to War: Steven Spielberg Makes *1941* a 'Stupidly Outrageous' Film," *Time*, April 16, 1979, 97.

FIGURE 2.1 "The loudest sound effects since World War II itself." *While the commercial failure of 1941 has often been blamed on the film's overemphasis on special effects and a deafening soundtrack, the lack of laughter from audiences may also reflect the nature of the film's surface mania, which functions as an overemphatic attempt to corral the film's much darker comedic impulses. (Universal/Photofest)*

Spielberg recalled that he had initially offered a role in the film to John Wayne, whom he had met at Joan Crawford's memorial service in 1977. According to Spielberg, after Wayne read the script, he called the director and "was outraged. He thought it was the most anti-American piece of drivel he had ever read in his life. He said, 'I'm so surprised at you. I thought you were an American. I thought you were going to make a movie to honor the memory of World War II, but this dishonors the memory of what happened.'" Wayne attempted to talk Spielberg out of making the film, and told him, "I'll be very disappointed in you if you wind up making this picture."[8] Spielberg never saw the film as "anti-American," preferring instead to see it as being "a pie in the face of America. It was like a pie fight from the old silent movie era. And what's wrong about sticking a pie in the face of the Statue of Liberty from time to time if it's in the spirit of humor?"[9] Of course, for some a pie in the face of anything sacrosanct in American culture (including World War

---

[8] Wayne may have very well been disappointed that Spielberg chose to continue work on *1941*, although he passed away on June 11, 1979, six months before the film was released theatrically.
[9] Bouzereau "The Making of *1941.*"

II), even if only from time to time, is verboten, and while Spielberg may not have been entirely intentional in making the film a subversive attack on the country's memory of World War II, it is clearly evident in the final product.

The story takes place in and around Los Angeles on December 13, 1941, six days after the bombing of Pearl Harbor. The screenplay by Robert Zemeckis and Bob Gale is loosely based on actual historical incidents, specifically the largely forgotten "Great Los Angeles Air Raid" (also known as "The Battle of Los Angeles") on February 24, 1942, in which anti-aircraft guns positioned in Los Angeles spent 45 minutes firing into the night sky after unidentified aircraft had been spotted flying over the city. Two nights earlier, a Japanese submarine had approached the California coast and shot approximately 20 shells at the Ellwood Oil Field 12 miles north of Santa Barbara, causing only minimal damage. Twisting those historical facts to suit their needs, Zemeckis and Gale wrote an initial draft and then worked with Spielberg and Milius to expand the sprawling "what if?" comedy around a large cast of characters responding to the perceived threat of a Japanese attack on American soil. The chaos and cacophony of Spielberg's big-budget slapstick action grows steadily bigger and louder throughout the film, moving from fisticuffs between individuals, to all-out brawls between hundreds of people, to large-scale scenes of destruction that culminate with a plane crashing on Hollywood Boulevard, an enormous Ferris wheel rolling off its axis into the ocean, and an entire house sliding off its foundation and crashing onto the beach below. Yet, despite the thunderous effects and frantic, exhausting nature of the film's comedy, the darker, more subversive elements are still clearly evident.

Budget and critical reception

At a final cost of $31.5 million[10] that was borne by two major studios (Universal and Columbia), *1941* went $5 million over its $26 million budget, which itself

---

[10] The ultimate cost of the film varies depending on the source. Joseph McBride reports the final cost as $31.5 million in his well-documented biography of Spielberg. Vincent Canby's review in the *New York Times*, however, cites the cost as being as high as $40 million (which, even when combining production costs and marketing costs, still sounds inflated), while an article published in *Rolling Stone* shortly after the film's release (Chris Hodenfield, "*1941*: Bombs Away!" in *Steven Spielberg: Interviews*, Lester D. Friedman and Brent Notbohm (eds), (Jackson: University Press of Mississippi, 2000) sets the "eventual price tag" at $26.5 million (which likely mistakes the original budget with the actual final cost). In his book *Lost Illusions: American Cinema in the Shadow of Watergate and Vietnam*, David A. Cook also reports the budget as $26.5 million (143), and Glenn Erickson and Mary Ellen Trainor report somewhat tongue-in-cheek that producer Buzz Feitshans "watch[ed] more than twenty-six million dollars leave the kitty" (10) in the promotional tie-in *The Making of 1941*.

was more than $20 million over initial cost estimates and $14 million more than Spielberg had vowed it would cost.[11] It was, at the time, one of the more expensive films produced by Hollywood,[12] and its pricey nature fed directly into its negative critical reception, which, as noted earlier, frequently tied this "wasteful" monetary expenditure to the failure of its comedy.

The critics were decidedly vicious in their treatment of *1941*, and while their points were often valid, the scorn and poisonous invective heaped on the film was likely fueled by a backlash against Spielberg, who at 33 already had two of the decade's highest grossing films in *Jaws* and *Close Encounters of the Third Kind* and a seemingly unassailable reputation. As Joseph McBride puts it, "the unusually hostile reaction of some critics also may have reflected a gleeful desire to see its precociously successful young director receive his comeuppance."[13] The hostility is clear in some of the most oft-reprinted slams of the film, including *Los Angeles Times* critic Charles Champlin calling it "the most conspicuous waste since the last major oil spill, which it somewhat resembles,"[14] while Stephen Farber, writing in *New West*, declared it "the most appalling piece of juvenilia yet foisted on the public."[15] Despite the negative critical notices and general air of failure surrounding the film, it was not an outright flop as it has often been described. While it did not do particularly well in the United States, grossing only $31 million domestically, it turned a profit during its theatrical release due to the $60 million it made in foreign countries, whose audiences tended to be more appreciative of the absurdist manner in which the film mocked American jingoism.

Lester D. Friedman suggests that part of the film's failure with American audiences stemmed from their inability to enjoy a film that ridiculed American military institutions "during a difficult national crisis" that

---

[11] Three months prior to the film's production, Spielberg had vowed, "I will not make this movie if it costs a penny over $12 million," a statement that production crew later made into gag T-shirts (McBride, *Steven Spielberg: A Biography*, 305). This was not the first time Spielberg had gone over-budget, as both *Jaws* and *Close Encounters* incurred substantial cost overruns, and the experience of all these films hardened Spielberg's resolve to bring his next film, *Raiders of the Lost Ark*, in on time and on budget.

[12] Adjusted for inflation using the Bureau of Labor Statistics' CPI Inflation Calculator, *1941* would have cost roughly $85.4 million to produce in 2013, which, while expensive, does not compare with the extraordinary budgets of modern blockbusters. It was even far below the cost of the previous year's hit *Superman* (1978), which was produced simultaneously with *Superman II* (1981) at a cost of $55 million ($197.3 million in adjusted dollars). Nevertheless, *1941* still cost more than four times the average $7.5 million negative cost for a film in 1979. See David A. Cook, *Lost Illusions: American Cinema in the Shadow of Watergate and Vietnam, 1970–1979* (Berkeley: University of California Press, 2000), 349.

[13] McBride, *Steven Spielberg: A Biography*, 309.

[14] Charles Champlin, "Spielberg's Pearl Harbor," *Los Angeles Times*, December 14, 1979, H1.

[15] Stephen Farber, "Nuts!," *New West*, January 14, 1980, 59.

included the humiliation of U.S. citizens imprisoned in Iran and "the Carter administration's feeble attempts to rescue them."[16] If, as Michael T. Isenberg suggests, "Comedy plays an innately social function as a salve to soothe society's wounds,"[17] *1941* did the opposite by enflaming them. It may have also been a case of genre fatigue after a decade of explicitly anti-war films that were made largely in reaction to American involvement in Vietnam: *Kelly's Heroes* (1970), *Soldier Blue* (1970), *Little Big Man* (1970), *M*A*S*H* (1970), *Catch–22* (1970), *Johnny Got His Gun* (1971), *Slaughterhouse-Five* (1972), *Coming Home* (1978), *The Deer Hunter* (1978), *Apocalypse Now* (1979). Yet another explanation for its box office disappointment is that, unlike Spielberg's subsequent war films—*Empire of the Sun* (1987), *Schindler's List* (1993), *Saving Private Ryan*, and *War Horse* (2011)—*1941* lacks a crucial sense of humanity to balance its carnivalesque mockery of both war itself and war movies, leaving the audience with a lingering sense of loss that mitigates the humor of the wild antics on-screen (nine years earlier a similar fate befell Mike Nichols' *Catch–22*, another ambitious war comedy and one of the great underrated films of the era).

In fact, *1941* is one of the least reassuring of Spielberg's films. Rather than restoring order at the end, as is frequently the case in romantic comedy, or celebrating the victory of its anarchic heroes, as *Animal House* and its cinematic progeny did, *1941* gives the viewer no assurance that anything will be better or that anything has been accomplished. Thus, the film largely rejects the traditional role of antiauthoritarian comedy, which Michael T. Isenberg explains via sociologist Hugh Dalziel Duncan's *Communication and Social Order* (1958):

> We begin by laughing at others only to end by laughing at ourselves. The strain of rigid conventions, of majestic ideals, of deep loyalties, is lessened, for now they are open to examination. They can be questioned, their absurdities can be made plain. Now that we can openly express our vices, there is hope for correction. At least we now have company in misery; we are no longer alone and can take heart for another try. For when all is said and done, what do we have but each other? So long as we can act together we have all the good there is in life.[18]

---

[16] Lester D. Friedman, *Citizen Spielberg* (Champaign: University of Illinois Press, 2006), 191.
[17] Michael T. Isenberg, "World War I Film Comedies and American Society: The Concern With Authoritarianism," *Film & History* 5, no. 3 (1975): 7.
[18] Ibid., 8.

Because the Americans in *1941* spend most of the film fighting themselves, rather than acting together, there is no space in the film to confirm "all the good there is in life."[19]

In the aftermath of the critical lashing and disappointing box office receipts, Spielberg was uncharacteristically apologetic about the film in interviews, swearing that he would spend the rest of his career disowning it. In an interview with *Rolling Stone*, he said, "It wasn't a film from my heart. It wasn't a project I initiated, dreamed about for ten years, although I have shed blood over it as if it were my own."[20] It has long been assumed that Spielberg's apologetic tone following *1941* was directly tied to the film's failure to please his audience, especially since his comments about his not initiating the film could just as easily describe *The Sugarland Express* and *Jaws*. However, it might also be the case that Spielberg was unconsciously apologizing for how *1941* reflected more about him than he cared to reveal, suggesting a darker, more cynical, and less congruent view of life that, while having punctuated his previous films, had never taken one over entirely.

Narrative perversity and incongruity in *1941*

The hostile critical reception that greeted *1941* upon its theatrical release was due in part to its lack of congruity and blatant refusal to adhere to classical norms of narration, which struck some critics as simple incompetence on Spielberg's part. Of course, such incongruity was not a new development in American cinema during the 1970s; in fact, many of the most critically lauded and successful films of the decade by filmmakers such as Francis Ford Coppola, Martin Scorsese, Robert Altman, Woody Allen, John Cassavetes, and Bob Rafelson challenged cinematic conventions narratively, aesthetically, and ideologically. However, the incongruities in *1941* were so pronounced, so loud, and so downright perverse that they demanded a completely different viewing strategy that critics and viewers at the time simply were not willing to adopt. Such incongruities are clearly incompatible with the comforting, coherent worldview that Spielberg is often accused of creating in his films[21],

---

[19] In this regard, *1941* is a particularly sharp rebuke to Robert Kolker's insistence in *A Cinema of Loneliness* (4th edn, New York: Oxford University Press, 2011) that "[Spielberg's] films create for their viewers comfortable surrogates for an uncomfortable world, satisfying desire, clarifying, indeed forging relationships between the individual and the world within their own imaginative structures" (274). Not surprisingly, Kolker's discussion of Spielberg's work studiously avoids even a single mention of *1941* outside of the filmography at the back of the book.
[20] Hodenfield, "*1941*: Bombs Away!," 76.
[21] See Robert Kolker, *A Cinema of Loneliness*.

thus the great irony of *1941* is that, even though it is Spielberg's only outright comedy, it is one of his darkest and least reassuring films.

Despite its narrative linearity (the story unfolds chronologically over a clearly defined 24-hour period), *1941* is one of the more exaggerated instances of the new forms of storytelling that arose in 1970s American cinema in response to both the influx of European art cinema during the previous decade and various industrial conditions that broadened filmmakers' narrative and stylistic options. The manner in which Hollywood began incorporating incongruous narrative and stylistic devices into otherwise classical narratives was arguably the most momentous formal transformation since the industry converted to synchronized sound in the late 1920s, thus making the 1970s "the defining period separating the storytelling modes of the studio era and contemporary Hollywood."[22] Film scholar Todd Berliner uses the term "narrative perversity" to describe the unorthodox elements that helped shape this new form of storytelling:

> ... [it was] a counterproductive turn away from a narrative's linear course ... Narrative perversities manifest as story detours and dead ends, ideological incongruities, logical and characterological inconsistencies, distracting stylistic ornamentation and discordances, irresolutions, ambiguities, and other impediments to straightforwardness in a film's narration, and they jeopardize an artwork's narrative and conceptual coherence. Narrative perversity adds something incongruous to an artwork—something out of harmony with the work as a whole.[23]

In this context, "perversity," which typically has a negative connotation, even within the field of film studies, is not to be understood negatively but rather in the literal sense of being "turned around": "Perversity denotes a disposition to act contrary to what is reasonable or expected."[24] *1941* is therefore doubly perverse. Textually, it violently rejects "reasonable" and "expected" classical norms of narration and style, while extratextually it marks an unexpected and, to date, unrevisited detour in Spielberg's career.

Narrative perversities frequently create moments of narrative incoherence, a term that Berliner uses "not in its common metaphorical sense of irrationality or meaninglessness but rather in the literal sense to mean a lack of connectedness or integration among different elements."[25] Use of the term

---

[22] Todd Berliner, *Hollywood Incoherent: Narration in Seventies Cinema* (Austin: University of Texas Press, 2010), 4.
[23] Ibid., 10.
[24] Ibid.
[25] Ibid., 25.

"incoherent" immediately connects Berliner's argument to Robin Wood's seminal essay "The Incoherent Text: Narrative in the '70s,"[26] although Berliner separates his argument by noting that he is focusing primarily on the poetics of narration, whereas Wood is focused intently on ideology. Both approaches are useful in understanding the various challenges posed in *1941*.

Although Wood was largely dismissive of Spielberg's films, particularly in his writings published in the late 1970s and throughout the 1980s (after which point he generally ignored him), his discussion of "incoherent texts" could have very well been written in response to a screening of *1941*. Originally published as an essay in *Movie* in 1980–81 and later republished in a slightly revised version as a chapter in *Hollywood From Vietnam to Reagan* (1986), "The Incoherent Text: Narrative in the '70s" argues that there is a richness of experience to be had in films that are functionally and ideologically incoherent. In using the term "incoherent," Wood is not referring to explicitly experimental or avant-garde works that operate by a set of assumptions and reading strategies that deviate from the classical, mainstream norm and are revealed as coherent once the reader has mastered their "rules." Such films, characterized by the work of Jean-Luc Godard and Luis Buñuel, feature "consciously motivated incoherence" as a means of expressing the artist's views of the world as absurd, arbitrary, and chaotic.[27] Rather, Wood is interested in exploring "films that don't wish to be, or to appear, incoherent but are so nonetheless, works in which the drive toward ordering experience has been visibly defeated."[28]

Wood proceeds from the assumption that art is the artist's attempt to order experience for the viewer, and an incoherent text arises when that order unintentionally breaks down or falters. True to his psychoanalytic critical lens, Wood attributes such a breakdown to factors that are usually beyond the artist's conscious control, both personally and socially: "The reason why any work of art will reveal—somewhere—areas or levels of incoherence is that so many things feed into it which are beyond the artist's conscious control—not only his personal unconscious (the possible presence of which even the most traditional criticism has been ready to acknowledge), but the cultural assumptions of his society."[29] Wood, following Marcuse and Freud, argues that civilization is built on repression (both basic and surplus), and art thus gets caught in a fundamental dualism in which it must satisfy the urge to reaffirm and justify that repression, as well as "the urge for rebellion, the

---

[26] Robin Wood, "The Incoherent Text: Narrative in the '70s," *Movie* 27–28 (1980–1).
[27] Ibid., 46.
[28] Ibid., 47.
[29] Ibid.

desire to subvert, combat, overthrow."[30] That dualism is present in virtually all of Spielberg's films to some degree, although it is most clearly evident in *1941*, a film that is the very definition of an incoherent text.

Wood writes of films in which "incoherence is no longer hidden and esoteric: the films seem to crack open before our eyes,"[31] an apt description of the experience of watching *1941*. Like the films Wood examines,[32] *1941* is a film whose "interest lie[s] partly in [its] incoherence … [it] achieve[s] a certain level of distinction, [has] a discernible intelligence (or intelligences) at work in [it] and … exhibit[s] a high degree of involvement on the part of [its] makers."[33] *1941* also fits with Wood's incoherent films temporally, as all were products of Hollywood in the late 1970s, a period that Wood describes as one of "generalized crisis in ideological confidence": "Society appeared to be in a state of advanced disintegration, yet there was no serious possibility of the emergence of a coherent and comprehensive alternative," a "quandary … [that] can be felt to underlie most of the important American films of the late 60s and 70s."[34] Despite being consistently marginalized in the ensuing decades, *1941* nevertheless intrigues and compels due to its incongruities, confusion, and cynicism, all qualities that Wood ascribes to incoherent texts and all of which were derided by critics during the film's initial theatrical run.[35]

Narrative incoherence

1941's incoherence begins with its plot—or, to be precise, its unbalanced jumble of subplots. The film features no fewer than nine plot strands involving civilians and military personnel, both American and Japanese, all of which eventually intertwine in the film's final act and all of which share in common frustrated desires and interpersonal conflict. There are the three main subplots involving civilians who live in and around Los Angeles:

1   A romantic triangle comprised of Wally Stephens (Bobby Di Cicco), a Hispanic working-class youth who has been practicing to win a local

---

[30] Ibid.
[31] Ibid., 48.
[32] The films Wood examines in the essay are Martin Scorsese's *Taxi Driver* (1976), Richard Brooks's *Looking for Mr. Goodbar* (1977), and William Friedkin's *Cruising* (1980).
[33] Ibid., 47.
[34] Ibid., 48.
[35] For example, writing in the *Los Angeles Times*, Charles Champlin criticized the film for what he saw as its "abiding cynicism, which arises, however, not in a considered contempt for the world's follies but out of an apparent indifference and withdrawal from anything but spliced celluloid. It offers a nihilism based not on a rejecting rage but on an arrogant indifference to values" (H1).

jitterbug contest; Betty Douglas (Dianne Kay), his blonde, blue-eyed girlfriend who has been ordered by her father to stay away from Wally after he stole her father's car; and Corporal Chuck "Stretch" Sitarski (Treat Williams), an aggressive soldier who lusts after Betty and harbors a deep animosity toward Wally following an altercation at a roadside diner where Wally works.

2. Tensions in the Douglas home, which sits on a strategically advantageous bluff overlooking the Pacific Ocean. The family's bespectacled, bow-tied paterfamilias Ward Douglas (Ned Beatty) is determined to protect the homestead despite the protestations of his wife Joan (Lorraine Gary), who doesn't want guns in the house. This tension is mirrored by the conflict next door, where Ward's neighbor Angelo Scioli (Lionel Stander) has incited the wrath of his wife by turning their car into an armored vehicle, and it climaxes when Ward decides to shoot at the Japanese submarine with an anti-aircraft gun that has been installed in his front yard.

3. Odd-couple comedy between Claude Crumm (Murray Hamilton), a local man with a fear of heights, and Herbie Kazliminsky (Eddie Deezen), an obnoxious, overly chatty ventriloquist, who are working for the civil defense and have been stationed atop a Ferris wheel to watch for enemy aircraft.

Intercut throughout the subplots involving local civilians are six additional subplots involving military personnel:

4. Activity aboard the Japanese submarine, which is led by Cmdr. Akiro Mitamura (Toshiro Mifune). Mitamura's goal of finding an "honorable" target in Los Angeles to destroy is hampered by both his conflicts with Cpt. Wolfgang von Kleinschmidt (Christopher Lee), a Nazi officer aboard the submarine, and the need to extract information from Hollis P. Wood (Slim Pickens), a country yokel his soldiers have kidnapped.

5. Commanding American officer Major General Stilwell's (Robert Stack) attempts to maintain order in and around Los Angeles and "take his mind off things" by watching a screening of Walt Disney's *Dumbo* (1941) at a theater on Hollywood Boulevard.

6. The numerous endeavors by Capt. Loomis Birkhead (Tim Matheson), Gen. Stilwell's aide, to seduce Donna Stratton (Nancy Allen), the general's secretary, by exploiting her intense sexual arousal around aircraft by getting her inside a plane.

7   The various activities of the 10th Armored Division commanded by Sgt. Frank Tree (Dan Aykroyd). Sgt. Tree's division is responsible for installing the anti-aircraft gun at the Douglas home and is later stationed on Hollywood Boulevard, which becomes a locus of conflict. The division is also a site of racial conflict between the racist Pvt. Foley (John Candy) and a newly added black soldier, Pvt. Ogden Johnson Jones (Frank McRae).

8   The paranoia of Col. "Madman" Maddox (Warren Oates), a deranged colonel in charge of the 501st Bomb Disbursement Unit who is convinced that Japanese fifth columnists are being parachuted in at night and are amassing in the fields around Barstow.

9   The havoc created by Wild Bill Kelso (John Belushi), a captain in the U.S. Army Air Corps who is tracking "two squadrons of Jap zeroes" that he believes tried to bomb San Francisco the night before.

All of these interrelated subplots are built largely around characters whose desires are constantly confounded and frustrated, which is perhaps best illustrated by the Douglas family: Joan's desire to distance her family from the violence of impending war is undermined not only by the revolver she finds in the sofa while vacuuming and the shotgun Ward brings in from the garage, but by the Army's 40mm anti-aircraft gun that literally breaks down the front door right after she asserts, "I will not have guns in this house!" Meanwhile, Ward's desire to play the role of dutiful protector of hearth and home turns disastrous when his manning of the anti-aircraft gun results in substantial damage to his own property while consistently missing the Japanese submarine.

Some characters' desires are simply delusional, such as Wild Bill Kelso's pursuit of non-existent Japanese planes and Colonel Maddox's intention to protect Barstow from non-existent Japanese fifth columnists (the extent of Maddox's delusion is exemplified in his ordering one of his soldiers to kick Birkhead in the shins to ensure that he is not a Japanese soldier on stilts). And, in some cases, characters may have legitimate desires, but then misperceive that those desires have been met. We see this in Mitamura's double misperception in thinking that he has destroyed an "honorable" target. Not only is Hollywood not an "honorable" target (or, really, a target at all since it is an industry, not a specific location), but he actually destroys an amusement park along the Santa Monica pier and sails away with delusions of glory.

Yet, despite the presence of a thematic connection among all of these subplots, they still produce an incoherent experience in terms of audience identification and focus. The film reflects what Berliner calls "conceptual incongruity": "a discordance of concepts, ideas, or principles."[36] The Wally–Betty–Stretch romantic triangle was the narrative focus in early drafts of the screenplay, but that focus was repeatedly diminished in later drafts as subplots were stacked on top of it. Wally's presence in the film was further minimized in the editing process following the film's preview screening in Dallas, as several sequences focused on his character were removed in order to shorten the film and increase its tempo.[37] The subsequent narrative incoherence in terms of balance among subplots and characters thus began with the screenplay, which became increasingly bloated with input from both Spielberg and executive producer John Milius; was intensified by the production itself, which Spielberg candidly admitted was a disaster in which he was unable to corral his cast and maintain order in the performances;[38] and was finally entrenched in the editing room as Spielberg tried desperately to save what he saw as an unfunny film by making it loud, fast, and raucous. The result is a narrative that has no central protagonist or protagonists with whom the audience can identify, a rarity for a mainstream studio production and confusing for audiences accustomed to classical Hollywood narrative's insistent focus on a singular, psychologically defined, goal-oriented protagonist. As Spielberg himself described it, "it was like a nightmare [Robert] Altman."[39]

Spielberg's reference to director Robert Altman is apt, as Altman's 1970s films provide a key point of comparison to *1941*. While there are numerous similarities with *1941*, Altman's kaleidoscopic narrative and genre experiments in films like *M*A*S*H* and *Nashville* (1975) are routinely celebrated while Spielberg's work in *1941* is viewed as a failure. This is because Altman's films, despite their various complexities, ultimately find coherence both individually and within the larger canon of Altman's work, while *1941* remains defiantly incoherent and disjointed. Formally, *1941* has quite a bit in common with *M*A*S*H* and *Nashville*. From a narrative perspective, all of these films studiously ignore classical Hollywood conventions and spread

---

[36] Berliner, *Hollywood Incoherent*, 26.
[37] The scenes cut from the 146-minute version of the film involving Wally take place mostly during the film's opening half. These scenes include a brief bit in which Wally and his friend Dennis DeSoto (Perry Lang) are thrown out of the diner following an altercation with Stretch; a long sequence in which Wally and Dennis connive to steal an expensive "zoot suit" from a department store by having Dennis blow an air-raid siren, thus creating panic in the store; and a scene outside the USO dance hall where Wally and other "Zoot Suiters" are denied entrance, followed by another altercation with Stretch that leads to a brawl between the Zoot Suiters and the various servicemen. In additional to minimizing Wally's presence in the film, the removal of these scenes also diminishes the role that racial tensions play in the film.
[38] Hodenfield, "*1941*: Bombs Away!," 78.
[39] Ibid., 79.

FIGURE 2.2 "Nightmare Altman." *The romantic triangle comprised of Hispanic working-class Wally Stephens (Bobby Di Cicco), his girlfriend Betty Douglas (Dianne Kay), and aggressive soldier Corporal Chuck "Stretch" Sitarski (Treat Williams), which culminates in fisticuffs during the film's chaotic jitterbug sequence, is one of the film's nine desperately random and intertwining plot strands. Originally intended to be the film's central narrative focus, it was diminished significantly in later screenplay drafts and in the editing of the film following its disastrous sneak preview in Dallas. (Universal/Photofest)*

the viewer's attention across multiple interconnected subplots and a large cast of characters. Visually, they are all extraordinarily "busy," filling the wide 2.35:1 Panavision frame with an overabundance of visual information that is decidedly more than any one viewer could process in a single viewing, although Altman's films tend to utilize the telephoto lens to flatten and compress space while Spielberg primarily uses wide-angle lenses to create a sense of depth that emphasizes activity in all three planes of action. The films are also as overwhelming aurally as they are visually, although Altman's soundtracks favor a continuous sonic onslaught in the form of overlapping dialogue and intrusive environmental sounds, while the soundtrack in *1941* engulfs the spectator with intensity and volume: characters shouting at and over each other, John Williams' epic orchestral score, the roar of various engines, and the escalating cacophony of destruction (explosions, collapsing buildings, gunfire, etc.).

Yet, despite these structural and aesthetic similarities, Altman's films work in the conventional sense of form and content functioning in unison, rather than against each other. As Robert Kolker notes in his extended analysis of Altman's body of work, "What Altman creates is not the conventional structure of a whole that is analyzed into its parts, but a simultaneity of the whole *and* its parts, a simultaneity the viewer must always attend to."[40] Thus, in a film like *Nashville*, the intertwining subplots are dramatically engaging individually, but also cohere to form a tapestry of American culture in the mid–1970s—a microcosm of a country in cultural and political flux, which gives the film's unresolved ending thematic weight and meaning. In other words, the film is conceptually congruent. The subplots in *1941*, on the other hand, feel almost desperately random and disengaged from each other, interrelated only to the extent that their characters eventually cross each other's paths and interact, which leaves no room for the film to make any kind of coherent thematic statement beyond a general mocking of all pretenses toward control and authority (which will be discussed in more detail later in the chapter).

Incongruence between comedy and realism

The incoherence in *1941* also relates directly to the conflict between its tone of anarchic comedy and its rigorously controlled, beautifully realized visuals; unlike Altman's films, there is a discrepancy, rather than simultaneity, between the whole and its parts. Although staged as a frenzied "comedy spectacular," Spielberg and veteran cinematographer William A. Fraker used a stylized, yet determinedly realistic aesthetic of desaturated colors and heavily diffused light that produces internal friction between tone and image. The film's realism is also heightened by diegetic elements such as the Japanese and German characters speaking their native languages, the massive presence of actual military hardware, and the impressive special effects that rarely if ever draw attention to themselves as constructed elements. Nigel Morris goes so far as to suggest that the film's failure might be attributable to this unresolved tension: "If *1941* had abandoned realism and looked more like *Helzapoppin'* or even *The Wizard of Oz* it might have proven acceptable."[41] Of course, we will never know if that is the case, leaving us with a film of impeccable visual design that nevertheless feels "like having your head inside a pinball machine for two hours," a quote that is regularly

---

[40] Kolker, *A Cinema of Loneliness*, 366.
[41] Nigel Morris, *The Cinema of Steven Spielberg: Empire of Light* (London: Wallflower Press, 2007), 69.

misattributed to Pauline Kael,[42] one of the few critics who thoroughly appreciated the film.[43]

If one were to focus solely on the mechanics of its cinematic presentation, *1941* would rank high among Spielberg's most visually accomplished films. Kael proclaimed that the jitterbug dance sequence in the USO was "one of the greatest pieces of film choreography" she had ever seen, and she described the film as a whole as "an amazing, orgiastic comedy, with the pop culture of an era compacted into a day and night."[44] Of course, Kael's voice in support of *1941* (which appeared in print nearly a year after its theatrical release) represented a tiny minority, but even those who derided the film overall had to concede the impressiveness of Fraker's cinematography and visual effects (both of which were nominated for Oscars). Fraker shot in the wide Panavision 2.35:1 aspect ratio, which Spielberg had previously used to great effect in *The Sugarland Express*, *Jaws*, and *Close Encounters of the Third Kind*, with a heavily diffused lens that gives the film a soft, hazy, slightly bleached appearance by emphasizing reflections off shiny surfaces and creating large blooms of light that contrast against darker areas of the frame (flashlights in the dark, for example, or light coming through a window into a dark garage). Fraker was directly responsible for helping to pioneer this heavily diffused look, which was accomplished with wider lenses, smaller light sources, and "flashing" and overexposure in the lab, in films like *Rosemary's Baby* (1968) and *Bullitt* (1968). It went on to become the most distinctive visual style of 1970s American cinema and helped break the studio-era practice of each studio having its own "look."[45]

In addition to Fraker's cinematography, *1941* was one of the first American productions to utilize a new innovation called the Louma crane, a small, flexible camera crane. Initially developed in France, the Louma crane used remote control servo motors to allow for unprecedented precision of movement in even the tightest of spaces.[46] With this innovation, Spielberg could move the camera in and around the film's frenetic action in ways that would have been impossible with a conventional crane, which had to leave enough room for the camera, the operator, the focus puller, and usually the director. The fluidity and dexterity of the Louma crane is best exemplified in the jitterbug

---

[42] The quote, which appears in Kael's review of *Used Cars* (1980), Robert Zemeckis and Bob Gale's second feature film, was spoken by a friend of hers who hated *1941*.
[43] Pauline Kael, "The Current Cinema: Dizzy, Dizzy, Dizzy," *The New Yorker*, November 10, 1980, 212.
[44] Ibid., 214.
[45] Cook, *Lost Illusions*, 358–9.
[46] See David W. Samuelson, "Introducing the LOUMA Crane," *American Cinematographer* (December 1979).

FIGURE 2.3 Incongruence between comedy and realism. *Cinematographer William A. Fraker's use of a stylized, yet determinedly realistic aesthetic of desaturated colors and heavily diffused light, as seen in this shot of Wild Bill Kelso (John Belushi), produces internal and unresolved friction between tone and image in 1941. (Universal/Photofest)*

dance sequence at the USO, where Wally attempts to dance with Betty while evading Stretch. The camera moves about the enormous dance hall in a series of long takes, gliding over tables and stairs and all around the dozens of jitterbugging extras, which gives the sequence a sense of weightless exuberance. True to the film's form, though, the precise choreography of the dance sequence culminates in cacophony as a massive brawl breaks out among the various servicemen, which Spielberg then match-cuts to a shot of Pvt. Jones trying to strangle Pvt. Foley back at the barracks, thus conflating and intensifying multiple instances of "Americans fighting Americans."

The manner in which the dance sequence deteriorates into a brawl is indicative of the film's overall impact, which is one of order constantly giving way to destruction. Within the film's narrative, all the authority figures prove to be incapable of maintaining order as various characters wildly pursue their own agendas at the expense of unity and cohesion. The film's numerous subplots are often at odds with each other, just as there is disunity between the impeccable cinematography and the violent slapstick comedy on screen, which produces a chaotic, potentially overwhelming viewing experience that does nothing to reassure the viewer of anything other than the reigning power of disorder.

Reflexive self-awareness

Given the narrative and tonal chaos of *1941*, it is not surprising that the film also displays a high level of reflexive self-awareness, particularly regarding its own status as a "disaster." "Allusionism" was a distinguishing feature of 1970s American filmmaking; as David A. Cook notes, "Shaped by auteurism, the recent availability of classical films on television, and the gradual institutionalization of film study in the academy, this new historical film consciousness enabled both the knowing revision of classical genres ... and a new category of self-reflexive films that fetishized the practices of 'lost Hollywood'—either through parody or memorialization."[47] Nigel Morris has argued that *1941* is loaded with various forms of intertextuality, primarily to other films that it is either parodying or paying homage to, including Stanley Kramer's *It's a Mad, Mad, Mad, Mad World* (1963), Stanley Kubrick's *Dr. Strangelove, or How I Learned to Stop Worrying and Love the Bomb* (1964), and even some of Spielberg's earlier films. The opening sequence is a virtual shot-for-shot pastiche of the opening of *Jaws*, although this time the naked female swimmer (played again by Susan Backlinie) finds herself attacked from below not by a shark, but by a Japanese submarine periscope, and Wild Bill Kelso later lands his plane at the same desert gas station presided over by the same woman from *Duel* (1971), Spielberg's first television movie. More generally, the chaotic, at times surreal tone of the film is clearly indebted to the era of silent comedy, especially the one- and two-reelers churned out by Mack Sennett's Keystone Studio, which courted the "low-brow" working-class audience by lampooning authority figures and prizing overt physicality and hectic action over more subtle and rarefied forms of humor. *1941* follows in the Keystone tradition of subverting plot to slapstick: "The story was sometimes merely a framework for the outlandish sight gags, chases and non-stop action that were the Sennett trademark."[48] The only real difference is that Sennett typically maintained his surreal madness for 5 to 20 minutes, while Spielberg attempted to maintain his for 146 minutes.

Morris notes that one form of intertextuality in *1941* is intratextuality, when "films refer to themselves through mirroring, microcosmic, and mise-en-abyme structures."[49] While Morris cites visual mirrors like a rolling drum in the dance hall and the rolling Ferris wheel in the film's climax, the most striking form of intratextuality in the film is the manner in which it appears to demonstrate consistent self-awareness of its own disastrousness, which

---

[47] Cook, *Lost Illusions*, 284.
[48] Brent Walker, *Mack Sennett's Fun Factory* (Jefferson, NC: McFarland, 2009), 10–11.
[49] Morris, *The Cinema of Steven Spielberg*, 66–7.

creates dissonance for the viewer in the way it blurs the line between the diegetic world of the film's action and the non-diegetic world of its production and reception. This is particularly the case for modern viewers who watch the film knowing the history of its initial failure with audiences and critics.

As a result, much of the dialogue in *1941* that comments on events within the world of the story takes on an amusing secondary meaning when one understands how the film is perceived as a flop and Spielberg himself was trying to distance himself from the project before it was even completed.[50] During the film's opening moments, which begin with a black screen and a solemn march by composer John Williams, a seriously written opening crawl informs the audience about the historical context against which the film is set. Describing the aftermath of the attack on Pearl Harbor, the crawl tells us "American citizens were stunned, shocked, and outraged at this treacherous attack," which seemingly describes the response to the film itself, from John Wayne's initial reading of the script, to the disastrous initial test screening at the Medallion Theater. Similarly, when Sgt. Frank Tree tells Wally to "get rid of" his Pearl Harbor shirt because "it's in bad taste," he might as well be referring to the film's fast and loose take on history.

General Stilwell, who is the primary representative of order and reason in the film, regularly speaks in ways that seem to be commenting on the film: "Madness. It's the only word to describe it," he says as he's being driven to Daugherty Field in Long Beach to address the press corps about the fears of potential Japanese invasion (the fact that there is no "madness" on screen at this point and that the dialogue follows directly the scene in which Wild Bill Kelso accidentally blows up a gas station in Death Valley only reinforces the extra-diegetic nature of the comment). Later, as he stands on Hollywood Boulevard in front of a movie theater after much of the downtown area has been reduced to ruin during an all-out brawl, he intones, "What a mess! What a goddamned mess!" as a car flips over behind him.

Some of the dialogue even seems to address specific criticisms of the film long before said criticisms could be made. After the horny Capt. Loomis Birkhead finishes what he thinks is a clever monologue addressed to Donna Statton that is laced with double entendres linking airplane lingo to his own sexual desire for her, she laughs and then pointedly undercuts him by saying, "I don't like your immature sexual innuendos!," which presages numerous critical barbs aimed at the film's juvenile sexual attitudes. Thus, *1941*, despite

---

[50] According to Joseph McBride, "Spielberg's disenchantment with *1941* was evident long before its first exposure to an audience. 'Comedy is not my forte,' he admitted during the shooting. While editing the film, he bluntly called it an 'utter horror'" (*Steven Spielberg: A Biography*, 307).

its narrative and tonal incongruities, displays a surprisingly consistent recognition of its own chaotic nature.

1941 as animal comedy

While arguably incoherent by classical Hollywood standards, the abject lunacy in *1941* abides by the centuries-old inverse logic of the carnivalesque, overturning convention and making mockery of hierarchies and attempts at order. Nigel Morris has cogently noted that Mikhail Bakhtin's concept of the ancient tradition of the carnival,[51] which "counters hegemony by pitting comedy and bodily pleasure against constraints" and "reverses logic, challenges aesthetics, hierarchies, and barriers, and waives prohibitions"[52] is an apt approach for understanding *1941*, even though he views the film as "a pale, sanitised carnivalesque."[53] And, while the film is not as "obscene, scatological and offensive" as the medieval carnivals invoked by Bakhtin, neither is it the modern carnival of "mild frivolity [that] marks the triumph of reason and control."[54] Instead, *1941* sits uncomfortably in the middle, its reception infinitely confused by the cognitive dissonance resulting from our concomitant recognition of the behind-the-scenes military-like precision required to deliver the film's still-impressive feats of spectacle and the manner in which those feats of spectacle refuse to cohere into something recognizable or rational. Reason and control are nowhere to be found

One of the carnivalesque's most visible modern manifestations is what William Paul has termed "animal comedy," a comedic subgenre that flourished in the 1970s and 1980s.[55] Paul coined the term after one of the genre's defining entries, *Animal House*, a film that Spielberg greatly admired and was clearly attempting to emulate in *1941*, not just in its irreverent spirit, but in the casting of *Animal House* stars John Belushi and Tim Matheson.[56] Blake Edwards helped pioneer this form of cinematic comedy in the mid–1960s with *A Shot in the Dark* (1964), *The Great Race* (1965), and *What Did You Do*

---

[51] Mikhail Bakhtin, *Rabelais and His World*, trans. Helene Iswolsky (Bloomington: Indiana University Press, 1984).
[52] Morris, *The Cinema of Steven Spielberg*, 69.
[53] Ibid., 70.
[54] Ibid.
[55] William Paul, "The Rise and Fall of Animal Comedy," *Velvet Light Trap* 26 (1990). This essay was expanded into a chapter in Paul's subsequent book *Laughing Screaming: Modern Hollywood Horror and Comedy* (New York: Columbia University Press, 1994).
[56] The following year he cast Karen Allen, another alumnus of *Animal House*, as Marion Ravenwood in *Raiders of the Lost Ark* (1981).

in the War, Daddy? (1966), although Paul cites Robert Altman's *M*A*S*H* and George Lucas's *American Graffiti* (1973) as "the two clearest progenitors of later Animal Comedy."[57] Animal comedy thus emerged in the 1970s as the popularity of the romantic comedy was in temporary decline, "represent[ing] a return to screen slapstick on a fairly grand and insistent scale."[58]

Paul usefully links animal comedy to the distinction classical scholars make between Old Comedy and New Comedy, with films like *Animal House* and *1941* reflecting a return to the former after a 40-year domination of Hollywood cinema by the latter. New Comedy is "essentially what we have come to know as romantic comedy, what Hollywood in its infinite wisdom has succinctly formulated as 'Boy meets girls [sic], boy loses girl, boy gets girl.'"[59] A definition of Old Comedy, which derives chiefly from the plays of Aristophanes and can also be seen in the works of Chaucer and Shakespeare, sounds very much like a direct description of *1941*: "very loosely plotted, episodic, developing through a series of contests or battles in which one character or group of characters triumphs over another."[60] Furthermore, Paul notes that, while "Old Comedy may be ruthlessly satiric in spirit ... satire is not really the essential matter of Old Comedy. More striking is its sense of license, an almost total lack of inhibition in its view of both sexual and social relations."[61]

1941 has been criticized in part for its failure to achieve a coherent sense of perspective and satire; as Nigel Morris puts it, "*1941* is both indiscriminant and arbitrary, proffering no subject position for the spectator other than largely un-amused detachment."[62] Yet, the film's indiscriminant and arbitrary nature—the core of its animal comedy—could very well be understood as part of its unique strength. What sets the film apart is its refusal to abide by the dominant dictates of Hollywood screen comedy while celebrating the more uncivilized impulses that drive animal comedy, which, when unleashed within a historical military setting, inherently undermines traditional notions of order, patriotism, and respect. Thus, in order to fully appreciate the subversiveness of *1941*, it is important to understand several of the key features of the animal comedy—the characters' sexual desire, the use of grotesquerie, and a group focus—and how the film both fits into and deviates from them.

---

[57] Paul, "The Rise and Fall of Animal Comedy, 75.
[58] Ibid., 73.
[59] Ibid., 74.
[60] Ibid.
[61] Ibid.
[62] Morris, *The Cinema of Steven Spielberg*, 65.

Animal characters and sexual desire

Befitting its status as animal comedy, *1941* is filled with sexually driven characters, and entire subplots are built around the unabashed pursuit of sexual gratification.[63] Most striking in this regard is the subplot involving Birkhead, who we first see entangled with a female member of the press inside his car, and his attempts to seduce Donna Stratton. Despite Donna's initially icy response to Birkhead's sexual advances, he knows via previous experience that Donna "has planes on the brains," meaning she is sexually aroused by airflight.[64] Therefore, he spends most of the film conspiring to create situations in which he can get her inside an aircraft, even though he has only a rudimentary knowledge of how to fly one. Birkhead's pursuit of Donna is mirrored in Stretch Sitarski's pursuit of Betty Douglas, albeit in an even more intense fashion. While Birkhead's pursuit of Donna is played comically, often at his expense, Stretch is depicted as an angry, violent character whose unrelenting desire for Betty very nearly turns him into a rapist at one point as he tries to drag her beneath an armored car while Sgt. Tree and his men, thinking they are targets of a Japanese air raid, machine-gun all of the lights along Hollywood Boulevard. The tone of the scene is genuinely unnerving, as Stretch toys sadistically with Betty while she screams like a victim in a horror movie ("That's my kinda girl," he says as he holds her down by her hair underneath the car. "It's the end of the line, kid. No more games"). Her escape from the situation by slamming his head against the underside of the car does not play as slapstick, but rather as the necessarily violent means required of someone trying to escape her rapist.

In this regard, *1941* reverses the character typology of the animal comedy in that the less sexually inhibited characters are not necessarily viewed positively. Stretch is portrayed as a romantic villain and would-be rapist, while Birkhead is a comical figure whose single-minded embrace of his animal nature drives him into foolish situations (when he finally gets Donna up in the air, he is so consumed with the operation of the plane that he can't be distracted by her airborne desire, and when he is, the plane ends up crashing into the La Brea Tar Pits). The other most sexually ravenous character in the film is Maxine (Wendie Jo Sperber), Betty's heavyset best friend who displays a voracious lust for men in uniform, particularly Stretch, after whom

---

[63] See Paul, "The Rise and Fall of Animal Comedy," 78.
[64] A similar plot strand appears in *Porky's* (1981) in which a female gym teacher played by Kim Cattrall is known to become voraciously sexually aroused whenever she is inside the boy's locker room.

FIGURE 2.4 "Planes on the brains." *Befitting its status as an animal comedy, 1941 is filled with sexually driven characters and subplots revolving entirely around the pursuit of sexual gratification, including the one involving Capt. Loomis Birkhead (Tim Matheson), who spends most of the film conspiring to create situations in which he can get Donna Stratton (Nancy Allen) inside an airplane even though he has only a rudimentary knowledge of how to fly one. (Universal/Photofest)*

she is continually running throughout the film (as Paul notes, sexual desire in animal comedy is democratically spread across both male and female characters).

In contrast, Wally Stephens, the film's nominal romantic hero, is hardly a sexually liberated animal. Rather, his interest in Betty is decidedly old-fashioned in its chaste romanticism and revolves largely around his wanting to dance with her at the jitterbug competition. He is very much the "little guy" who frequently plays the role of comic war hero in war comedies: "average guys with no distinguishing characteristics, save perhaps their ethnic personalities and their ability to become entangled in absurd situations."[65] Wally is clearly depicted as an individual who resists authority, which fulfills the role of comic war heroes acting as "mouthpieces for depicting concern over and exasperation with authority and the claims of social class,"[66] while also playing into the animal comedy's celebration

---

[65] Isenberg, "World War I Film Comedies and American Society," 14.
[66] Ibid., 14.

of anti-authoritarianism. Wally's conflict with Stretch, the film's symbol of violent militarism at its worst, begins at the roadside diner where Wally works as a dishwasher and busboy. Stretch, disgusted by Wally's jovial attitude and dancing while waiting tables, asks him why he isn't in uniform, to which Wally replies off-handedly, "I just don't take orders from anybody." Later, when Wally has commandeered a tank, he deliberately shoots up the patrol car of Capt. Miller, the "flatfoot" who "sent him up the river," presumably for stealing Ward Douglas's car. These acts of both verbal and physical social rebellion ensure that Wally, despite being a relatively bland character, is not mistaken for a conformist, but rather someone who lives by his own rules.

The film's conflicted view of liberated individuality is most prominent in the attention it gives to Captain Wild Bill Kelso, who spends most of the film tracking "two squadrons of Jap zeroes" that he believes tried to bomb San Francisco the night before. These enemy aircraft are, of course, a figment of his overheated imagination, and he winds up causing significantly more harm than good throughout the film. Thinking he is shooting at the Japanese, he winds up shooting down Birkhead and Donna's plane, the pursuit of which causes panic throughout downtown Los Angeles. At the end of the film he drives a motorcycle into the ocean, swims out to the Japanese sub, and crawls inside it as it submerges. The last we see of him he is standing alone inside the sub, surrounded by Japanese soldiers with drawn weapons, ordering them to take him to Tokyo and then asking for a light for his soaked cigar.

Thus, despite his wild antics and animalistic behavior, Wild Bill runs contrary to the typical characteristics of the animal comedy in appearing to be completely uninterested in sex. The only time he displays any kind of sexual urge is when he pulls over his motorcycle to pick up Maxine, who has hiked up her dress and stuck out her leg to grab his attention. Unlike Birkhead, whose energy is focused entirely on sexual gratification, Wild Bill's energy is focused exclusively on shooting down enemy planes (his sexual energy is displaced into violent action). Thus, while Wild Bill is a clearly defined animal character, one who does whatever he wants whenever he wants and engages in constant crude behavior like guzzling soda and soup in his plane while in flight, he is ultimately, like most everyone else in *1941*, a complete failure. As he is unable to achieve any of his goals and is successful only in wreaking unintended havoc, beginning with his accidental destruction of a gas station and ending with his plane crashing in the middle of Hollywood Boulevard, he makes for an odd point of audience identification in an animal comedy. He is, then, very much the opposite of John "Bluto" Blutarsky, the slobbish hero Belushi played in *Animal House*, who wreaks havoc in his "war" against authority at the fictional Faber College, but intentionally and successfully.

Aside from the desires of specific characters, the overall tone of *1941* is charged with sexual energy, although it is just as often frustrated as consummated. The film is visually obsessed with revealing women's undergarments, from bras, to hosiery and garters, to panties. The film's opening *Jaws* pastiche culminates with the explicitly phallic gag of Susan Backlinie's naked female swimmer being hoisted out of the ocean on top of the Japanese submarine's lengthy periscope. The film relentlessly parodies the military by constantly associating men in uniform with ravenous, animalistic sexual desire, best demonstrated in the Tex Avery-like moment when the USO dance hall is suddenly swarmed with a crowd of leering, hooting soldiers and sailors who must be held back from the group of USO hostesses assembled there. Sexual politics are foregrounded as one of the girls stands up and protests, "These men in uniform only want one thing!" to which Miss Fitzroy (Penny Marsall), their chaperone, responds, "I don't want to hear any more about your precious morality. Morale: *that* is what is important." This lesson in sexual duty is strangely reinforced in a later scene by Betty's father, who pulls her aside that evening for a little "father–daughter talk" and tells her in all seriousness, "You're going to be meeting a lot of strange men. Men in uniform. Boys a long way from home. Lonely, desperate. They really have one thing on their minds. Show 'em a good time." Ward may very well think that he is simply instructing his daughter to dance with the soldiers, but the implication of his speech (evidenced by Betty's confused look when he leaves) is that he has told his virginal daughter that she is obligated to perform sexually for the larger good of the American war effort.

Crucially, it is not just American men in uniform who are obsessed with sex. A key scene shows the Japanese crew crowded on top of the surfaced submarine leering and cheering as they watch through binoculars as Joan Douglas takes a bath. This scene takes place immediately after the air raid sirens begin wailing in downtown Los Angeles and we see Stretch pursuing Betty and then Maxine pursing Stretch. Thus, the visual objectification and insatiable sexual desire form a common ground between both unrelated characters and the film's warring armies, which are otherwise linked only by their mutual incompetence. This incompetence (or, we might say, impotence) is visually reflected later in the film when Spielberg match cuts between Ward loading the anti-aircraft gun in his yard and the Japanese loading the cannons on their sub. Both attempts at aggression fail miserably, as all of Ward's shells fall short of the sub, and the Japanese are distracted from Ward's house by the amusement park, which they mistake for the "honorable target" of Hollywood.

Elements of the grotesque

Grotesquerie is a key element of *1941*, particularly in Wild Bill Kelso, whose boorish physical behavior and complete lack of inhibtion mark him as an anti-authoritarian "hero," even though his primary drive is the nationalistic desire to destroy "the enemy," and he fails in all of his endeavors. There are also elements of the grotesque in the portrayal of Hollis Wood, the uncouth, but patriotic country bumpkin who is kidnapped by the Japanese and forced to tell them where Hollywood is located. When Hollis swallows a compass the Japanese need to navigate, they force him to drink prune juice and then sit him in the latrine and wait for nature to take its course. The explicitly scatological nature of the scenario is adeptly verbalized by Hollis when he proclaims, "You ain't gettin' shit outta me! I've been constipated all week and there's nothin' you can do about it!" Although there is no direct scatological imagery beyond Hollis tricking his captors by dropping his boots into the toilet to make a splashing noise, the whole sequence runs blatantly against any sense of "good taste" and "decorum."

Befitting its narratively and thematically incongruous nature, *1941* is not specifically engaged in turning authority figures into grotesque caricatures of repression à la Dean Wormer (John Vernon) in *Animal House*, Judge Elihu Smails (Ted Knight) in *Caddyshack* (1980), or Miss Balbricker (Nancy Parsons) in *Porky's* (1981). In fact, the only characters who maintain any semblance of dignity amid the film's chaos are the official authority figures, General Stilwell and Cmdr. Mitamura, both of whom were cast with actors who brought with them the weight of decades of serious dramatic roles (Robert Stack was still best known for playing the unimpeachable FBI agent Eliot Ness in the television series *The Untouchables*, while Mifune was an international legend due to his roles in Akira Kurosawa films). Rather than becoming objects of derision, these authority figures play the role of straight men against which the mania around them is contrasted. Nevertheless, these authority figures are made to be the objects of ridicule at various points in the film. For example, General Stilwell's insistence on watching Walt Disney's *Dumbo* (1941), his tearing up during the scene in which Dumbo and his mother are reunited, and his anger when he is taken away from the screening to deal with the chaos erupting outside play as humorous counterpoint to the expectations of a stern military general.[67] Nevertheless, both General Stilwell and Cmdr. Mitamura fail in their respective objectives. For Stilwell, the goal is to maintain order, while

---

[67] Although it is historical fact that General Stilwell went to see *Dumbo* in a theater in Washington, DC, on December 25, 1941, the manner in which the film depicts his complete absorption with the film to the detriment of what is happening outside plays as comic exaggeration.

FIGURE 2.5 "You ain't gettin' shit outta me!" *Elements of the grotesque can be seen in the portrayal of Hollis Wood (Slim Pickens), the uncouth but patriotic country bumpkin who swallows a compass the Japanese need to navigate and is forced to drink prune juice and then sit in the latrine and wait for nature to take its course. (Universal/Photofest)*

for Mitamura the goal is to destroy something "honorable" in Los Angeles so that he may share "in the victories of our Imperial Navy." Stilwell and the men under his command maintain no order, and Mitamura succeeds only in the meaningless destruction of an amusement park. Other military figures are also presented as objects of ridicule for various reasons: Capt. Birkhead is sexually obsessed, Col. Maddox is literally insane, Pvt. Foley is an unabashed racist, Sgt. Tree is full of information, but ultimately pedantic and ineffective, and Capt. Wild Bill Kelso is erratic, unhinged, and causes more harm than good. As all of these characters are representative of different elements of the U.S. military, the film is clearly making a mockery of the military system itself—the whole fails because of its parts. This is perhaps best demonstrated in a sequence late in the film in which two soldiers are firing at planes over Hollywood Boulevard. When their captain asks them "What are you shooting at?" one of the soldier replies, "I don't know, whatever they're shooting at!" The lack of discipline, order, and purpose in the soldier's actions and his comical lack of concern plays as a metonym for the film's overall tone of disorder and chaos.

Group focus

As noted earlier in this chapter, *1941* lacks an identifiable protagonist, a problem that was initiated with the addition of multiple subplots in various drafts of the script and intensified when Spielberg cut the film from its initial running time of 146 minutes to 118 minutes. Chris Hodenfield notes that "Even with great character actors … the audience barely has a character to hold onto or identify with."[68] In his lengthy analysis of the film, screenwriter Todd Alcott asserts that the film's flaws can be isolated to the moment when "the director took his eye off the protagonist. Everything wrong with *1941* stems from a decision made, early on in the process, to stick a bunch of stuff in the narrative that has nothing to do with the protagonists' pursuit of their goals."[69]

From the perspective of classical Hollywood narrative, the lack of a psychologically defined, clearly delineated protagonist pursuing a specific goal *is* a liability. Yet, classical Hollywood narrative is only one narrative mode, and *1941* reacts against it by taking the animal comedy's focus on groups, rather than individuals, to its nadir. In animal comedy, characters are typically associated with an institution, which downplays the role of individuals in favor of groups. This affects the narrative structure, which Paul describes as "episodic, contingent, always retaining the possibility of veering off with a character who might have previously seemed minor."[70]

In *1941*, the characters are drawn together by the panic and fear of invasion that has enveloped Los Angeles, and the individual characters are interesting only insofar as they represent different aspects of the larger whole coming apart at the seams. That is, the film is not interested in individual psychology, but rather in group psychology—the way in which otherwise normal, rational human beings lose their minds and individuality to group-think and panic. Each character is essentially a variation on the same theme about the failure of maintaining control—militarily, domestically, romantically, and sexually— and the interconnected "contests" in the film see only repeated failure. The lack of focus on individual characters in *1941* makes particular sense given that, as Paul points out, the emphasis in animal comedy on heterogeneous groups made up of distinct character types aligns them with the generic tradition of the World War II combat film.[71] Citing Jeanine Basinger, Paul notes how the "'unique group of mixed individuals'" is the key feature that sets

---

[68] Hodenfield, "*1941*: Bombs Away!," 72.
[69] Todd Alcott, "Spielberg: *1941* Part 1," *Todd Alcott: What Does the Protagonist Want?*, http://toddalcott.livejournal.com/184028.html (accessed April 30, 2013).
[70] Paul, "The Rise and Fall of Animal Comedy," 78–9.
[71] Ibid., 75.

these films apart from all earlier war films, creating a new form that both invokes and exalts "'the melting pot tradition' and democracy."[72]

With its chaos and constant depictions of "Americans fighting Americans," *1941* does quite the opposite, playing as a clear parody of the cohesive ideology of the World War II combat film. Rather than depicting men of different walks of life coming together and fighting for a common cause, *1941* shows how the threat of attack induces panic and pandemonium, which in turn incites, rather than downplays, differences. While not always overt, racial tensions play a substantial role in the film. Pvts. Foley and Jones are literally at each other's throats, and Spielberg includes an almost throwaway gag in which the two characters are racially "reversed" inside a tank when Pvt. Foley's face is smeared black with soot from a blown exhaust manifold and Pvt. Jones's face is made white with flour, which suddenly emboldens him to inflict Jim Crow-era oppression on his adversary by demanding that he get in the back of the tank. In a less disconcerting comedy, this racial tension would be eased at some point, if not made into its own reconciliatory subplot, but in *1941* the conflict between Pvts. Foley and Jones is left unresolved. Although the film has been criticized for dismissing the real-life racism of its period, particularly the internment of Japanese Americans during the war and the underlying racial conflict that fueled the "zoot suit riots" to which the film alludes during the mayhem on Hollywood Boulevard, it does make various nods toward the realities of racial violence, if obliquely and comedically. It is hard to imagine, for example, that Spielberg was not consciously using the scenes from *Dumbo* in which crows play as anthropomorphic stand-ins for stereotypical black characters (General Stilwell laughs, sings along, and applauds during their song "When I See an Elephant Fly"). Similarly, in the aftermath of the riot inside the USO hall, Sal Stewart (Joe Flaherty), the radio announcer who has hosted the jitterbug competition, concludes his broadcast by saying, "I hope you enjoyed tonight's program. I'd like to thank all the GIs for helping make tonight's evening such a—memorable occasion. Maybe in the future we can have some Negroes come in and we'll stage a race riot right here." While Sal, whose accent suggests that he is Italian (although his real name, Raoul Lipschitz, is a mix of Italian and Czech), is delivering this dialogue, the camera pans across the destruction on the floor (overturned tables, broken chairs, smashed bottles) and finds Stretch's prostrate body, with a gaudy neon American flag flashing in the background, thus conflating racial violence with Stretch's attempts at sexual violence and all the forms of racial oppression that were legally operating in the United States at that time. Thus, rather than depicting a "melting pot" version of

---

[72] Ibid.

America, *1941* posits a country wracked with unresolved (and irresolvable) inner turmoil and conflict.

The film's inversion of the democratic group dynamic reaches its climax in the film's final moments, which also undercut the animal comedy's use of a revenge plot. Paul notes that animal comedies typically feature "a revenge motif in at least one plot strand, the resolution of which, marked by the triumph of the group of animals, signals the end of the plot for the entire film."[73] While there are elements of revenge in the various American characters fighting amongst themselves (particularly the Wally vs. Stretch subplot), there is no overriding revenge motif except in Mitamura's desire to attack something on the U.S. mainland in order to join in the honor of the Japanese Navy. And, while in a typical animal comedy the successful resolution of the revenge motif, such as the Delta Chis' assault on the town parade in *Animal House*, provides resolution for the film as a whole, the tensions in *1941* are left completely unresolved.

The final sequence of the film finds all of the major characters together at the Douglas house, most of whom are exhausted and sleeping in the early morning light on the various pieces of furniture that now sit in the front yard. The house is a wreck, having been shot up not by the Japanese, but by the anti-aircraft gun that Ward used to shoot at the enemy submarine. When General Stilwell arrives and is given a report by Sgt. Tree that the Japanese sunk their tank and the Ferris wheel, Ward makes an impassioned, inspirational speech that fully embodies the "us-versus-them mentality" that pervades animal comedy[74] while also playing ironically against what we have witnessed throughout the film: "We've been though a lot, all of us. We faced the enemy for the first time last night right in our own backyards, and we came together, put our differences aside, and carried on in the true sprit of America. I think no matter what happens, what sacrifices we have to face, we can carry forward like Americans." Taken on its own, it is a perfectly concise evocation of the democratic ideal of all Americans pulling together and fighting for a common cause, but when set against the destruction of the Douglas house and the previous 137 minutes of American ineptitude and internal strife, it plays as a sharp ironic barb. That barb is fully pushed home when Ward declares that he is going to nail a Christmas wreath to his front door, saying "this symbol of Christmas, this symbol of peace. I just want to remind us all that we're not going to let a bunch of treacherous enemy killjoys ruin our Christmas."

He then hammers the wreath into the door, which causes not the door to fall down, as one might reasonably expect in a slapstick comedy, but rather

---

[73] Paul, "The Rise and Fall of Animal Comedy," 79.
[74] Ibid.

the entire house, which slides cartoonishly off its foundation and crashes onto the beach below, a final, literal indignity to the hearth and home that Ward tried so earnestly to protect and a metaphoric indignity to the ideals of American patriotism and togetherness. Not surprisingly, the film then descends into more chaos, with Claude ripping the head off Herbie's dummy, Pvt. Foley hitting Pvt. Jones (who is now wearing an Indian headdress, thus conflating the oppression of American Indians and African Americans) with a stuffed toy, and Maxine finally grabbing Stretch long enough to kiss him on the mouth, to which General Stilwell says, "It's gonna be a long war." Thus, chaos continues to reign, Americans continue fighting Americans, and there is no sense of closure or reassurance anywhere in sight.

3

"What Exactly Are We Applauding?"

Indiana Jones and the Ideologies of Heroism and American Exceptionalism

Of all of Steven Spielberg's films, *Raiders of the Lost Ark* (1981) and its three sequels featuring the archaeologist-adventurer Indiana Jones—*Indiana Jones and the Temple of Doom* (1984), *Indiana Jones and the Last Crusade* (1989), and *Indiana Jones and the Kingdom of the Crystal Skull* (2008)—are perhaps the most telling in terms of both Spielberg's astounding international popularity and the critically underappreciated complexities and contradictions that twist and turn beneath the surface of even his most overtly commercial films. The status of Indiana Jones as a storied cultural icon with broad international appeal is similar to Spielberg's in that both are so roundly familiar, popular, and ubiquitous that they are frequently taken for granted, dissuading us from scratching beneath the surface pleasures into the darker catacombs beneath.

In terms of sheer commercial popularity, the numbers for the *Indiana Jones* series are duly impressive: *Raiders* grossed $209 million at the domestic box office in 1981, making it the highest grossing film of the year (grossing almost twice that of the next closest film, *On Golden Pond*) and the highest grossing film ever distributed by Paramount Pictures.[1] The film's sizeable domestic box

---

[1] All box office figures cited here are from Box Office Mojo (http://www.boxofficemojo.com; multiple access dates).

office take was particularly impressive and noteworthy given that it came at a time of economic inflation and high unemployment and helped reinvigorate the industry's faith in theatrical distribution in the face of emerging new media developments such as cable and satellite television and home video. Adjusted for inflation, it is still in the top 20 all-time domestic hits, just ahead of Spielberg's *Jurassic Park* (1993). Three years later, *Indiana Jones and the Temple of Doom* grossed $179 million in the U.S., making it the third highest grossing film of 1984, and *Indiana Jones and the Last Crusade* grossed $197 million four years after that, making it the second highest grossing film of 1989. Given the nature of the storyline in *The Last Crusade*, not to mention the prominent placement of the word "last" in the title, most audiences assumed that the series would end as a trilogy, but in 2008 it was resurrected with *Indiana Jones and the Kingdom of the Crystal Skull*, which grossed $317 million, placing it third at the U.S. box office that year. Even more astounding are the international box office revenues: $141 million for *Raiders*, $153 million for *Temple of Doom*, $277 million for *The Last Crusade*, and $469 million for *The Kingdom of the Crystal Skull*. The fact that the latter two films in the series grossed more abroad than they did in the U.S. is indicative of both the rising importance of foreign sales in Hollywood's shifting economic practices and the success Spielberg has found in speaking to audiences across cultural and geographic barriers.[2] All told, the four *Indiana Jones* films have grossed $902 million domestically and $1.04 billion overseas—a total of $1.9 billion. And this does not take into account the various home video releases of the films, as well as the vast, decades-spanning ancillary market of both spin-off consumer products (toys, video games, role-playing games, clothing, collectibles, etc.) and the numerous transmedia extensions of the saga, which include the television series *The Young Indiana Jones Chronicles* (1992–3), several comic book series published by Marvel and Dark Horse Comics, and the 12 prequel novels published by Bantam Press between 1991 and 1999. Thus, Indiana Jones's place in popular culture has been firmly cemented by both box office success and the transmedia universe it has engendered.

Although his physical appearance is an amalgam of numerous familiar figures from the movies and television, including Alan Ladd's war profiteer Mr. Jones in *China* (1943), Humphrey Bogart's desperate gold prospector Fred C. Dobbs in *The Treasure of the Sierra Madre* (1948), Charlton Heston's fortune hunter Harry Steele in *Secret of the Incas* (1954), Johnny Weissmuller's

---

[2] As Frederick Wasser notes in *Spielberg's America* (London: Polity Press, 2010), in the late 1980s, "in contrast to his rivals, [Spielberg] was moving more adroitly to build a global audience and to become the US's biggest filmed entertainment export" (144).

eponymous adventurer from the *Jungle Jim* films (1948–54) and subsequent television series (1955–6), and any number of western heroes and outlaws, Indiana Jones almost immediately entered the pantheon of eminently recognizable cinematic icons. In the American Film Institute's 2003 poll of the 100 Greatest Heroes and 100 Greatest Villains, he ranked second behind *To Kill a Mockingbird*'s beloved father figure Atticus Finch and just ahead of British secret agent James Bond. A little less than a decade later, he ranked 10th in Fandomania's poll of "The 100 Greatest Fictional Characters"[3] and fifth in ABC News/*People* magazine's "Best Movie Character" online poll, which garnered more than half a million votes over a three-month period.

Yet, the great irony of Indiana Jones is that his broad popularity tends to obscure the darker elements that make him and the film franchise built around him so compelling and contribute to his long-lasting appeal. The surfaces of the *Indiana Jones* films (heavily informed by their massive marketing campaigns) boast of the kind of escapist fun that audiences love to lose themselves in and progressive critics like Andrew Britton,[4] Patricia Zimmerman,[5] and Robin Wood[6] bemoan as both political obfuscation and a coarsening of film art. The surface, however, is really a thin veneer that tends to distract from, but can never entirely obscure, the darker themes beneath that challenge conventional notions of heroism and question ideals of American exceptionalism. While the films certainly engage in and, in some respects, reinforce conservative cultural values and reactionary colonialist traditions that cast the Third World as an undeveloped place of savagery in need of rescue from and domination by the West, they also mitigate and frequently undermine those values and traditions.

Like Spielberg's other films, *Raiders of the Lost Ark* and its sequels are more ideologically complex than they are frequently given credit for, and this chapter will explore some of those darker elements with a particular focus on *Raiders*, as it was the originating film and a crucial turning point in Spielberg's career where he transcended the perceived disaster of his farcical comedy *1941* (1979) and re-established himself as one of the pre-eminent filmmakers of the era. Although Robin Wood saw the *Indiana Jones* series as endemic of various threats of repressive conservative culture in the 1980s, he hit the nail on the head in asking, "what exactly are we applauding as we cheer on the

---

[3] Jason Dorough, "The 100 Greatest Fictional Characters of All Time," *Fandomania*, August 31, 2009, http://fandomania.com/100-characters (accessed November 13, 2013).
[4] Andrew Britton, "Blissing Out: The Politics of Reaganite Entertainment," *Movie* (Winter 1986).
[5] Patricia Zimmerman, "Soldiers of Fortune: Lucas, Spielberg, Indiana Jones, and *Raiders of the Lost Ark*," *Wide Angle* 6, no. 2 (1984).
[6] Robin Wood, *Hollywood From Vietnam to Reagan* (New York: Columbia University Press, 1986).

exploits of Indiana Jones?"[7] Wood meant the question to be rhetorical, calling the appreciative viewer out for cheering what he viewed as something just short of fascist entertainment, but the question can also draw our attention to the darker nature of Indiana Jones and the series he inhabits.

Blockbuster (anti)heroism

Because it was well known prior to the release of *Raiders of the Lost Ark* that Indiana Jones was originally inspired by the adventurous heroes who populated children's matinee movie serials in the 1930s, '40s, and '50s, there has been a tendency to read his character in similar terms, which feeds into misconceptions that Spielberg's films uncritically celebrate the simplest ideals of American male heroism. However, far from the flat, one-dimensional cipher he is often accused of being, Indiana Jones is a complex, compelling entity—simultaneously a superhero and an ordinary, flawed human being. While his origins are rooted in the classical movie serials, he was also deeply shaped by the New Hollywood of the 1970s, whose protagonists were often flawed, antisocial, disturbed outcasts who were rarely victorious or in any sense heroic and who also inhabited the landscapes of reworked genres from the classical Hollywood era. Viewing Indiana through such a lens forces us to recognize the deeper ideological, narrative, and characterological complexities of the film series, regardless of how it was framed commercially as popcorn escapism.

Roots of the character

The character of Indiana Jones was first concocted by executive producer George Lucas in the early 1970s as "'a shady archaeologist' who wears a 1930s-style fedora and carries a bullwhip, like Zorro or Lash La Rue."[8] Although that fundamental concept remained essentially unchanged, the character went through numerous refinements over the next half-decade as Lucas worked out the details in collaboration with Spielberg, who joined the project after Lucas shared the idea with him during a Hawaiian vacation in 1977, just as *Star Wars* was being released and *Close Encounters of the Third*

---

[7] Ibid., 170.
[8] Joseph McBride, *Steven Spielberg: A Biography* (Jackson: University Press of Mississippi, 2010), 312. Douglas Brode gives in *The Films of Steven Spielberg* (New York: Citadel Press, 1995) a more specific date of inception in noting that Lucas first had the idea for "a series of archeology-based adventure films" in 1973 (88).

Kind was in post-production. Prior to Spielberg's involvement, the character had been shaped in collaboration with filmmaker Philip Kaufman, whom Lucas first approached about directing the film and who introduced the idea of Indiana chasing after the Ark of the Covenant of Hebraic Law (his contributions were enough that he earned co-story credit with Lucas on *Raiders*). In 1978, Indiana was formally put to paper by screenwriter Lawrence Kasdan, who met with Lucas and Spielberg for five days of intensive story conferences during which time the story and the major action set pieces were laid out. These meetings also resulted in further refinement of Indiana's character, particularly the elimination of Lucas's idea that, in his private life, he was a suave, Cary Grant-like playboy given to tuxedoes and womanizing. That idea was dropped at the insistence of Spielberg, Kaufman, and actor Harrison Ford.[9]

The descriptions of Indiana Jones in the reviews that appeared during *Raiders'* initial theatrical release are unsurprisingly uniform, defining him primarily by his dual professions of "archaeologist" and "professor," modified with various adjectives such as "daring," "globe-hopping," and "adventurous" and usually paired with at least one reference to his penchant for getting caught in dangerous, seemingly inescapable situations. To wit, Vincent Canby's succinct description in the *New York Times*: "a two-fisted professor of archeology with a knack for landing in tight situations in some of the earth's more exotic corners."[10] That Indiana's defining traits are so consistently evoked by different critics and writers is a direct product of the film's tightly woven structure, which, in the style of the western, draws immediate and sustained attention to Indiana's most obvious signifiers of masculinity, adventurism, and daring. As film scholar Lane Roth notes, *Raiders*, as a "particularly popular product of [the Hollywood] dream factory … employs cross-cultural, durable symbols to establish quickly a locus of motives with a large, differentiated movie audience."[11]

In addition to noting the iconic elements of Indiana's character, virtually all of the critics noted his metacinematic positioning as a modern version of the adventurous heroes of the movie serials of the 1930s, '40s, and '50s. Movie serials during the early sound era ran the gamut of action-oriented genres, including westerns, aviation stories, jungle adventures, and science fiction (all of which are present to some extent in the *Indiana Jones* films) and were produced primarily by three studios: Universal, Columbia, and Mascot

---

[9] Janet Maslin, "How Old Movie Serials Inspired Lucas and Spielberg," *New York Times*, June 7, 1981; McBride, *Steven Spielberg: A Biography*.
[10] Vincent Canby, "Movie Review: Raiders of the Lost Ark," *New York Times*, June 12, 1981, C10.
[11] Lane Roth, "Raiders of the Lost Archetype: The Quest and the Shadow," in *The Films of Steven Spielberg: Critical Essays*, ed. Charles L. P. Silet (Lanham, MD: Scarecrow Press, 2002), 59.

Pictures, the latter being a minor studio formed in 1927 that later merged with several other studios in 1935 to form the more well-known Republic Pictures. Serials typically ran between 10 and 15 "chapters," beginning with an opening 30-minute episode followed by subsequent 20-minute episodes that were shown weekly. Although the assumption has long been that serials were aimed primarily at children and juvenile audiences attending Saturday matinees, film scholar Guy Barefoot has argued otherwise using the discourse surrounding exhibition strategies and audience conceptions contained in press books, trade papers, and newspapers: "the evidence … confirms that the film serial's survival into the 1930s and beyond was not restricted to Saturday children's matinees. Serials were made with children in mind and attracted a sizable child audience, but that audience was not limited to screenings marked as exclusively for children, nor were serials only made with children in mind or only watched by children."[12] This misconception of serials being attractive to and watched only by children has contributed to the critical and academic community largely ignoring the role they played in cinema history, and it would not be a stretch to imagine that the same holds true for the academic view of the *Indiana Jones* films, whose deeper implications and contradictions have generally been ignored in favor of a surface characterization as childish at best, but more frequently as regressive and filled with "reprehensible political and ideological positions."[13]

The connection between the *Indiana Jones* films and classic film serials was heavily influenced by both the film's obvious allusions to the cinematic past[14] and the numerous press interviews with Spielberg and Lucas, both of whom regularly referred to their childhood experiences watching serials, including *Flash Gordon Conquers the Universe* (Universal, 1936), *Don Winslow of the Coast Guard* (Universal, 1943), *Blackhawk: Fearless Champion of Freedom* (Columbia, 1952), and *Commando Cody: Sky Marshal of the Universe* (Republic, 1953).[15] Throughout these interviews they also expressed their desire to reinvigorate the cinematic traditions of their childhood with state-of-the-art special effects and an increased intensity that would suit a contemporary audience of all ages—a film simultaneously old-fashioned and modern. *New York Times* film critic Janet Maslin, writing in anticipation of the film's June 12, 1981, theatrical release, quoted Lucas in helping explain the character's origins:

---

[12] Guy Barefoot, "Who Watched That Masked Man? Hollywood's Serial Audiences in the 1930s," *Historical Journal of Film, Radio, and Television* 31, no. 2 (June 2011): 183.
[13] Zimmerman, "Soldiers of Fortune," 34. See also Wood, *Hollywood From Vietnam to Reagan*.
[14] Omar Calabrese in *Neo-Baroque: A Sign of the Times* (Princeton, NJ: Princeton University Press, 1992) claimed that he could identify 350 references to other films in *Raiders of the Lost Ark*.
[15] McBride, *Steven Spielberg: A Biography*, 312.

FIGURE 3.1 A modern serial. *With their daring action sequences and narrative cliffhangers,* Raiders of the Lost Ark *and its sequels were recognized as a modern version of the adventure movie serials of the 1930s, '40s, and '50s, which have long been associated with children and juvenile audiences attending Saturday matinees. As a result, the deeper implications and contradictions in the Indiana Jones films have generally been ignored. (Digital Frame Enlargement)*

"With both 'Star Wars' and 'Raiders,' I started out by asking myself, 'Gee, when I was a kid what did I really like?' Mr. Lucas recently explained. He liked the derring-do of the serials, and the unbeatable courage of their characters, not to mention the 30's settings. "Practically every movie star of the 30's has one movie like this, be it Alan Ladd or Clark Gable or whoever—playing a soldier of fortune in a leather jacket and that kind of hat," Mr. Lucas said, referring to Mr. Ford's snap-brim. "That's a favorite period of mine, but it was more the character we were after than the period, although they're obviously both rooted in the same ground."[16]

Media scholar Patricia Zimmerman argues that the exhibition strategies around *Raiders*, which relied heavily on promoting Indiana's roots in adventure movie serials of the distant cinematic past in both press materials and interviews, functioned primarily "to eradicate any political reading of the film's jingoism, Third World exploitation, spectacle and backlash against feminism."[17] While it is certainly true that the manner in which Paramount framed the film encouraged a generally apolitical approach to its adventurism, it also functioned to obscure how Indiana's character was not just a modern version of Flash Gordon or Commando Cody, but was deeply shaped by the more recent cinematic past, namely the New Hollywood of the 1970s and its rogue's gallery of misfits, outcasts, and losers. The fact that Lucas's initial

---

[16] Maslin, "How Old Movie Serials," D19.
[17] Zimmerman, "Soldiers of Fortune," 34.

idea for Indiana Jones emerged in the early part of the 1970s, a time when Hollywood antiheroes such as the aging outlaws of Sam Peckinpah's *The Wild Bunch* (1969) and the failed detectives in Robert Altman's *The Long Goodbye* (1973) and Roman Polanski's *Chinatown* (1974) were flourishing and the American culture at large felt adrift in a sea of scandal, an unpopular foreign war, and a tanking economy suggests some level of influence on the character, even if Lucas was deliberately trying to create a nostalgic throwback to a simpler, more directly heroic lineage, similar to his wistful depiction of early 1960s teenage car culture in *American Graffiti* (1973).

And, even if that were Lucas's sole intention, we cannot ignore the fact that the other filmmakers with whom he collaborated were not necessarily likeminded given their clear affinities with characters decidedly less heroic than Flash Gordon and Zorro. While Philip Kaufman was working with Lucas on the character and story, he was also involved in several revisionist westerns in the vein of Peckinpah and Altman. He wrote and directed *The Great Northfield Minnesota Raid* (1972), which focuses on a failed bank robbery by the Jesse James gang, and he co-wrote Clint Eastwood's *The Outlaw Josey Wales* (1976),[18] which added layers of emotional vulnerability to Eastwood's otherwise uncompromising "Man With No Name" screen persona. Although *Raiders* was Lawrence Kasdan's first screenwriting assignment, he had previously sold a script to Spielberg titled *Continental Divide* that self-consciously emulated the sharp wit and lack of sentimentality characteristic of Howard Hawks's romantic comedies of the 1930s. He had also been hired by Lucas to do a fast rewrite on *The Empire Strikes Back* (1980), which was decidedly darker in tone than *Star Wars*. He would soon go on to write and direct *Body Heat* (1981), a modern updating of Billy Wilder's classic film noir *Double Indemnity* (1944) that replaces the original's Production Code-mandated moralistic ending with a darkly ironic denouement that finds Kathleen Turner's femme fatale not only victorious in the end, but literally basking in the rewards of her successful manipulations.

Of course, Spielberg also contributed substantially to the character and narrative in meetings with Lucas and Kasdan, and he brought to the table a proclivity for stories about ordinary, average men like *Jaws*' Chief Martin Brody and *Close Encounters*' Roy Neary who are thrown into extraordinary circumstances. Spielberg's view of Indiana as stated in interviews often contrasts sharply with Lucas's, suggesting that, despite their successful collaboration, they were working from decidedly different viewpoints. Lucas, whose worldview is steeped in mythology and archetypes, tended to view

---

[18] Kaufman was originally supposed to direct the film as well, but Eastwood replaced him several days into production.

Indiana with an undifferentiated heroic sheen, to the extent that he once said, "If I could be a dream figure, I'd be Indy."[19] Spielberg, on the other hand, had a much more humanistic and down-to-earth conception of Indiana, which helped add significant layers of complexity and contradiction to what could have been a two-dimensional action figure. In fact, according to journalist and biographer Frank Sanello, the recurring criticism of Indiana being such a character brings out a rare display of anger in Spielberg, who argues that "Indiana Jones is not a cardboard hero but rather a human being with ordinary frailties."[20]

In shadows and darkness

The opening minutes of *Raiders of the Lost Ark*, which find Indiana deep in the South American jungle leading a team of local Indians in search of a hidden Mayan temple, are designed in virtually every respect—visually, tonally, musically—to establish a sense of mystery around the character of Indiana Jones. Starting with the iconic Paramount logo dissolving into a shot of a similarly shaped Andean mountain, John Williams's musical score is low and foreboding, establishing a tense mood that is heightened by Indiana's first on-screen appearance. With his back to the viewer and shrouded entirely in shadow, he walks into the frame from behind the camera, for a split second filling the frame entirely and making the screen go black. In hindsight we recognize his iconic shape with the fedora on his head and bullwhip at his side, but for a first-time viewer this shadowy introduction is anything but heroic; *ominous* would be a more apt descriptor.

It is the first of many times Indiana will be associated with shadow, which Lane Roth reminds us is a powerful Jungian archetpe "that represents 'the dark side of our nature.'"[21] Roth goes on to quote Jung's student Frieda Fordham in defining the shadow as "all those uncivilized desires and emotions that are incompatible with social standards and our ideal personality, all that we are ashamed of, all that we do not want to know about ourselves."[22] It is precisely these qualities that critics usually find lacking in Spielberg's (and Lucas's) early films, which are often described as "infantalizing" the sophisticated adult audience by encouraging them to identify with characters who are

---

[19] McBride, *Steven Spielberg: A Biography*, 312.
[20] Frank Sanello, *Spielberg: The Man, the Movies, the Mythology* (Dallas, TX: Taylor Publishing, 1996), 99.
[21] Roth, "Raiders of the Lost Archetype," 63.
[22] Ibid.

either children or "childlike," particularly in terms of their innocence.[23] Writing about the *Star Wars* trilogy, which is frequently discussed in tandem with the *Indiana Jones* films given their many similarities and overlapping productions and personnel, cultural critic and film historian Peter Biskind notes that "grown-ups in these films are shrouded in darkness, in mystery; they're opaque and filled with secrets."[24] This is an apt description of Indiana, who is the very opposite of a transparent, innocent, childlike character. Although he is frequently misread as an "ideal personality"—hence his high ranking on all the "greatest hero" polls and the efforts made by some critics to describe him as a conventional movie hero—he is better defined by his uncivilized desires and lack of social standards, which Spielberg emphasizes visually throughout the film with an expressive use of darkness and shadow that is more film noir than Saturday morning serial.

The use of Indiana's shadow to indicate his presence (similar to the use of John Williams's theme music to indicate the presence of the shark in *Jaws*) is particularly powerful in a later scene when he arrives at a bar in Nepal. Here his shadow does not just convey mystery and intrigue, but instead introduces arguably the most unsavory aspect of Indiana's character: the inappropriate affair he had with Marion Ravenwood (Karen Allen) ten years earlier that led to the "falling out" between him and her father, Abner Ravenwood, who mentored him at the University of Chicago. "I was a child, I was in love," Marion says. "It was wrong and you knew it!" While the exact details of the relationship are left vague, Marion makes it clear that the relationship was illicit and deeply hurtful to her. Describing herself as a "child" rather than simply "young" is particularly disturbing in this regard, and Spielberg emphasizes the egregiousness of Indiana's sin via his shadow, which looms enormously on the wall of the bar when he enters, hovering ominously over Marion's disproportionately small body as she stands with her back to the camera.[25] Spielberg holds the shot as she turns and faces the man she has "learned to hate" and then walks forward toward the camera until she is larger than his shadow, thus suggesting the maturity and independence she has developed since their affair.

What is most striking, however, is how stoic Indiana remains in the face of Marion's accusations. There is no hint of actual regret, just a stubborn refusal

---

[23] Peter Biskind, "Blockbuster: The Last Crusade," in *Seeing Through Movies*, ed. Mark Crispin Miller (New York: Pantheon, 1990); Wood, *Hollywood From Vietnam to Reagan*.
[24] Biskind, "Blockbuster," 126.
[25] Spielberg visually echoes Indiana's shadow on the wall with Toht's shadow when he enters the bar a few minutes later. The two shadows look surprisingly similar given the characters' hats, which is then reinforced by the accompanying music as Toht enters the bar, which sounds just like the music that introduced Indiana in the earlier South America sequence.

to face his past sins. "You knew what you were doing," he counters bluntly, and later, "I did what I did. You don't need to be happy about it" (he only apologizes when he discovers that Abner has died). It is a startlingly frank depiction of emotional cruelty and refusal to take responsibility for one's actions, which is reinforced later in the film when Indiana has the opportunity to rescue Marion from the clutches of the Nazis and chooses not to because it would risk his chances of being the first to find the Ark. Film scholar Douglas Brode puts it succinctly in noting that "Spielberg's portrait of the American male value system is more complex and critical than has been generally acknowledged."[26] Even though Indiana finds some sense of redemption in the last reel by finally choosing Marion over the Ark (a symbolic choice of selfless humanity over personal victory), the emotional and relational darkness of the Nepal scene haunts the film.

The use of darkness and shadow in the opening sequence of *Raiders* to enhance Indiana's mystery and intrigue is further complemented by Spielberg's use of a low camera when Indiana discovers a barbed arrow lodged in a tree trunk. He shows Indiana only from the chest down, thus continuing to obscure his face and make him seem more foreboding (especially since we see the faces of all the Indians working for him), an aesthetic device Spielberg would later use to dehumanize the government agents in *E.T.* (1982). The viewer doesn't actually see Indiana's face until several minutes into the film right after he has used his bullwhip to disarm Barranca (Vic Tablian), a mutinous porter who was about to pull a gun on him. Spielberg depicts this action—the first moment of violence in the series—in ten quick cuts, which formally emphasize Indiana's speed, agility, and sense of presence (he hears Barranca cocking the gun from behind him). However, those seemingly heroic qualities, which are comparable to the "disciplined and pure" violence of the gunslinger in westerns,[27] are given a darker sheen when Indiana steps out of the shadows into the shafts of light breaking through the trees above and Williams's score shifts into a menacing series of low horns that we will hear again later in the film with the introduction of Toht (Ronald Lacey), one of the film's villainous Nazis. The music works in concert with the mutually reinforcing elements of Harrison Ford's performance and the cinematography. When his face is revealed, we are held by his intense, angry expression, which is heightened by the interplay of light and shadow on his countenance (half his face is visible, while the other half is still shrouded in darkness) and the swirling mist behind him. In describing this "ominous"

---

[26] Brode, *The Films of Steven Spielberg*, 94.
[27] John G. Cawelti, *The Six-Gun Mystique*, 2nd edn (Bowling Green, OH: Bowling Green University Popular Press, 1984), 88.

shot, Nigel Morris suggests that it conveys a level of dangerousness comparable to Robert Mitchum's appearance in *Night of the Hunter* (1955).[28] At this point, all the film's formal elements have indicated that Indiana could reasonably be construed as a villain, rather than the film's hero, which establishes from the outset the complex interplay of good and bad in his character.

The opening scene also establishes Indiana's driven, single-minded relentlessness. Sapito (Alfred Molina), the only porter who has not run or been driven away at this point, pleads with him not to go into the temple—"Señor, nobody has come out of there alive. *Please*"—but Indiana ignores his words, brusquely turns him around, and starts stripping his backpack off him, thus confirming both his determination to follow through with his pursuit and his complete disregard for those he is employing. This relentlessness is also apparent in Indiana's conception of archaeology. He speaks his first lines of dialogue when he discovers the opening to the temple hidden in an embankment, telling Sapito, "This is it. This is where Forrestal cashed in."[29] "A friend of yours?" Sapito asks, to which Indiana responds, "A competitor. He was good. He was very, very good." Thus, while the opening moments contribute to the idea of archaeology as an adventure, Indiana's dialogue and the later revelation of Forrestal's rotting corpse impaled on a booby trap of retracting pikes inside the temple confirm it to be a blood sport[30] in which different archaeologists compete against each other and those who fail lose not only "fortune and glory," a refrain heard repeatedly throughout *The Temple of Doom*, but also their lives. Forrestal may have been "very, very good," but he wasn't good enough. The competitiveness of the archaeological enterprise is further cemented with Indiana's response to Forrestal's corpse. While Sapito screams in abject horror when it comes flying out of the wall after the booby trap mechanism is sprung, Indiana remains steely and almost disturbingly unfazed, a stance that Spielberg emphasizes by framing Indiana and the corpse in a two-shot locking eyes. After Indiana successfully retrieves

---

[28] Nigel Morris, *The Cinema of Steven Spielberg: Empire of Light* (London: Wallflower Press, 2007), 78.

[29] In the third draft of Kasdan's screenplay, dated August 1979, Indiana has four lines of dialogue prior to this point. Three of the lines of dialogue were cut completely and the fourth line was kept, but given to Barranca ("If they knew we were here, they would have killed us already"). Whether the decision to eliminate Indiana's initial dialogue was made during the writing, production, or editing stage, it results in making his character seem even more remote and ominous, detached from those with whom he is working and focused solely on his personal endeavor. It also means that his whipping the gun out of Barranca's hand has more force as it is an action from a shadowy, unknown figure who has yet to utter a word.

[30] While the term *blood sport* has historically referred to either the sport of hunting or entertainment in which various animals fight, sometimes to the death (e.g. cockfighting, bear-baiting), I am using it here in its broadest definition to signify any form of competition involving bloodshed.

FIGURE 3.2 Interplay of good and bad. *The introduction of Indiana Jones (Harrison Ford) in* Raiders of the Lost Ark, *which is set against low, foreboding music, builds with a series of ominous shots before finally revealing his face, the intense, angry expression of which is heightened by the interplay of light and shadow on his countenance, suggesting that Indiana could reasonably be construed as a villain, rather than the film's hero. (Digital Frame Enlargements)*

the object of his quest—a golden statue of a Mayan fertility goddess—and navigates additional dangers, which include swinging over a vast chasm, avoiding poisoned darts that shoot from the walls, and outrunning the collapse of the temple itself and a giant boulder that rushes down the tunnel, the film pulls a reversal by introducing René Belloq (Paul Freeman), a French archaeologist and Indiana's arch-nemesis who takes the hard-won statue away from him and then commands an entire tribe of Hovitos Indians to kill him.

The film's concept of archaeology as blood sport puts a new and darker twist on popular cultural conceptions of archaeological science, which Mark A. Hall notes is frequently motivated by "[t]he quest for treasure ... a central strand of cultural appropriations. It is a cultural concept with deep routes springing from European mythology and story telling as evidenced in tales such as *Beowulf*, the *Volsung Saga* and the *Mabinogion*."[31] In previous cinematic depictions of archaeological adventurism, particularly the Universal *Mummy* series from the 1930s and the Hammer remake in the 1950s, horrors emerge primarily from the findings themselves; according to Hall, "Since the 1920s not a decade has passed without at least one film dealing with the horror possibilities of Egyptian archaeology."[32] *Raiders of the Lost Ark* ups the tension in the way the archaeological pursuit itself turns violent, with competing scientists (including Indiana Jones) willing to not only risk "life and limb" in the archaeological pursuit, as he later tells his students, but to kill each other in order to claim the prize and the potentially dangerous secret it holds.

Between a loser and a hardbody

As the opening sequence of *Raiders of the Lost Ark* demonstrates, Indiana is first introduced as a mysterious, ominous character. And, even though his cynical humor and personal charm soften him throughout the film and its subsequent sequels, he is nonetheless far from a one-dimensional cardboard hero, but rather a fascinating amalgam of multiple, conflicting points of influence: the pop heroism of the classic serials and the bleak despondency of the revisionist 1970s antihero, with Lucas's desire for silver-screen gallantry tempered by Kasdan and Spielberg's urge for humanity and flaws. In this regard, then, we can read Indiana as a transitional figure between the cynical

---

[31] Mark A. Hall, "Romancing the Stones: Archaeology in Popular Cinema," *European Journal of Archaeology* 7, no. 2 (2004): 164.
[32] Ibid., 161.

antiheroes of the 1970s New Hollywood and the jingoistic hardbody heroes of the Reagan era.

The "hardbody film," a term that was first coined by Susan Jeffords[33], is defined by Drew Ayers as:

> ... those (usually very violent) Hollywood action films made chiefly between the 1980s and early 1990s that feature a central male hero as the lone protagonist charged with "saving the day." What is unique to this cycle of films is the focus on the body of the male hero, a body that is fetishized for its hard and sculpted muscularity and/or its athletic skill and physical prowess. These films also fetishize the weapons, vehicles, and other objects used by the heroes in their quests. Of interest as well is that many of these films have a very limited supporting cast and an underdeveloped or completely nonexistent parallel romantic storyline.[34]

Raiders of the Lost Ark and the other *Indiana Jones* films are never included in the lists of films that comprise this subgenre of action/adventure cinema[35] primarily because Harrison Ford's physique, while certainly athletic and toned, is a far cry from the commanding, hyper-masculine, muscle-bound hardbodies of bulked-up actors like Arnold Schwarzenegger, Sylvester Stallone, Chuck Norris, and Jean-Claude Van Damme. Indiana is never visually objectified in the same manner as the hardbody heroes; he is never, for example, depicted in stylized and fragmented close-ups, and he is rarely unclothed in any manner, while most hardbody films "are notable for their insistence on depicting the unclothed male form."[36] In *Indiana Jones and the Temple of Doom*, which was released just as the hardbody cycle was starting to gain momentum, there is greater visual attention paid to Ford's body, as he spends a significant portion of the film's second half without a shirt, and when he later puts it back on, it is tattered across the back, mostly open in the front, and eventually has one of the sleeves torn off, thus allowing for more physical display than in *Raiders*.

Despite the physical disparities in terms of both size and visual treatment, Indiana shares with the hardbody heroes a relentless punishment of his physical body, although the ideological functions of this punishment are quite different. In separate essays, film scholars Steve Neal, Susan Jeffords, and David Savran argue that such explicit and pointed violence is a necessary

---

[33] Susan Jeffords, *Hard Bodies: Hollywood Masculinity in the Reagan Era* (New Brunswick, NJ: Rutgers University Press, 1994).
[34] Drew Ayers, "Bodies, Bullets, and Bad Guys: Elements of the Hardbody Film," *Film Criticism* 32, no. 3 (Spring 2008): 42.
[35] See, for example, the Appendix at the end of Ayers' listing of the hardbody "film corpus."
[36] Ayers, "Bodies, Bullets, and Bad Guys," 41.

counterbalance and corrective to the objectification and homoerotic suggestiveness that results from the heroic (and often minimally clothed) male body on display.[37] As Savran notes, "Any delight that the male spectator might derive from watching [the hardbody hero's] rippling flesh is mitigated by the fact that that same flesh is insistently brutalized and turned into a spectacle of pain which the spectator might be expected, if not to avert his eyes from, at least to wince at."[38] Because Indiana's flesh is not on display in this manner, the violence against it does not perform the same de-eroticizing function; rather, it emphasizes Indiana's physical vulnerability, a key means by which *Raiders* differentiates itself from both the hardbody movies that followed it and the classic serials that inspired it.

The bodily punishment that Indiana suffers is often more intense and for longer periods of time than the suffering of characters like John Rambo, whose displays of physical anguish are evident only in the immediate moment of violence, such as when he is being tortured on an electrified box-spring by Soviet agents in *Rambo: First Blood Part II* (1985), or in a scene of explicit self-care, such as when he stitches his lacerated bicep in *First Blood* (1982) or uses gunpowder to cauterize a shrapnel wound in his side in *Rambo III* (1988). In all four *Indiana Jones* films, although particularly in *Raiders* and *Temple of Doom*, Indiana's body is repeatedly beaten, cut, shot, and even whipped, and unlike the heroes of the classic film serials, it displays the ravages of this violence in no uncertain terms, which complicates Robert Kolker's claim that Indiana's survival of such physical abuse "presag[es] the body resilience that becomes a mark of the male action and superhero film."[39] In *Raiders*, Spielberg emphasizes the brutal physical ramifications of the film's action, particularly the extended truck chase sequence through the desert in which Indiana is shot in the arm and later dragged behind the truck. The emphasis on the physical is achieved not just through the make-up effects that depict broken and bruised skin, but also in a lengthy scene in which Marion attempts to tend to his numerous wounds. The muscular weakness, joint stiffness, and intense amounts of pain he suffers—"It's not the years, it's the mileage," he tells her—are not reminiscent of the serial movie heroes after which he is modeled, who tended to be all but invincible and whose bodies were rarely marked by violence, or the hardbody heroes, whose pain and bleeding function primarily as obstacles to be quickly surmounted and forgotten. After the truck chase in *Raiders*, we are not allowed to forget its lingering physical

---

[37] Steve Neale, "Masculinity as Spectacle: Reflections on Men and Mainstream Cinema," *Screen* 24, no. 6 (1983): 2–17; Susan Jeffords, *Hard Bodies*; David Savran, "The Sadomasochist in the Closet: White Masculinity and the Culture of Victimization," *Differences* 8, no. 2 (1996): 127–52.
[38] Savran, "The Sadomasochist in the Closet," 135.
[39] Robert Kolker, *A Cinema of Loneliness*, 4th edn (New York: Oxford University Press, 2011), 316.

effects, even when Spielberg plays it for wince-inducing comedy when Sallah (John Rhys Davies), Indiana's Egyptian ally, gives him a big, painful bear hug before sending him off on a tramp steamer. Indiana's clearly marked physical suffering humanizes him, reminding us explicitly that his feats, however superhuman they may appear in the moment of action, come with an all-too-human physical cost—a powerful example of the complex multimodal address that deftly interweaves fantasy and reality throughout the series.[40]

Thus, despite sharing certain commonalities with the hardbody heroes who would come to dominate the American action movie throughout the 1980s, Indiana's heroism is not so clearly drawn; rather, it is touched with shades of disrepute and physical vulnerability. This gives us a different perspective on one of the most memorable and controversial moments in *Raiders* when Indiana, abruptly challenged during a hectic chase in Cairo by an enormous, black-clad, scimitar-wielding Arab swordsman, simply pulls out his revolver and shoots the man dead. Frederick Wasser views this sequence as evidence that Spielberg had "absorbed some of the new win-by-any-means definition of heroism" and cast Indiana as a "mean-spirited hero" who helped inspire similar masculine (hardbody) heroes of 1980s action cinema.[41] The scene, which was reportedly improvised on set by Spielberg and Harrison Ford because the actor was exhausted from a bout of dysentery, also bothered screenwriter Lawrence Kasdan, who had written a more conventional fight scene that was storyboarded but never filmed. "It disturbed me," Kasdan said. "I thought that was brutal in a way the rest of the movie wasn't."[42]

But, is it? Part of the complexity of Indiana's status as a hero is his use of violence, which is crucial to differentiating him from the traditional icon of masculine American heroism: the gunslinger. As John Cawelti writes in *The Six-Gun Mystique*, the ritual of the draw is a quintessential component of the western and key to the proper gunslinger's heroism: "This controlled and aesthetic mode of killing is particularly important as the supreme mark of differentiation between the hero and the savage."[43] In casually gunning down the Arab swordsman, Indiana betrays "the qualities of reluctance, control and elegance,"[44] thus fatally compromising his status as a hero not so much because he is "mean-spirited" or cruel in his method of killing, but because he places simple practicality above proper heroic behavior. Discussion of this killing typically takes place outside the context of the larger sequence, in which Indiana is desperately trying to find Marion, who has been kidnapped

---

[40] Morris, *The Cinema of Steven Spielberg*, 103–4.
[41] Frederick Wasser, *Steven Spielberg's America* (London: Polity Press, 2010), 97.
[42] McBride, *Steven Spielberg: A Biography*, 317.
[43] Cawelti, *The Six-Gun Mystique*, 87.
[44] Ibid.

FIGURE 3.3 "It's not the years, it's the mileage." *Throughout the Indiana Jones films, Spielberg emphasizes the brutal physical ramifications of the action sequences on Indiana's body, particularly the extended truck chase sequence through the desert in* Raiders of the Lost Ark *in which Indiana is shot in the arm and later dragged behind the truck. (Digital Frame Enlargement)*

(right before the crowd parts to reveal the swordsman, Indiana has climbed on top of a cart and is desperately yelling Marion's name). He is already physically exhausted (note how his shirt is drenched with sweat and he is breathing heavily) and time is of the essence, so to engage in a "fair fight" with the swordsman would be the height of absurdity given the situation— the kind of thing that only happens in the movies. Thus, Indiana's decision to quickly dispatch his adversary is eminently practical, even as it flies in the face of audience expectations and undercuts his association with the mythology of American heroism. Douglas Brode recognizes this in arguing that "Spielberg redeems the gag ... through meaningful context. We are meant to see the Indiana Jones image as just that, a self-conscious caricature, mounted by a man who needs just such bravado to cover his own deep insecurities. Harrison Ford is playing Dr. Jones, while Dr. Jones is playing at being Indiana. There are times when the role-playing must give way to imperatives of reality."[45] It is not surprising, then, that audiences tend to burst out with laughter at the surprising move, not because Indiana displays some kind of great physical or intellectual superiority in shooting the swordsman, but because he breaks cinematic convention and acts *practically*, rather than *spectacularly*.

At other points in the film, Indiana's use of violence is surprisingly brutal and unrestrained, which again conflicts with the myth of the gunslinger to which his character owes a great debt. A good example can be found in the extreme ferocity of the desert truck chase sequence. After an intense

---

[45] Brode, *The Films of Steven Spielberg*, 96.

sequence of events in which Indiana is thrown through the truck's windshield onto the hood, crawls underneath the truck along its chassis and is temporarily dragged behind it, and then crawls back into the cab, he goes after the Nazi driver with a kind of vengeful anger that is atypical of mainstream action movies of the era, although quite common in 1970s vigilante films like *Walking Tall* (1971), *Dirty Harry* (1971), and *Death Wish* (1974). Indiana's face is a bitter grimace of fury as he repeatedly slams the driver's head into the dashboard and then delivers the *coup de grace* by hurling him out of the broken windshield, a literal eye-for-an-eye repayment for the earlier violence inflicted on him. It is telling that, after the driver is killed by being run over by the truck and Indiana runs Belloq's staff car off the road, Spielberg delivers a brief denouement in which Indiana grimaces in agony and grips the arm in which he was been shot, further reminders of his all-too-human physicality.

The killing of the Arab swordsman and the truck chase are but two examples of moments in the series that posit Indiana as functionally triumphant (albeit also wounded and exhausted), yet he also suffers more than his fair share of failures throughout *Raiders* and its sequels, is subject to explicit satirizing, and is depicted as being just a step away from outright villainy. Most of Indiana's flaws and contradictions are evident in the opening sequence of *Raiders of the Lost Ark*. As mentioned earlier, although he escapes the underground temple alive with the statue he sought, it is immediately taken from him by Belloq, a foreshadowing of both Belloq's later taking the Ark from him at the dig outside of Cairo and the film's cynical conclusion in which the U.S. government reneges on its promise to allow Indiana and Dr. Marcus Brody (Denholm Elliott), a fellow academic and museum curator, to maintain possession of the Ark and study it. And, while Indiana's dashing exploits in navigating the temple's many booby traps have their fair share of conventional swashbuckling and derring-do (the very fact that he survives them is evidence of his physical and intellectual superiority to Forrestal, his competitor), there is also a clear tone of humor and satire that Spielberg carried over from his previous film, the historical slapstick farce *1941*.[46] It should not escape notice that the first use of John Williams's triumphant Indiana Jones theme music accompanies a shot of him swinging awkwardly from a vine and splashing into a river well short of the escape plane floating in the middle (a humorous homage to the many Tarzan movies of the 1930s and 1940s and, as Douglas Brode points out, a similar sequence on a beach in Disney's *20,000 Leagues*

---

[46] Specifically, the visual gag in which Toht appears to threaten Marion with an instrument of torture that turns out to be a collapsible hanger for his overcoat was actually filmed for *1941* when Christopher Lee's Capt. Wolfgang von Kleinschmidt is trying to coerce Slim Pickens' Hollis Wood in the Japanese submarine. The piece was never used in either the original theatrical version or the subsequent director's cut released on laser disc in 1996, although it was included as an outtake.

Under the Sea). This follows several long shots of him running for his life across an open field with the Hovitos chasing after him, screaming to his pilot Jock (Fred Sorenson) to start the engines as dust flies comically off his clothes. While Peter Biskind (1990) reads these shots as "bring[ing] to mind the myriad of naively racist jungle movies of the thirties,"[47] such a reading requires that Indiana be depicted as somehow superior to the "bunch of spear-chucking natives" from whom he is escaping, which is clearly not the case. Once in the river, Indiana is made to look pointedly ridiculous swimming through the water with the brim of his soaked fedora drooping into his face while dozens of Hovitos fire poisoned darts at him—a visual better suited to Bob Hope than Charlton Heston. The final assault on Indiana's dignity comes with the revelation of his abject fear of snakes when he finds Jock's pet python in the seat with him. When he yells with a mix of fear and anger, "I hate snakes, Jock, I hate 'em!," Jock responds, "C'mon—show a little backbone, will ya?," a pointedly humorous demand given what Indiana has just gone through.

Spielberg's tendency to temper Indiana's bravado with awkward and even buffoonish behavior is evident in the subsequent films, as well. For example, the first time we hear Williams's signature theme music in *The Temple of Doom* is when Indiana is being sped away from a disastrous encounter with Chinese gangsters at a Shanghai night club and is swigging antidote to poison he drank in what he thought was a moment of triumph. *The Last Crusade* is even bolder in playing Indiana's actions for laughs, beginning with the opening sequence of a young Indiana Jones (River Phoenix) trying valiantly to steal the Cross of Coronado from a group of grave robbers. The sequence is replete with failed actions, starting with Indiana attempting to jump from a ridge onto his horse, only to have it step forward just before he lands. In the ensuing chase across the top of a moving train, he grabs hold of a rig on a water tower and swings not to safety, but instead makes a complete circle and winds up right back on the train in front of his adversary (a gag that is repeated later in the film when Indiana and his father are tied to a chair in a burning room and discover a secret revolving door that takes them 360 degrees right back into the inferno).

Not incidentally, the opening action sequences in all three of these films end in failure for Indiana: he loses the statue to Belloq in *Raiders*, he is never able to retrieve the diamond that was his payment in *The Temple of Doom*, and he has the Cross of Coronado taken away from him and returned to the grave robbers by the local sheriff in *The Last Crusade*. In each sequence Indiana is betrayed, humiliated, and barely escapes with his life, which is

---

[47] Biskind, "Blockbuster," 119.

quite the opposite of the structurally similar pre-credits sequences of the later James Bond movies, which tend to reinforce 007's power and authority via spectacular stunts and narrow escapes.[48] And, while there are elements of triumph at the end of all four films, it should be noted that Indiana's quest to find the Ark of the Covenant and keep it away from the Nazis in *Raiders* is an abject failure and the Ark protects itself by annihilating the Nazis who open it, suggesting that all of Indiana's efforts have been in vain.

It is also important to note that, similar to the antiheroes of 1970s American cinema, Indiana Jones is an individualistic, self-interested hero whose actions typically benefit others only incidentally. Like Basie in *Empire of the Sun* (1987), Indiana is "a darker version of the American adventurer; he is a self-centered survivor."[49] Philosophers Michel Le Gall and Charles Taliaferro discuss Indiana as a "prodigal son" character and emphasize how he betrayed the trust of his adoptive father figure Abner Ravenwood with his inappropriate relationship with Marion ten years earlier.[50] They also refer to his behavior as "reckless (a far cry from the calculating and dispassionate heroics of standard-fare action movies) and, on occasion, cavalier and unheroic."[51] Susan Aronstein recognizes Indiana's selfish individuality in comparing him to the knights of Arthurian legends, noting that, especially in the earlier films, he is "adamantly nonconstructed, dangerously individual ... a mercenary out for his own gain, uninterested in 'right' and uncontrolled by any sort of chivalric or cultural code."[52] He is therefore quite distinct from the swashbuckling heroes of Hollywood adventure films in the 1930s and 40s, who Vivian Sobchack describes as "men who take pleasure in their grace and skill, who often brag—yet their final allegiance is not to themselves but to their society."[53]

The title of *Raiders of the Lost Ark* is crucial in this regard. A "raider," as defined by the *Oxford English Dictionary*, is "a person who raids or mounts a hostile and predatory incursion; a marauder"—a perfect description of

---

[48] The primary exception is the most recent Bond film, *Skyfall* (2012), in which James Bond (Daniel Craig), following a lengthy chase sequence in Istanbul, is accidentally shot from atop a moving train by another British agent and falls hundreds of feet into a river below. This pre-credits sequence, rather than reinforcing Bond's physical and mental superiority, shockingly emphasizes his physical vulnerability, albeit in a way that provides an opportunity for a rebirth of the character.
[49] Wasser, *Steven Spielberg's America*, 132.
[50] Michel Le Gall and Charles Taliaferro, "The Recovery of Childhood and the Search for the Absent Father," in *Steven Spielberg and Philosophy: We're Gonna Need a Bigger Book*, ed. Dean A. Kowalski (Lexington: University Press of Kentucky, 2008), 38–49.
[51] Ibid., 40.
[52] Susan Aronstein, "'Not Exactly a Knight:' Arthurian Narrative and Recuperative Politics in the Indiana Jones Trilogy," *Cinema Journal* 34, no. 4 (Summer 1995): 9.
[53] Vivian Sobchack, "Genre Film: Myth, Ritual, and Sociodrama," in *Film/Culture: Explorations of Cinema in Its Social Context*, ed. Sari Thomas (Metuchen, NJ: Scarecrow Press, 1982), 161.

Indiana Jones. When the title was altered to *Indiana Jones and the Raiders of the Lost Ark* on the video box art when it was re-released on VHS in 1999, the intention was to bring the film's title in line with the other films in the series, but it functionally destroyed the symmetry between the title and the film's content.[54] Indiana is, in his own words, a grave robber. In *Raiders of the Lost Ark*, we hear an important fragment of one of his class lectures as Marcus Brody opens the classroom door: "... don't confuse that with robbing, in which case we mean the removal of the contents of the barrow." This scene immediately follows the opening sequence in the Mayan temple in which we saw Indiana doing almost exactly that: removing the contents, not of a barrow, but of a sacred temple. A bit later in the classroom scene, Marcus tells Indiana somewhat casually and almost sarcastically, "I'm sure everything you do for the museum conforms to the International Treaty for the Protection of Antiquities," a statement that flies in the face of everything we saw in the opening ten minutes. His reputation as something less than an ethical scientist also crops up in *Temple of Doom*, when the Prime Minister of Pankot Palace reminds him of an incident in Honduras in which he was accused of being "a grave robber rather than an archaeologist" and another incident in Madagascar that resulted in the sultan threatening to castrate him if he ever returned. The original title of *Raiders of the Lost Ark* therefore makes sense in implying in no uncertain terms that Indiana is one of the "raiders," along with Belloq and his Nazi employers, as well as Indiana's employer, the U.S. government. In other words, the title lumps both heroes and villains into a singular category, emphasizing the "hostile" and "predatory" nature of their pursuits—further emphasis on the idea of archaeology as a blood sport.

Thus, it is not surprising that Indiana and Belloq are visually and thematically connected throughout *Raiders* in different and fascinating ways. Visually, they are opposites, their different modes of dress suggestive of class antagonism, particularly when they are contrasted in South America: Indiana is resolutely working class in his rough leather jacket, loose trousers, and workboots, while Belloq is marked as the gentleman on safari: high boots, riding pants, a safari hat, and a well-pressed shirt. Their opposition is made even more striking given that Indiana is covered with dirt and cobwebs after narrowly escaping from the temple and is sitting on the ground while Belloq stands over him; the visual implication is that Indiana has been

---

[54] The official title of the film remains *Raiders of the Lost Ark*, despite the change in all box art since 1999. The title has remained unchanged in the film's opening credits, and the American Film Institute still lists it as *Raiders of the Lost Ark* in its database (http://www.afi.com/members/catalog/DetailView.aspx?s=&Movie=55226; accessed February 15, 2012).

reduced to unwittingly playing the role of Belloq's assistant, performing the dirty, dangerous work inside the temple while Belloq awaits outside to retrieve the prize without sullying his clothes. Although critics have identified Indiana as a representative and agent of Western colonialism, Belloq is the film's true colonialist: his distinctive French accent, insistence on surface formality (he calls Indiana "Dr. Jones" and says "At least we can behave like civilized people"), and fashionable clothes (particularly the Panama Jack hat and white suit he dons in Cairo) play as convenient shorthand for European colonial smugness and aristocracy. He mocks Indiana several times for "choosing the wrong friends," which suggests that he is the superior colonialist for being able to control and manipulate both the Hovitos tribe and the local Egyptians while Indiana is betrayed over and over again. Despite their visual distinctions, though, Indiana and Belloq are presented as essentially two sides of the same coin, particularly in their conversation in a Cairo hookah bar after Indiana has been led to believe that Marion was killed in a truck explosion. Continuing the idea of archeology as a blood sport, Belloq calls Indiana "an adversary so close to my own level" and laments that their years of competition may be coming to a close. To further connect the two men, Spielberg frames them in a compelling two-shot, with Belloq fully lit and in focus occupying the middle ground on the right-hand side of the screen while Indiana, who is drunk and angry over Marion's presumed death, remains primarily in shadow and slightly out of focus in the immediate foreground, taking up roughly two-thirds of the left-hand side of the screen. While framed in this manner, Belloq says, "You and I are very much alike. Archaeology is our religion. Yet we have both fallen from the purer faith. Our methods are not different as much as you pretend. I am a shadowy reflection of you. It would take only a nudge to make you like me, to push you out of the light." Spielberg's lighting and framing plays as adroitly ironic visual counterpoint to Belloq's dialogue about "shadowy reflections" and "light" as Indiana is the one shrouded in darkness; it looks like *he* is the shadowy reflection who has already been pushed out of the light, not Belloq. Indiana's only response is to growl, "Now you're getting nasty," to which Belloq replies, "You know it's true." This exchange confirms what the film has already implied visually and narratively. There is only a small divide between Indiana and Belloq, a recurring motif in Spielberg's films that frequently focus on pairs of characters—Jamie and Basie in *Empire of the Sun* (1987), Oskar Schindler and Amon Goeth in *Schindler's List* (1993), Carl Hanratty and Frank Abagnale Jr. in *Catch Me If You Can* (2002)—who are, to greater and lesser degrees, "shadowy reflections" of each other. Far from a pure hero, Indiana functions as one only in comparison to those he is fighting against.

FIGURE 3.4 "I am a shadowy reflection of you." *To visually connect Indiana and his nemesis, the French archaeologist Belloq (Paul Freeman) in* Raiders of the Lost Ark, *Spielberg frames them in a compelling two-shot, with Belloq fully lit and in focus occupying the middle ground while Indiana, who is drunk and angry over Marion's presumed death, remains primarily in shadow and slightly out of focus in the immediate foreground. (Digital Frame Enlargement)*

Redeeming the raider

Indiana's self-interestedness and darker shades gradually recede over the course of the series as he is reincorporated into traditional family and social structures, ultimately confirmed by his repaired relationship with his absent father, Dr. Henry Jones (Sean Connery), in *The Last Crusade* and his marriage to Marion and realization of his own fatherhood in *The Kingdom of the Crystal Skull*, even though his full submission to something other than himself in the final moment of the series is mitigated by his symbolic refusal to give up his fedora. His actions in *The Temple of Doom*, although chronologically set before *Raiders*, suggest a willingness to forgo "fortune and glory" for the greater good of returning the stolen Sankara stones and the village's children from a villainous Thuggee cult, with whom Indiana is clearly distinguished even if his behavior is still frequently self-interested and crude. We see this most clearly in the film's opening sequence where Indiana is introduced in a Shanghai nightclub finalizing a shady deal to sell the remains of Nurhachi, the first Emperor of the Manchu Dynasty, to a Chinese gangster named Lao Che (Roy Chiao). Indiana's willingness to deal with organized crime if it means a profit (his payment is a huge diamond) is testament to his self-serving, opportunistic nature. By *The Last Crusade*, the divide between him and the villains is decidedly sharper, particularly in the case of Dr. Elsa Schneider (Alison Doody), who, like Belloq, is a driven archaeologist who sells her soul by working for the Nazis. Her villainy is even more personal, however, as she is first presented as an ally before being revealed as a Nazi who double-crosses Indiana after sleeping with him. However, an exchange similar to the one between Indiana and Belloq in *Raiders* is telling: "Don't look at me like that," Elsa says of the disgusted grimace on Indiana's face while in her presence. "We both wanted the Grail. I would have done anything to get it. You would have done the same," to which Indiana replies, "I'm sorry you think so." In *The Kingdom of the Crystal Skull* there is no attempt made to associate Indiana, now a much older man stepping into the paternal role he has largely resisted, with any of the Soviet villains, who are resolutely cartoonish. Thus, Indiana develops from his character in *Raiders* who essentially agrees with Belloq that the difference between their drives and methods is little more than a self-delusion, to boldly asserting his moral separation from Elsa in *The Last Crusade*, to being so clearly separated from Soviet villainy in *The Kingdom of the Crystal Skull* that it no longer needs to be addressed.

The sense of idealism that is studiously lacking in *Raiders* and much of *The Temple of Doom* is addressed in the opening sequence of *The Last Crusade*, which explicitly depicts how Indiana lost it. Here we meet Indiana as a teenager taking a trip through Utah's Monument Valley with his Boy Scout troop in 1912. When Indiana and a friend explore a cave and discover a group of looters in the cavern below them digging up the Cross of Coronado, the idealistic young Indiana is incensed. "It's an important artifact and it belongs in a museum!" he says, which plays ironically against his later exploits as an adult in which he travels the globe raiding "important artifacts" and selling them for his own profit. At this point in his life, archeology has not become a blood sport. Importantly, Spielberg sets up the sequence to trick the viewer into misrecognizing the leader of the dig, who is identified in the credits only as "Fedora," as Indiana Jones. We first see him from behind, wearing the iconic leather jacket and fedora hat, just as we saw Indiana in the opening of *Raiders*. Even when he turns around to look at the just unearthed artifact, his unshaven face is partially obscured by the shadow cast by the brim of his hat, and we don't see his countenance fully until he raises his face into the light and the camera moves in to reveal that he is not, in fact, Indiana Jones. We thus learn that Indiana's signature look was explicitly adopted from Fedora, the villain in this opening sequence, signaling the loss of his boyish idealism and adoption of a harder, more cynical worldview that informs his actions throughout the series. When Indiana finally reclaims the Cross of Coronado as an adult in *The Last Crusade*, it is not so much out of faithfulness to his boyhood idealism, but rather revenge for his adolescent humiliation.

Indiana Jones and the Temple of Doom differs from *Raiders of the Lost Ark* in that Indiana's quest to retrieve the lost Sankara stones is not driven by a nationalist or monetary agenda, but rather by a plea from the shaman of a starving Indian village that has been ransacked by a revived Thuggee cult. This would seem to indicate that Indiana has had a change of heart and is acting in a purely heroic manner in trying to save the village and retrieve their children who have been kidnapped and forced into slavery. Yet, Indiana's initial motives are entirely self-interested. When his adolescent sidekick, a Chinese orphan named Short Round (Ke Huy Quan), asks him what the Sankara stones are, Indiana replies, "Fortune and glory, kid." At this point, Spielberg has framed Indiana and Short Round in a wide shot standing on a ridge on the left-hand side of the screen; in the far background of the right-hand side of the frame we can barely make out the decimated village feebly lit against the dark of the night sky. Thus, Indiana's association of the lost stones with his own fortune and glory is visually counterpointed against the village's genuine need of the stones for survival, and Spielberg drives the point home by cutting to a close-up of Indiana's face as the music swells ironically and he repeats, "Fortune and glory." Indiana's decision to risk life and limb to retrieve the stones is therefore framed within his own self-interest, and it is entirely ambiguous as to whether he even intends to return the stones to the village if he finds them. This selfish desire extends well into the film, and it is not until he hears the screams of the kidnapped children being beaten in the mines that he makes the decision to rescue them. However, whatever selflessness Indiana demonstrates in rescuing the children from slavery is essentially short-lived since the action in *The Temple of Doom* takes place in 1935, thus situating it chronologically before the action in *Raiders of the Lost Ark*, which is set in 1936.[55]

In *The Last Crusade*, Indiana does demonstrate a significant amount of personal growth, and his view of archaeology as a "win at all costs" blood sport is leavened with both familial ties and spiritual growth. When Indiana is first offered the chance to track down the clues that might lead to the discovery of the Holy Grail, he turns it down. It is only when he discovers that his father has disappeared while pursuing the Grail that he agrees to "pick up the trail." Thus, his immediate motivation for the quest is driven by saving his father, rather than accumulating more fortune and glory, as in *Raiders* and *The Temple of Doom*. When Kazim, a member of the Brotherhood of the Cruciform

---

[55] There is some debate regarding if and how Indiana Jones develops as a character over the films. Susan Aronstein ("Not Exactly a Knight") argues that the series, "as do all Arthurian romances, uses the process by which Indiana Jones, as hero, allows himself to be hailed and recognizes his place within the structure of the tale's dominant 'American' ideology to affirm that ideology" (3). Lester D. Friedman (*Citizen Spielberg*, Urbana: University of Illinois Press, 2006) views the series as a kind of coming-of-age story, "an evolutionary bildungsroman with Indiana Jones at its core" (76–7). Andrew M. Gordon (*Empire of Dreams*) sharply disagrees and instead views the films as inherently unrelated monomyths in which Indiana learns "the same moral lesson—to value people over sacred objects—each time: that is repetition rather than growth" (110–11).

Sword, a centuries-old group dedicated to protecting the Grail's secret location, tells Indiana, "Ask yourself, why do you seek the Cup of Christ? Is it for His glory, or yours?," Indiana makes explicit the purpose of his quest: "I didn't come for the Cup of Christ. I came to find my father." His motivation is further delineated in the film's climax when he agrees to recover the cup only because the film's villain, a millionaire with delusions of eternal life named Walter Donovan (Julian Glover), has shot Henry in the stomach, thus necessitating the cup's healing power. Indiana's willingness to take on three deadly challenges to recover the Grail becomes not only a fully selfless action, but a fundamentally spiritual one, as well. As Donovan says, "The healing power of the Grail is the only thing that can save your father now. It's time to ask yourself what you believe." The decision by Indiana, who has throughout the series professed consistent skepticism about religion, mysticism, and magic, to retrieve the Grail in order to heal his father is definitive proof of his faith in its supernatural power. In both *Raiders* and *The Temple of Doom*, he expressed consistent doubt about the otherworldly nature of the objects of his quest—the "artifacts" that would bring him "fortune and glory." In *The Last Crusade*, he finally recognizes and submits completely to something outside his own self-interest and control. While he appeared to do this at the end of *The Temple of Doom*, his admonition in the final moments that "Anything can happen on the way to Delhi" suggests that his intervention in India resulting in the restitution of the village and the salvation of its children was a detour in his otherwise relentless pursuit of "fortune and glory." In *The Last Crusade*, the former raider is effectively redeemed.

Disturbing our "Morning in America"

The most persistent and troubling criticism of the *Indiana Jones* series, particularly *Raiders of the Lost Ark* and *Indiana Jones and the Temple of Doom*, is that it functions as a thinly disguised, mutually reinforcing cultural corollary to the neoconservative political agenda, increased militarization, and aggressive U.S. foreign policy of the 1980s by emphasizing the supposed right of a superior American nation to dominate the Third World in its own interests. As J. Hoberman put it, "Together with his commercial ally and fellow infantilizer George Lucas, Spielberg produced the quintessential entertainments for Ronald Reagan's Morning in America."[56] Similarly, Frank P. Tomasulo argues that "in making *Raiders of the Lost Ark*, Spielberg implicitly endorsed the

---

[56] J. Hoberman, "Laugh, Cry, Believe: Spielbergization and Its Discontents," *Virginia Quarterly Review* 83, no. 1 (2007): 123.

new Reagan administration's policies in the Middle East, Central and South America, as well as the new regime's positions on women's rights, laissez-faire capitalism, CIA covert operations, the Moral Majority, and America's renewed stature in the world of nations."[57] According to Patricia Zimmerman, the film is not just politically dangerous in setting back the clock on American foreign policy, feminism, and domestic politics, but fundamentally disingenuous in hiding its agenda with extra-filmic appeals to its clever and efficient production strategies and diegetic appeals to cinematic nostalgia:

> The manufacture of consensus around [*Raiders*] is based on employing references to film history and filmmaking to: decenter the immediate political questions of a film which destroys Third World people at a time when U.S. intervention in Central America is mounting; get a feisty woman entrepreneur out of a bar and into a skirt at a time when the advances of the second wave of feminism are threatened by a resurgence in the ideology of the traditional nuclear family; and mix up control of religious power with politics at a time when the New Right has molded this alliance into a powerful political tool. By effacing its own historical context, this film tries to deny that it in fact advocates the ideology of the New Right. History, as witnessed in *Raiders*, disguises political polarization. It is, instead, a vacation spot away from conflict.[58]

Susan Aronstein takes a different approach in arguing that the first three films in the series have the same underlying structure and ideology of the ancient Arthurian legends: "The tales of Indiana Jones are tales of knighthood, modernizations of medieval chivalric romances in which America stands in for the Arthurian court, the Third World becomes the forest of adventure, and the Nazis or Thuggees function as hostile knights to be defeated in an effort to recuperate and reaffirm America's cultural destiny."[59] And, while Robin Wood deliberately falls short of referring to *Raiders* as a "fascist film," he does write that it and other films like it are "precisely the kinds of entertainment that a potentially Fascist culture would be expected to produce and enjoy."[60] The consistency of this ideological critique of the *Indiana Jones* series is powerful enough that it also appears with regularity in the writings of those scholars and critics who are otherwise even-handed, if not admiring, in their critical treatment of Spielberg's films. For example, Frederick Wasser argues that

---

[57] See Friedman, *Citizen Spielberg*, 109.
[58] Zimmerman, "Soldiers of Fortune," 37.
[59] Aronstein, "Not Exactly a Knight," 3.
[60] Wood, *Hollywood From Vietnam to Reagan*, 170.

"[*Raiders*], more than [Spielberg's previous films], melded the blockbuster into the Reagan ideology of resurgent America. A larger metaphor behind the action in *Raiders* was the American emotional desire to never lose again."[61]

Like much of the negative criticism geared toward Spielberg's films, the general critical consensus around the reactionary ideological implications of the *Indiana Jones* series has calcified with repetition into apparent fact beyond question. That even Spielberg's admirers tend to distance themselves from the films' surface politics, rather than question and interrogate them, is testament to the enduring power of this interpretive frame. Thus, the following section is not meant to thoroughly debunk arguments about the films' neoconservative leanings, but rather to interrogate them by suggesting that any such appeal the films might offer is only one layer of meaning and that the films can sustain more nuanced and contradictory readings that are decidedly darker and more critical of dominant ideology. As Nigel Morris eloquently argues, "That a movie relates to social discourses does not automatically mean it condones or reproduces one particular stance."[62]

There is no doubt that, on the surface at least, there is a tempting coherence to the ideological charges that the *Indiana Jones* films fit all too neatly into the New Right politics of the Reagan era, and it is no wonder that progressive critics who were already leery of Spielberg's work immediately tried to put those pieces together. Yet, the fit is largely illusory in that it works only if certain elements of the films are emphasized (the centrality of a male hero, the settings in mostly Third World nations, the secondary role of female characters, etc.) while other elements are conspicuously ignored or downplayed while crucial assumptions remain unquestioned. One of the biggest assumptions, which has already been interrogated earlier in this chapter, is the idea that Indiana Jones is a successful hero whose quests end in triumph. For example, Ella Shohat and Robert Stam argue that the films are "premised on an imperialized globe, in which archeology professors can 'rescue' artifacts from the colonized world for the greater benefit of science and civilization."[63] While this premise is essentially valid in examining the diegetic fantasy world of the *Indiana Jones* series, Shohat and Stam assume that there is follow-through on that premise when, in fact, there is not. Throughout the series the artifacts sought by Indiana are rarely if ever "rescued," and they never in any way benefit (Western) science and civilization. At the end of *Raiders*, the Ark of the Covenant is kept out of the

---

[61] Wasser, *Steven Spielberg's America*, 97.
[62] Morris, *The Cinema of Steven Spielberg*, 109.
[63] Ella Shohat and Robert Stam, *Unthinking Eurocentrism: Multiculturalism and the Media* (London: Routledge, 1994), 124.

Nazis' hands and ends up with the U.S. government, but as we will see in more detail later, it is ironically crated up and hidden away, its power clearly beyond human control. At the end of *The Temple of Doom*, Indiana loses two of the three Sankara stones in the river and returns the third to the small Indian village from which it was originally stolen by the Thuggees. At the end of *The Last Crusade*, Indiana again keeps the Holy Grail from Nazi clutches, but at the end his very survival requires that he *not* retrieve it from where it has fallen into a crevice, arguably to be lost for all time. And, finally, at the end of *The Kingdom of the Crystal Skull*, an alien flying saucer that Indiana and others discover buried for millennia beneath a temple in the Amazonian jungle flies off into another dimension and disappears. For Indiana Jones, every major discovery he makes is only a prelude to his losing it or giving it up.

Similarly, the argument that the *Indiana Jones* films are upbeat, regressive fantasies about American exceptionalism and the general superiority of Western culture over the Third World is premised on an unquestioned collapsing of Indiana Jones, paternalistic values, and the United States government in a way that turns him into a literal and figurative representative of an idealized, if not divine, America. However, there is plenty of evidence within the films to not only call this assumption into question, but also to suggest that the series as a whole takes a frequently satirical stance toward the idea of American exceptionalism and the nation's role in policing the world.

There is no question that Indiana Jones *is* an American and has been and will continue to be viewed as such by virtually all audiences. His clothing and demeanor evoke a long list of earlier American heroes from adventure movies and serials. He is explicitly located in *Raiders of the Lost Ark*, *The Last Crusade*, and *The Kingdom of the Crystal Skull* as living and working in northern California, and *The Last Crusade* confirms that, despite his globe-hopping as an adult, he grew up in Utah or some other western state, thus fully associating him with the western frontier. Nevertheless, he is in no way a particularly committed American; his nationality is more of a happenstance than a defining characteristic. He is neither a patriotic Captain America nor a Boy Scout-like Superman. Rather, as noted earlier, Indiana is a mercenary, an archeological gun for hire whose only consistent employer is the museum housed at the university where he teaches. Because museums are viewed as storied cultural institutions, it would seem that Indiana's association with one would endow him with respectable cultural capital. Yet, the depiction of archeology as a blood sport, especially in *Raiders*, leaves a stain that calls into question the museum's legitimacy. When Marcus Brody tells Indiana after he brings back several artifacts from the South American adventure at the beginning of *Raiders*, "Yes, the museum will buy them as usual, no questions asked," it clarifies both Indiana's monetary incentive in hunting the said artifacts and the willingness of a trusted cultural institution to "look the other way" and ignore his questionable methods as long as it delivers artifacts for their shelves (one could imagine that there is a museum in France somewhere willing to do exactly the same thing for Belloq). Because this particular line of dialogue otherwise serves no narrative purpose, it stands out as an explicit effort to both shade Indiana's adventures with a darker sheen of opportunism and implicate the museum for which he works in potential international criminality.[64]

Although the connections between Indiana and the U.S. government are regularly emphasized in critical writings about the *Indiana Jones* films,[65] such connections are tenuous at best, and frequently combative. Unlike the heroics of James Bond, who helped inspired Lucas's initial conception of the character and spurred Spielberg's interest in the project,[66] Indiana never earns the respect of his government when he is in their employ. Instead, he is either used and discarded, as in *Raiders*, or viewed with deep suspicion, as in *The Kingdom of the Crystal Skull*. In the latter film, Indiana is revealed as having worked as a spy during and after World War II, a strange occupation given the antagonistic nature of his dealings with the U.S. government in *Raiders* and the government's complete absence in the other two films. On the one hand, this would seem to imply that Indiana is no longer the rogue agent he once was, having run 20 to 30 missions in Europe during the war, spied on the Soviets in the Cold War aftermath, and been involved at least tangentially in the infamous "cover-up" around the Roswell flying saucer crash. Yet, he is still viewed with distrust by the government, which appears in the form of two traditionally black-suited federal agents who are suspicious of his earlier kidnapping and forced cooperation with Soviet agents. Thus, despite years of service, he is still a potential enemy "of great interest" to the Bureau.

In *Raiders of the Lost Ark* he also functions as an official American agent working directly for the U.S. government, yet he accepts the assignment to beat the Nazis to the Ark not so much out of national pride, but rather because the government is willing to foot the bill for his adventure. The phrase "fortune and glory" is not used explicitly until *The Temple of Doom*, but it is certainly implied in Indiana's reaction when Marcus informs him that

---

[64] Film critic Gary Arnold seemed to pick up on this in his review in the *Washington Post* when he called Indiana an "archaeologist and soldier of fortune" and described his relationship with Marcus Brody as "somewhat shady" ("The Blazing Cinematic Sensation of 'Raiders of the Lost Ark,'" June 12, 1981, E1).
[65] See, for example, Aronstein, "Not Exactly a Knight"; Zimmerman, "Soldiers of Fortune."
[66] McBride, *Steven Spielberg: A Biography*, 309, 316.

the government wants him to "go for it." For Indiana, ever the self-interested hero, the quest feeds his own desire to bring back "a find of incredible historical significance," not promote American exceptionalism and "save" the Third World. It is also telling that the discussion between them never once references any kind of nationalistic duty, but rather their own financial and scholarly benefit: "They're prepared to pay handsomely for it," Marcus says proudly and then assures Indiana that the university's museum will get possession of the Ark afterwards, a promise that is crucially broken at the end of the film.

The adventure in *Raiders* ends not in some exotic location, but rather in a well-appointed government office at the end of a long table (made all the more imposing by the low angle and slow tracking of Spielberg's camera), with government agents informing Indiana and Marcus that the Ark has been placed somewhere "very safe" and that there are "top men" working on it. The vagueness of these assertions is typical political doublespeak, and the deeply ironic final shots reveal them to be outright lies. The film's two hours of rollicking adventure are brought to a close not in a moment of triumph for Indiana, but in loss and frustration as the Ark of the Covenant is secretly crated up and rolled away into the depths of a seemingly endless warehouse of similar-looking crates, reduced from a fabled historical and religious artifact to the label stenciled on the side of its wooden container: "TOP SECRET ARMY INTEL 9906753." While the United States is technically "in possession" of the Ark, the government and the military are clearly afraid of it and simply want to hide it away along with thousands of other government/military secrets, rather than follow through on their promise to allow Marcus and the museum to take possession of it for further research, which is confirmed in *Kingdom of the Crystal Skull* when a shot reveals that the Ark is still there in the mid–1950s. Like so much else in history, the Ark is hidden away, labeled "DO NOT OPEN!" and rendered functionally meaningless except as fodder for conspiracy theorists (the warehouse at the end of *Raiders* is nothing if not a vast symbol of all the information and knowledge that is withheld from the American people by its government).

This broken promise between the government and Indiana, the ironic sour note on which the film ends, is key to the film's often satirical view of the U.S. government, and yet the ending is regularly misread in an attempt to align it with the argument that *Raiders* totes a Reagan-era ideological agenda of American resurgence. Susan Aronstein, for example, describes Indiana's mission as "divine" and that "Indiana and, through him, the American government, inherits the Ark of the Covenant."[67] Later, she describes the government as depicted in the film as an "idealized American government, a government that

---

[67] Aronstein, "Not Exactly a Knight," 7.

FIGURE 3.5 *"Fools. Bureaucratic fools." The adventure in* Raiders *ends not in some exotic location, but rather in a well-appointed office with government agents giving Indiana and Marcus Brody (Denholm Elliott) vague assertions that are typical of political doublespeak, which the deeply ironic final shots reveal to be outright lies. Thus, the film's two hours of rollicking adventure are brought to a close not in a moment of triumph for Indiana, but in loss and frustration.*

is ultimately vindicated as the Ark 'chooses' Indiana and America in *Raiders*' apocalyptic light show."[68] Despite this assertion (necessitated by Aronstein's comparison of the *Indiana Jones* series to Arthurian legends), there is no evidence in *Raiders* that the government is "idealized." Rather, it is quite the opposite. The government is critically viewed with skepticism and even satirical humor in a way that aligns *Raiders* with roughly contemporaneous paranoid conspiracy theory films like Alan J. Pakula's *The Parallax View* (1974), Francis Ford Coppola's *The Conversation* (1974), and Brian De Palma's *Blow Out* (1981). While conspiracy theories and fears about governmental abuses of power and control are rarely associated with Spielberg's films in the popular imaginary, Barna William Donovan in his book *Conspiracy Films: A Tour of Dark Places in the American Conscious* (2011) cites *Raiders of the Lost Ark* and *E.T.* as examples of the kinds of films on which Generation X was raised that explain why so many of them have a conspiratorial mindset.[69]

The only government figures present in *Raiders* are the two intelligence agents, Colonel Musgrove (Don Fellows) and Major Eaton (William Hootkins), who arrive at Indiana's university and request a meeting with him regarding an intercepted Nazi communiqué that mentions his former friend and mentor Abner Ravenwood. There is nothing "idealized" about them, and dialogue

---

[68] Ibid., 9.
[69] Barna William Donovan, *Conspiracy Films: A Tour of Dark Places in the American Conscious* (Jefferson, NC: McFarland, 2011), 145. One might also note that *Close Encounters of the Third Kind* (1977) also prominently features government conspiracy and cover-up.

preceding their appearance on-screen is hardly reassuring. Marcus notes to Indiana that "They seem to know everything," the tone of his voice evoking not a sense of safety and security, but rather fears of unchecked governmental power and deception, fears that will be confirmed in the film's final scenes. Similarly, when Marcus tells Indiana that the agents want to see him, Indiana's response is decidedly skeptical and slightly paranoid: "What do I want to see them for? What, am I in trouble?"—hardly the response of a patriotic American agent working for an idealized government. This vocalized skepticism about the government agents creates a sense of trepidation, although there is something decidedly comical about them with their vaguely Laurel-and-Hardy-esque physical appearance and amusing lack of knowledge regarding the Ark, which seems to belie Marcus's intimation that they "know everything." "Any of you guys ever go to Sunday School?" Indiana asks with some exasperation after he has to explain to them what the Ark is—a pointed jab at the agents' lack of Judeo-Christian heritage that is confirmed with Indiana's last line of dialogue in the film: "Fools. Bureaucratic fools. They don't know what they've got there."

The apparent lack of knowledge on the part of the government's representatives calls into question how and why America would be "vindicated" by the Ark "choosing" it, as Aronstein argues. The Ark does not "choose" the U.S., but rather winds up there by default because Indiana and Marion close their eyes during the ceremony in which Belloq and the Nazis open it and are subsequently obliterated by the forces within. Robin Wood, in drawing a connection between the Ark's destructive power and depictions of nuclear energy in films of the 1980s, reads this as "a blatant invitation to deliberate ignorance; you'll be all right, and all your enemies will be destroyed, as long as you 'don't look.'"[70] Like Aronstein, Wood views the survival of Indiana and Marion as proof that God, like nuclear power, is on their (the Americans') side. Yet, although the Ark is described throughout the film as both a weapon and a supernatural transmitter, it is ultimately revealed to be something beyond human comprehension or control, which is why it has been "lost" for 3,000 years. This is foreshadowed twice in the film. Early on, Marcus expresses his concern about Indiana going after the Ark: "For nearly 3,000 years man has been searching for the lost Ark. That's not something to be taken lightly. No one knows its secrets—it's like nothing you've ever gone after before." More pointedly, in a later scene in Cairo, Sallah says: "Indy, there is something that troubles me. The Ark. If it is there at Tanis, then it is something than man was not meant to disturb. Death has always surrounded it. It is not of this Earth." The "apocalyptic light show" that follows Belloq's opening of the Ark

---

[70] Wood, *Hollywood From Vietnam to Reagan*, 168.

confirms both Marcus's fears about its "secrets" and Sallah's assertion that it was not meant to be disturbed by *anyone*—Indiana and the U.S government included. Thus, the fact that Belloq and the Nazis are destroyed while Indiana and Marion survive does nothing to confirm American superiority unless said superiority is predicated on little more than knowing when to leave something alone. Like the family at the end of *Poltergeist* (1982), Indiana and Marion live through the ordeal, but nothing more. The Ark is essentially "lost" again and nothing is gained.

The ironic final shot of the Ark being stored away in the government warehouse is often discussed as a visual homage to one of the final shots of Orson Welles's *Citizen Kane* (1941) in which the camera tracks slowly over the newspaper magnate Charles Foster Kane's lifelong accumulation of objects and artifacts from around the world. However, comparisons usually fall short of interrogating the sense of irony that joins the two shots beneath the visual similarities. The shot in *Citizen Kane* implies the fundamental meaninglessness of Kane's life pursuits, with the rows and rows of partially crated valuables providing no discernable answer to the film's great question: "Who was Charles Foster Kane?" It's just *stuff*. In *Raiders*, the final shot of the Ark being stored away brings to a stunning close the film's long-running critique of the U.S. government, its functionaries, and its policies. If John Williams's Indiana Jones theme music played with a tinge of irony in the opening South America sequence as Indiana clumsily swung from a vine into the river, it takes on full ironic force when it kicks in as the closing credits roll over the image of the warehouse of government secrets: the very opposite of a triumphant, heroic ending. Spielberg reworks this self-conscious "borrowing" of a famous shot from a Hollywood classic to drive home an unsettling political perspective—the truth is more often hidden than revealed by larger governmental and corporate power structures—thus illustrating how his cinematic allusions are not uniformly "self-congratulatory and narcissistic," as Peter Biskind charges.[71]

The government is not the only thing American that is viewed critically in the *Indiana Jones* films. Americans themselves and the presumptions they carry with them abroad are also fodder for pointed humor throughout the series. In *Raiders*, when Marion is carted off inside a wicker basket by hooded thugs, we can hear her yelling from inside, "You can't do this to me! *I'm an American!*"—as if that would make even the slightest amount of difference. Willie Scott (Kate Capshaw), the American singer who gets caught up in Indiana's adventures much against her will in *The Temple of Doom*, has long been a point of criticism, especially the shrill manner in which she plays

---

[71] Biskind, "Blockbuster," 124.

up fears, phobias, and materialistic values traditionally marked as feminine. When written about, Willie is usually identified as the series' worst offense against feminism—Robert Kolker describes her as "a conventionally dumb and hysterical woman companion"[72]—yet she is rarely called out for what she truly is: the proverbial ugly American. Constantly concerned about her appearance, rejecting of anything that is not to her taste, and assuming that the rest of the world is like the United States (while riding an elephant out of a starving, rural Indian village, she asks for a telephone), Willie embodies all of the worst caricatures of American impudence. The only time she is accepting of foreign culture is when it is associated with wealth. She tells Indiana that she enjoyed living in Shanghai (where she worked as a singer) because she had a house, her friends were rich, and they went to parties in limousines; in other words, she ensconced herself in Western materialism and sealed herself off from the foreign culture in which she was living. And, although she vocally resists Indiana's desire to travel to Pankot Palace to investigate the missing Sankara stones, she eventually warms to the idea once she witnesses the palace's extravagance first-hand and entertains the notion that she might marry the Maharaja who is, she says, "swimming in loot" (she loses interest only when she discovers that he is a prepubescent boy). From this perspective, then, the infamous banquet scene in which the guests of Pankot are served live eels that spill out of a sliced snake, the entrails of enormous beetles, eyeball soup, and chilled monkey brains still in the skull is more a satirical jab at Willie's inability to adapt to foreign cultures, rather than just an extended gross-out gag. The disgusting-to-a-Western-palette contents of the dinner are exaggerated for comic effect, with Spielberg's camera constantly tracking in on the culinary travesties as they are brought to the table while heightened aural effects underscore every gooshy sound, thus turning the entire sequence into an elaborate form of visceral punishment for Willie's self-centeredness and cultural short-sightedness. It is as if all of her worst nightmares about foreign cultures have been synthesized into a single meal. And, while the examples of Marion and Willie would seem to associate American presumption in the Third World exclusively with female characters, *The Last Crusade* engages in similar humor, using Marcus Brody bumbling through an Arab marketplace, his inappropriate Western attire and complete inability to speak any language other than English satirically encapsulating the assumption that the world is America's backyard.

So, to return to Robin Wood's question of "what exactly are we applauding as we cheer on the exploits of Indiana Jones?," the answer is as multifaceted as the films themselves. On a purely visceral level, we are applauding the

---

[72] Kolker, *A Cinema of Loneliness*, 322.

bravura of Spielberg's filmmaking prowess and ability to simultaneously evoke and transcend the earlier films that inspired him. On an emotional level, we are applauding the manner in which the film's cathartic rush of well-orchestrated action and suspense fulfills our primal desire to, as Hitchcock put it, be played like a piano. But, somewhere in there, beyond the many layers of immediate cinematic satisfaction, we are also applauding the series' fundamental ideological complexities, which are churning just beneath its gratifying surface pleasures and constantly threatening to erupt. Even if we don't immediately acknowledge them on first viewing, they are nevertheless present, shading Indiana's adventures with a slightly darker sheen that may very well explain why they have remained in the cultural imaginary long after so many other cinematic action-adventures have faded from memory.

4

"Lost and Done For"

The Rejection of War Fantasies in *Empire of the Sun* and *War Horse*

Like virtually every Spielberg film since *Jaws* (1975), the theatrical release of his World War II combat film *Saving Private Ryan* in the summer of 1998 was preceded by a flurry of publicity that marked it as a major media event. And, as with *Schindler's List* (1993) five years earlier, the media coverage turned *Saving Private Ryan* into more than just a summer event film, even one by the industry's most successful filmmaker. Rather, media coverage positioned the film as a locus of historical meaning, a center point around which the 1990s resurgence of interest in World War II and the so-called "Greatest Generation" now revolved. In addition to the usual studio-driven marketing practices involving theatrical trailers, TV commercials, newspaper ads, and billboards, there were dozens of stories on air and in print that made *Saving Private Ryan* part of the national consciousness weeks before its theatrical release. These stories tended to center on particular themes, especially the film's intense depictions of combat violence, which many commentators and historians declared the most "authentic" representations ever committed to celluloid, and the role the film played in the rising cultural memory of World War II.[1]

---

[1] The increased attention to World War II prior to *Saving Private Ryan* is evidenced by the publication of bestselling books like Tom Brokaw's *The Greatest Generation* (1994) and Stephen Ambrose's *D Day: June 6, 1944: The Climactic Battle of World War II* (1995) and *Citizen Soldiers: The U.S. Army From the Normandy Beaches to the Bulge to the Surrender of Germany* (1997), as well as the passage of legislation in 1993 to fund the construction of the U.S. National World War II Memorial on the National Mall in Washington, DC (it opened to the public in 2004).

However, another recurring theme in the coverage of *Saving Private Ryan* was Spielberg's childhood fascination with World War II and how many of his earliest cinematic attempts as an adolescent were war movies. The opening paragraphs of a feature story in *USA Today*, published four days prior to the film's release, are indicative:

> When Steven Spielberg was a movie-mad adolescent in Phoenix, his dad, Arnold, fed his only son's hungry imagination with tales of being a radio operator on a B–25 bomber in Burma.
>
> So it figures the first genre tackled by the fledgling filmmaker would be war flicks.
>
> And if *Fighter Squad* and *Escape to Nowhere* were to face the ratings board today, the director says that, despite a splat or two of ketchup, they would easily earn a G.
>
> "For 'gosh,'" the Hollywood hotshot says with a self-deprecating grin.
>
> Time marches on. With a brilliant career to bolster him, Spielberg at 51 revisits World War II in *Saving Private Ryan*, opening Friday, the story of an eight-man unit's search behind enemy lines for a soldier whose three brothers have died in battle.[2]

Newsweek's cover story on the film noted that "One of the young Spielberg's first efforts—he was 14—was a 40-minute, 8-mm movie called 'Escape to Nowhere.' (He used firecrackers for bullets),"[3] while A&E's special two-hour episode of its *Biography* series dedicated to Spielberg, which aired the week after *Saving Private Ryan* was released, noted within the first three minutes that Arnold Spielberg's "dramatic tales of wartime adventure would later fire his son's imagination."[4]

Spielberg described his adolescent war movies as being "like little mini-Hollywood films, filled with glory and storming the outposts and taking the hill and, you know, all the macho, gung-ho stuff that World War II movies kind of delivered to us."[5] The available footage from these early films bears out Spielberg's description, as they demonstrate the young filmmaker's

---

[2] Susan Wloszczyna, "Spielberg, Reel to Real Brutality of War 'Needed Telling,'" *USA Today*, July 20, 1998, 1D.
[3] Jon Meacham, "Caught in the Line of Fire," *Newsweek*, July 13, 1998, 50.
[4] The *Biography* episode, "Steven Spielberg: An Empire of Dreams," also features footage from Spielberg's early 8mm movies, including *Fighter Squad*, *Escape to Nowhere*, and *Firelight*, which for most viewers was their first chance to see evidence of his adolescent cinematic experiments. Footage from all these films now circulates widely on the Internet, although none of them are available in anything close to their complete form.
[5] Chris Harty, "Into the Breach: *Saving Private Ryan*," *Saving Private Ryan*, directed by Steven Spielberg (1998, Burbank, CA: DreamWorks Home Entertainment, 1999), DVD.

fascination with dynamic action both in front of the camera and with the camera itself (even at this young age he had internalized how choreographed camera movement can intensify on-screen action). Shot silently on 8mm color filmstock around Camelback Mountain in the desert outside Spielberg's home in Phoenix, Arizona, *Escape to Nowhere* (1962) creates an impressive sense of constant action heightened by innovative special effects (such as placing mounds of dirt or flour on a board over a hole in the ground that would "explode" like a grenade when someone ran over it). It also features a surprisingly large cast of more that 20 of Spielberg's classmates playing the various soldiers, which he expanded by having them run past the camera multiple times to increase the sense of scale.

Yet, despite the obvious allure of the excitement of battle—blazing guns, explosions of dirt, dramatically falling bodies, troops leaping over the camera—even at this young age Spielberg demonstrated a nascent conflict between his passion for the kinetic possibilities of the cinema and the lure of something darker. Haven Peters, a schoolmate who played a key role in *Escape to Nowhere*, described the film as "all action." Yet, the film ended with Peters' character as the only surviving American soldier from a platoon decimated by the Germans: "I was all alone at the end," Peters said, "lost and done for. It ends as I'm just sitting there all by myself. It was sad."[6]

While most conventional media narratives tend to portray Spielberg's professional career as the full flowering of the adolescent potential he demonstrated in the Arizona desert, his war films are most fascinating not as potential achieved, but rather as unique and explicit rebukes to his childhood fantasies of war as the ultimate adventure. Spielberg's fascination with war as a particularly dynamic cinematic subject has in no way diminished throughout his career; rather, he has been repeatedly drawn to both explicit battlefield narratives, such as *Saving Private Ryan* and *War Horse* (2011), and dramatic stories set against the backdrop of war and terrorism, such as *Empire of the Sun* (1987), *Schindler's List* (1993), *Munich* (2005), and *Lincoln* (2012). Spielberg has even incorporated elements of the war film into other genres, including the slapstick comedy in *1941* (1979), the action-adventure film in *Raiders of the Lost Ark* (1981), and science fiction in *War of the Worlds* (2005). Yet, Spielberg's war films, rather than celebrate the "glory" and "all the macho, gung-ho stuff" of his amateur films, complicate and expand on the image of Haven Peters' lone surviving soldier "lost and done for" in *Escape to Nowhere*.

This chapter will look at two of Spielberg's war films—*Empire of the Sun* and *War Horse*—and examine how they each consciously reject the

---

[6] Joseph McBride, *Steven Spielberg: A Biography*, 2nd edn (Jackson: University Press of Mississippi, 2010), 99.

war fantasies of an earlier era. The protagonist in both of these films is a conventional "innocent"—a child and a horse, respectively—which allows Spielberg to reflect in particularly powerful fashion his conflicted feelings about heroism and the inherent dehumanization of real bloodshed, especially on an epic scale. Both films also share a commonality in being aesthetically modeled on classical Hollywood cinema, particularly the epic films of David Lean, although *War Horse* also draws heavily on the visual iconography of John Ford. Each film is unique in the tension it produces between Spielberg's innate understanding of the exciting, kinetic possibilities of warfare captured on film and the horrors—physical, spiritual, and psychological—behind that surface excitement.

Empire of the Sun: Illusions of safety

Following the comically horrific *Indiana Jones and the Temple of Doom* (1984), Spielberg's next two films, *The Color Purple* (1985) and *Empire of the Sun*, marked a resounding declaration that he was transitioning into more conventionally adult material, proving that he was a filmmaker of growing maturity not confined to the forms of so-called "escapist entertainment" with which he was primarily associated by the mid–1980s. *The Color Purple* was a commercial hit when it was released in December of 1985, grossing $98 million at the domestic box office, which placed it fourth for the year. It was also a substantial critical hit, garnering mostly positive and many outright rave reviews for its deft cinematic treatment of Alice Walker's Pulitzer Prize-winning epistolary novel about three decades in the life of a black woman named Celie (Whoopi Goldberg) who endures physical, psychological, and sexual abuse and neglect, first from her incestuous father and then from her cruel husband, who is known only as Mister (Danny Glover). The critical accolades came despite skepticism in many quarters regarding Spielberg's ability to render a story about patriarchal violence, female subjugation, and the realities of racism in the Jim Crow South told from a black female point of view. *The Color Purple*'s 11 Academy Awards nominations were testament to Spielberg's cemented stature in the film industry a decade after *Jaws* (1975), although the fact that, as with *Jaws*, he failed to receive a Best Director nomination despite the film being nominated for Best Picture was a harsh reminder that many in Hollywood still resisted taking him too seriously.[7]

---

[7] Spielberg's fellow directors took him more seriously than the industry as a whole, as the Directors Guild of America awarded him Outstanding Directorial Achievement in Motion Pictures for *The Color Purple*.

Empire of the Sun continued Spielberg's move toward a more "adult" cinema, but also reinforced the difficulties he faced with a critical establishment that was resistant to viewing him as a serious-minded filmmaker. Spielberg inherited the project from the legendary director David Lean, who had initially asked him to acquire the rights to and produce a film version of J. G. Ballard's 1984 semi-autobiographical novel about a British boy who spends several years separated from his parents and confined to an internment camp following the Japanese invasion of Shanghai in December 1941. However, Lean ultimately deemed the material unworkable as a film, and Spielberg, who had secretly wanted to direct it all along, took over the reins. It was Spielberg's first true war film, not counting the screwball shenanigans of *1941* and the Saturday morning matinee portrayal of Nazis in *Raiders of the Lost Ark*, and he approached the story of a child caught in the crosshairs of war with a deeply challenging mixture of grim, gritty physicality and a tone that frequently borders on the surreal, to the point that film scholar Andrew Gordon has argued quite persuasively that "the film thrusts us into the distorted, dreamlike perceptions of [the protagonist's] war-induced neurosis, and we get not so much a realistic war movie as a study in mania: a boy's fantastic dream of war."[8] The film did not sit well with audiences, who were clearly looking for something more conventionally "Spielbergian," and, unlike *The Color Purple*, it failed commercially, at least by Spielberg's typical standards, bringing in only $22 million at the domestic box office, which was not even enough to place it in the top 50 films of the year. More curiously, the film received decidedly mixed critical responses, and its six Oscar nominations were all for technical categories (art direction, costume design, cinematography, editing, sound, and music), thus confirming the notion that, like Alfred Hitchcock in the view of his contemporaries, Spielberg was a master technician, but not a serious film artist.

Yet, with hindsight, it is clear that *Empire of the Sun* is one of Spielberg's most masterful and underappreciated films. It didn't so much pave the way for a more "mature" career as it synthesized many of the darker impulses and ideas that had been coiling throughout his earlier, more conventionally entertaining and allegedly reassuring films and set the stage for later projects focused on historical atrocity such as *Schindler's List*, *Amistad*, *Saving Private Ryan*, and *Munich*. At the time, Spielberg described *Empire of the Sun* as the darkest film he had yet made: "I don't think I've made a dark movie. But it's as dark as I've allowed myself to get, and that was perversely very compelling to

---

[8] Andrew Gordon, "Steven Spielberg's *Empire of the Sun*: A Boy's Dream of War." *Literature/Film Quarterly* 19, no. 4 (1991): 210.

me."[9] For Spielberg, the film was at heart about "the death of innocence" and thus the very opposite of the Peter Pan mythos that was so often attached to him. Rather than telling the story of a boy who refuses to grow up, it tells the story of a boy who finds himself in circumstances that force him to grow up too fast, shedding all vestiges of childish innocence and naïveté in the pursuit of mere survival. *Empire of the Sun*, in this regard, is a particularly primal film that explodes the suburban psychological traumas of *Close Encounters of the Third Kind* (1977) and *E.T.* (1982) by situating them within a larger world at war. It is no wonder, then, that so many critics have read its images of war-ravaged survival through a psychoanalytic lens.[10]

The story, which takes place entirely in China from 1941 to 1945, centers on Jamie Graham (Christian Bale), the 11-year-old son of a wealthy British textile factory owner. Having grown up entirely within the ensconced, rarefied protection of the International Settlement in Shanghai, Jamie's is a world of wealth and privilege, the product of decades of British colonialism in Asia. His life is exemplified in the Tudor-style home on Amherst Avenue where he and his parents live with a small crew of Chinese servants and the always glistening 1939 Packard in which he is chauffeured about the city, safely protected from the misery, poverty, and violence of the streets. His world is shaken and then literally destroyed with the invasion of Shanghai by the Japanese in December of 1941. Separated from his parents, he first tries to survive in his deserted home before setting off on his own in occupied Shanghai, where he is eventually taken in by two scheming American black marketeers, Basie (John Malkovich) and Frank (Joe Pantoliano), who see potential profit in a well-heeled British boy whose parents might be looking for him. They rechristen him "Jim" ("A new name for a new life," Basie says), and Basie becomes a teacher and surrogate father of sorts, mentoring Jim in the cutthroat means of staying alive in a world turned upside down even as he remains concerned first and foremost with his own survival.

It isn't long before Jim, Basie, and Frank wind up in a Japanese internment camp, where Jim spends the next three years learning to survive in the harsh, physically and psychologically degrading environment. His experience in survival is best summarized near the end of the film when Basie asks him, "Jim, didn't I teach you anything?," to which he replies wearily, "Yes, you taught me that people will do anything for a potato." He learns the hard lesson that people will do anything to survive, even if that means sacrificing

---

[9] McBride, *Steven Spielberg: A Biography*, 393.
[10] See Andrew Gordon, "Steven Spielberg's *Empire of the Sun*"; Lynn S. Lawrence, "War as a Holding Environment: An Analysis of *Empire of the Sun*," *Psychoanalytic Review* 78, no. 2 (1991); Nigel Morris, *The Cinema of Steven Spielberg* (London: Wallflower Press, 2007): 135–48.

their own humanity to hold on to physical life. The desperation for survival and the heavy cost often associated with it is a sentiment that cuts through many of Spielberg's films, including those that otherwise portray heroism and self-sacrifice. One might think of the panicked beachgoers in *Jaws* trampling over one another to get out of the water when the shark is supposedly spotted (one of the film's most disturbing images is not of a shark attack, but rather a low-angle shot in the surf of an apparently lifeless elderly man who has been trampled by fellow swimmers and is being dragged out of the water) or Corporal Upham (Jeremy Davies) freezing in the stairwell during the climactic battle in *Saving Private Ryan*, his paralyzing concern for his own life keeping him from stopping a German soldier who is slowly and painfully stabbing Private Mellish (Adam Goldberg) to death on the floor just above him. Spielberg has used characters' desperation for survival for dark humor, such as the scene in *Jurassic Park* (1993) when the Tyrannosaurus Rex breaks loose of its compound. Donald Genarro (Martin Ferrero), an officious lawyer, panics and hides in the bathroom, selfishly leaving behind two children in his care, only to be eaten anyway when the dinosaur crashes through the building, leaving him absurdly vulnerable sitting on a toilet. The driving idea of survival in Spielberg's films is neatly encapsulated by Dr. Iris Hineman (Lois Smith), the creator of the Precrime system in *Minority Report* (2002): "It's funny how all living organisms are alike. When the chips are down, when the pressure is on, every creature on the face of the earth is interested in one thing and one thing only: its own survival."

Thus, the lengths to which Jim goes in order to survive, which at times involves sacrificing some of his own humanity (although never to the extent that Basie does) is part of the human drive as seen over and over again in Spielberg's films. And, while Jim does survive the ordeal and, in the film's final moments, is reunited with his parents, there is little sense of cathartic joy, as we recognize that he has devolved from a chatty, cherub-faced boy of great imagination to a silent, hollow-eyed survivor who is neither man nor child. Like Haven Peters at the end of *Escape to Nowhere*, he is alive, yet "lost and done for," as there is no suggestion of what his future holds beyond merely being alive. Like so many of Spielberg's films, the trauma Jim has endured and the humanity that has been stripped from him far outweighs any sense of triumph that he has survived.

Without doubt, even before his wartime ordeal, Jim is one of Spielberg's most complex and troubling protagonists, hardly the one-dimensional symbol of childhood innocence he is often accused of perpetuating. Quite the opposite, in fact, since *Empire of the Sun* plays as a sustained critique of the limits of a child's imagination in a world of violence and conflict, with the film's narrative trajectory building around the slow but steady decimation of

FIGURE 4.1 "People will do anything for a potato." *The relationship between Jim (Christian Bale) and his surrogate father figure Basie (John Malkovich) in* Empire of the Sun *is built around the desperation for survival, a theme that cuts through many of Spielberg's films, including those that otherwise portray heroism and self-sacrifice. (Digital Frame Enlargement)*

Jim's fantasies. Jim is initially portrayed as a selfish child of privilege who exists largely inside his own head, which is fed with an idealization of war—the kind of "macho, gung-ho stuff" that Spielberg tried to emulate in his childhood 8mm war movies—that will eventually become his own personal nightmare. He is first introduced at the Cathedral School singing in a church choir with other British boys, all identically dressed in maroon secondary school uniforms, although Jim stands out via both his vocal solo and his evident boredom, which causes him to become distracted and stare off into the distance, making noises with his mouth and clicking his jaw, much to the consternation of both the choir director and his Chinese nanny. This introductory scene also doubles as a sharply etched depiction of colonialism at work, as the British children sing a traditional Welsh lullaby while their Chinese nannies sit in the pews and their Chinese chauffeurs polish the cars outside.

Even as a child of 11, Jim has already internalized his inherited position of power and authority, which brings into question whether we can ever see him as truly "innocent." Early in the film he tells his nanny that he wants to have butter biscuits, to which she replies in halting English with a slightly bowed head that his mother wouldn't want him eating right before bed. His steady, nonplussed response to her subservient attempt to manage his behavior is almost frightening in its directness: "You have to do what I say," he states without a trace of emotion. While Jim's sense of power is directly connected to the British colonialism that made men like his father extremely wealthy at the expense of the cultures he helped colonize, it is completely divorced from any sense of national pride, as he unabashedly tells his father that he plans to join the Japanese Air Force because they have better planes and braver pilots. However, Jim does possess a certain degree of self-awareness, demonstrated in an early scene in which he asks his father, "We are lucky, aren't we, living here?" He recognizes to some extent that his privilege is not entirely earned, but is rather the result of forces and events that preceded him, which helps explain his fascination with the violence and poverty he sees everyday outside the car window.

Jim's fascination with the darker forces from which he is insulated suggest that his world of protective privilege is ultimately illusory. If Jim is, in fact, an innocent child, it is not in the sense that he is pure and virtuous, but rather that he is naïve about the true nature of the world and that his place in it is safe. In fact, the idea that safety is an illusion could easily be read as the film's dominant theme, and Spielberg literalizes this quite brilliantly in the surreal sequence in which Jim and his parents are chauffeured to a lavish costume party at a friend's house on the other side of Shanghai. Dressed as Sinbad the Sailor, Jim looks out of the window at the throngs of hardscrabble humanity outside—prostitutes, homeless children, barterers, sailors—with a mix of awe and wonder. At one point a slab of meat a man is carrying on a pole slaps grotesquely against the window, leaving a bloody smear through which he continues to stare. Spielberg cuts to shots of other partygoers in similarly chauffeured cars, dressed as clowns and pirates, looking tentatively out of the windows as their cars glide past armed soldiers and rows of barbed wire, sandbag reinforcements, and tanks. It's a bizarre, striking juxtaposition of wealth and power rendered visually absurd in a world teetering on the brink of destruction, thus establishing early on that, in *Empire of the Sun*, no place is safe from the forces of war, violence, and chaos, which move from the margins of Jim's life to eventually engulf it.

Like many children (including Spielberg in his early years), Jim is fascinated by aviation and warfare, although his fascination is unique in that it borders on an obsession. Early on we see him in the backseat of the Packard immersed in an issue of *Wings Comics*, completely lost in his own romanticized fantasies about war, and we next see him riding his bike around the backyard with a flaming model plane in one hand making buzzing engine noises. It is typical child's play, to be sure, although the insouciant manner in which he takes pleasure in making his Chinese nanny chase after him is unsettling in the way it collapses the powers of economic privilege and war violence into a single image of childish "innocence."

Jim's playacting is eventually confronted by the realities of a world at war.[11] His first real encounter with the war occurs during the aforementioned costume party when he discovers a downed fighter plane in the field behind the house. He is immediately entranced by his proximity to "the real thing," and he approaches the plane like a mystical talisman as ethereal music soars on the soundtrack. He climbs in and playacts a dogfight with his glider,[12] and there is something decidedly disturbing about the unfettered sense of elation he feels when he puts his finger in the bullet holes in the side of the plane. Even in the presence of the detritus of war, violence and destruction are abstract, romanticized concepts that stir his imagination, but don't frighten his soul. His first real confrontation with the realities of war soon follows as he discovers a large group of Japanese soldiers stationed just on the other side of an embankment from the downed plane. The image of Jim, elaborately dressed in his Sinbad costume, first discovering the soldiers and then being directly approached by one of them, is one of the film's starkest literalizations of what is to come of Jim's life: a "moment of startled innocence [that captures] the transfer of the child from the playground to the battleground."[13] And, as he walks briskly away, his entrapment in a world of violence is eloquently evoked by his being visually framed between the downed fighter in the foreground, the hulking, bullet-ridden remnant of a past battle, and the Japanese soldiers, who are amassing for a new one. Jim is literally surrounded by the violence of war—past, present, and future.

---

[11] While first-time viewers will not necessarily notice, the cover of the *Wings Comics* issue, which was commissioned specifically for the film, acts as foreshadowing for the eventual destruction of Jim's illusions. The front cover features a smiling pilot who looks exactly like Basie, in terms of both his remarkable facial resemblance and his clothing, which include a khaki military cap and green-tinted aviator sunglasses. The fact that Basie takes his sunglasses from Jim when they first meet and the bomber jacket worn by the pilot looks like the one Jim wears later in the film at an internment camp foreshadows the merging of Basie and Jim, as the former instructs the latter in all means of self-preservation, often at the expense of both others and his own humanity (early on Basie instructs him on how to take advantage of the death of others to secure additional rations). In addition to the physical resemblance between the pilot on the comic book cover and Basie, who sees the comic book when he pulls it from Jim's jacket pocket, and the presence of clothing associated with Jim, it also features a tower in the background that is identical to the one at the Japanese airfield next to the Soochow Creek Internment Camp where Jim spends several years. Smoke is billowing behind the tower and an American P–51 fighter is diving out of the sky, both foreshadowing the American attack on the airfield late in the film that becomes, for Jim, a key moment in which his crazed enthusiasm for death and destruction finally give way to the mourning, depression, and sadness that he has been masking with his mania. Thus, the comic book provides the film's first foreshadowing of the coming destruction of Jim's romanticized notions of war, as he will come face to face with real violence, and the grinning, idealized pilot of his imagination will be replaced by a shady, opportunistic scoundrel whose life lessons reject sacrifice and heroism in favor of self-preservation at all costs.
[12] Spielberg's use of a moving camera while Jim sits in the downed plane harkens back to some of the techniques he used as an adolescent filmmaker in *Fighter Squad* to create the illusion of movement in stationary planes; see McBride, *Steven Spielberg: A Biography*, 91–2.
[13] Lawrence, "War as a Holding Environment," 302.

FIGURE 4.2 "From the playground to the battleground." *Jim's first real confrontation with the realities of war comes during a costume party when he inadvertently stumbles upon a large group of Japanese soldiers stationed on the other side of an embankment behind the house, thus literalizing the fragile illusion of safety under which he has been living. (Digital Frame Enlargement)*

His second confrontation with the world at war occurs that night when his use of a flashlight to jokingly signal through his hotel window at a Japanese vessel in the harbor is followed by a massive explosion that he mistakes as being his fault ("I didn't mean it!" he cries when his father bursts into the room. "It was a joke!"). This moment plays a double role in both showing the inexorable incursion of the violence of war into Jim's rarefied world and his continued childish preoccupation with himself. Even the following morning he is still fascinated, rather than horrified, as he looks out the window at the throngs of panicked people in the streets of Shanghai running ahead of marching Japanese soldiers and rumbling tanks. He is consumed with a desire to see the violence around him, which is predicated on the notion that he is somehow protected from it, perhaps even above it, a perspective that his parents clearly do not share (they may be wealthy, but they are aware of the danger in which they find themselves). As Jim excitedly moves about in the back seat of the car to get a better vantage point through the back window, his mother finally explodes: "Oh, Jamie, *for God's sake, sit down!*" she cries out in a mixture of exasperation and fear. But still Jim's recognition of the danger around him remains muted, which leads to a crucial and fateful chain of events.

Captivated by the sight of warplanes in the skies above Shanghai, he drops his favorite toy airplane and, rather than leave it, he lets go of his mother's hand to retrieve it, thus causing a separation that will last for the next three years. Jim's childish preoccupation with the fantasy of war directly causes him to become ensnared in its realities, which Spielberg emphasizes via his being immediately caught in the crossfire between the Japanese soldiers on the streets and Chinese rebels on the rooftops above. Jim's fate is sealed in a crucial image in which a Chinese civilian is shot right in front of him, quite possibly taking a bullet that otherwise would have hit him. It is Jim's first direct confrontation with death—and he is genuinely shocked and horrified, the romance of war eclipsed in an instant—but it will hardly be his last.

Death is everywhere in *Empire of the Sun*, to the extent that the film is bookended by haunting images of death—one literal, the other figural—both of which are scored to Jim singing "Suo Gân," a beautiful Welsh lullaby whose lyrics admonishing a child to sleep in his mother's embrace and fear nothing reflect precisely what Jim has lost.[14] The film opens with a literal image of death: following an opening crawl over the film's title that establishes the setting and historical context, the film fades in on an extreme high-angle shot looking down at the glistening water of Hangzhou Bay, the tranquility of which is interrupted first by a pair of white-flowered wreaths floating across the screen from bottom right to upper left, followed by a trail of broken flowers and then a wooden coffin, the top of which has been broken, thus revealing the pale corpse inside.[15] This initial shot dissolves to a higher matching shot that reveals five coffins floating in the water that are unceremoniously shoved aside by the prow of a Japanese military vessel (the open coffin with the exposed corpse is directly hit and then subsumed beneath the huge gray ship, literalizing the manner in which everything falls beneath the war machine).

The film's closing shot takes place in the same location, but depicts the figural death of Jim's childhood and any sense of innocence it may have entailed. After we see Jim reunited with his parents and two shots of the V-Day celebration in the streets of Shanghai, we see Jim's suitcase, which he kept with him throughout his internment and used as a repository for a

---

[14] The lyrics of the song's first two stanzas, translated into English, are: "Sleep, child in my embrace / Cozy and warm is this / The arms of mother are tight about you / The love of mother is in her breast / Nothing will disturb your nap / No one will do you wrong / Sleep quietly dear child / Sleep sweetly on the breast of your mother." For a detailed discussion of "Suo Gân" and its thematic relevance to the action in *Empire of the Sun*, see Lewis Stiller, "Suo Gân and *Empire of the Sun*," *Literature/Film Quarterly* 24, no. 1 (1996).

[15] Lynn S. Lawrence suggests that the coffins are "small burial coffins of children" (301), which makes their presence even more disturbing and evocative of Jim's eventual "death of innocence." However, after examining the shot frame-by-frame, I cannot confirm that they are children's coffins, and their length in relation to the military vessel suggests adult-sized coffins.

FIGURE 4.3 Haunting images of death. Empire of the Sun *is bookended with parallel images of death, both literal and figurative. The opening image is literal, as five coffins floating in the waters of Hangzhou Bay are shoved aside by the prow of a Japanese military vessel, while the closing image is figurative, as Jim's suitcase, in which he stored a small collection of treasures that helped remind him of his life before the war, is pushed aside by a boat. (Digital Frame Enlargements)*

small collection of treasures that helped remind him of his life before the war, floating in the water. It is briefly nudged aside by a boat moving in the same left–right direction as the Japanese military vessel in the opening shot, thus creating a visual parallel to the film's opening that links the coffins and the suitcase as images of death. This thematic merging of Jim's suitcase with the coffins suggests the final death and burial of his childhood. Even though he

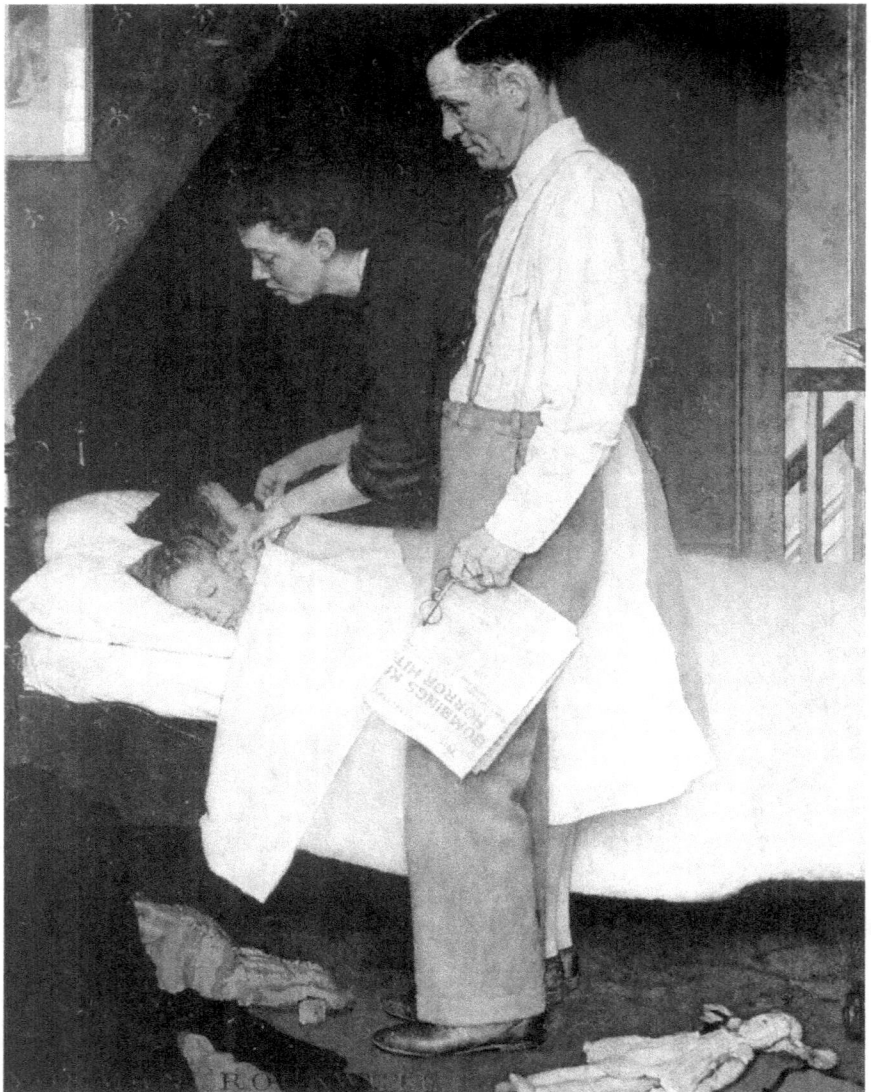

FIGURE 4.4 Freedom From Fear *(Norman Rockwell, 1943). Printed by permission of the Norman Rockwell Family Agency. Copyright © 2014 the Norman Rockwell Family Entities.*

has been "rescued" by his parents, in the end they cannot rescue and return to him what he has lost in the war.

While there are numerous other elements of the film that emphasize Jim's lost innocence amid the violence of war, the recurring presence of Norman

"LOST AND DONE FOR" 153

Rockwell's 1943 painting *Freedom From Fear* is one of the most intriguing as it comes to embody the film's melancholic sense of loss and symbolize the film's primary theme that safety is an illusion. Rockwell's painting depicts a mother and a father tucking their pre-adolescent boys into bed at night. The mother is leaning over the bed gently pulling up the sheet, both of the children's eyes are closed, and the father stands over them looking down at the poignant scene. The overall peacefulness of the image is put in stark relief via a folded newspaper the father is holding by his side, whose headline, despite being partially obscured, is clearly signaling the presence of war with the visible phrases "Bombings Ki[ll]" and "Horror Hit[s]."

Freedom From Fear was the final installment of Rockwell's "Four Freedoms" series, which he was initially inspired to paint after Franklin D. Roosevelt invoked what he called "the four essential human freedoms"—freedom of speech, freedom to worship, freedom from want, and freedom from fear—in his 1941 State of the Union address. The paintings were commissioned by *Saturday Evening Post* editor Ben Hibbs, who ran them as full-page illustrations in four consecutive issues of the magazine (February 20, February 27, March 6, and March 13, 1943), each paired with an essay about the freedom depicted. Rockwell then donated the paintings to the U.S. government, which used them to help raise $133 million in war bonds. While *Freedom From Fear* is arguably the least well known of the four paintings, Spielberg, who is a strong admirer of Rockwell's work and owns a substantial collection of his paintings,[16] was drawn to it as a young child when he discovered it in his father's pile of *Saturday Evening Post*s:

> I remember having a sense that when the mother and father both come into the children's bedroom to tuck in the boy, they must really love him. It must be a solidly happy family, a family unit, that hasn't been shattered by divorce or illness. That has always been the American dream, the great concept of the American unit, the American family. The fact that they are both there in the room, and the father's holding a newspaper with bad news about the war overseas—they're looking at the boy, thinking, if the war keeps going, in a few more years he could be drafted or enlist, and also thinking that we [are] here, living in freedom and at this moment our child is safe because our country is protecting all of us. But they're not smiling; they're not flaunting that freedom. They're very solemn, and very respectful of it.[17]

---

[16] Virginia M. Mecklenburg, *Telling Stories: Norman Rockwell From the Collections of George Lucas and Steven Spielberg* (Abrams, NY: Smithsonian Art Museum, 2010).
[17] Ibid., 111–12.

Spielberg's stated understanding of the painting emphasizes both the idealized notions of perfect familial love and the constant threat the world poses to it. He rightly recognizes the solemnity of the scene, which is ironic given that the painting was one of Rockwell's least favorite because, as he noted in his autobiography, he felt it was "based on a rather smug idea": "Painted during the bombing of London, it was supposed to say: 'Thank God we can put our children to bed with a feeling of security, knowing they will not be killed in the night.[']"[18] Spielberg, on the other hand, read into the image the underlying parental anxiety that, while their children were safe in that moment, that moment might not last. The title of the painting, then, is potentially ironic, in that the parents are *not* free from fear, and the children, while possibly unaware of the realities of war on the other side of the world, like Jim may very well be drawn into it at some point. Thus, the painting, quite contrary to Rockwell's intentions, embodies one of *Empire of the Sun*'s fundamental themes: the illusory nature of safety.

Freedom From Fear appears in *Empire of the Sun* in the form of a page ostensibly torn from the *Saturday Evening Post* that Jim keeps with him throughout his internment (although we never see when and where he comes into possession of it). It appears in the film five times, all of which take place while Jim is being held at the Soochow Creek Internment Camp during the film's second hour. The first time we see the painting, it is tacked onto the wall next to Jim's bed in the small corner he occupies in the British dorm, surrounded by other pictures cut from magazines: photos of various planes, an advertisement for a Buick, a portrait of Winston Churchill, and another Rockwell painting, *Who's Having More Fun?*, which depicts two children eating corn on the cob. Jim reaches out and straightens *Freedom From Fear*, which draws our attention to its presence and cements its thematic centrality among Jim's other reminders of his previous life. We see the painting again 15 minutes later as Jim watches in the middle of the night as Mr. and Mrs. Victor (Peter Gale and Miranda Richardson), a British couple who have dutifully (although not happily) taken on the role of surrogate parents at the camp, make love on the other side of the screen that divides their respective spaces. A violent air battle is raging in the skies outside, witnessed via fiery lights fading in and out of the clouds and the booming echo of explosions, which conveys to the entire scene a decidedly Freudian intertwining of sex and death. Spielberg cuts in to several close-ups of the painting fluttering against the wall, as the stillness of the air is presumably disturbed by the battle. The first close-up is of the children's peaceful faces

---

[18] Norman Rockwell, *Norman Rockwell: My Adventures as an Illustrator* (Garden City, NY: Doubleday, 1960), 342–3.

and the parents' hands above them; the second close-up, which focuses on the parents' faces, is quickly distorted and obscured by the moving page, creating an unsettling evocation of sudden parental absence, an experience all too familiar for Jim.

The next two times we see the painting, its presence is associated with Jim's failed surrogate parental figures. The painting first marks Jim's triumphal acceptance into the American dorm after successfully navigating the area outside the fence to set pheasant traps for Basie (actually a plot to use him in order to test for the presence of land mines), and later it marks his dismal return to Mr. and Mrs. Victor in the British dorm after Basie escapes the camp without him, explicitly violating his promise not to leave Jim behind. When Jim arrives in the American dorm, he opens his suitcase, revealing several important items inside, including the issue of *Wings Comics* (which we haven't seen since Jim and Basie first met in Shanghai) and the toy airplane he dropped during the invasion. However, he digs past those and pulls out the increasingly ragged magazine page with *Freedom From Fear* and tacks it on the wall next to his bed. Spielberg then composes an overhead shot of Jim lying in bed, his mud-caked face appearing strangely aged as his beaming sense of pride slowly gives way to a look of growing ambivalence. Jim's head and shoulders fill the right-hand side of the screen, a hanging lamp fills the middle of the composition, and the Rockwell painting can be seen on the left-hand side of the screen. On the one hand, the painting seems to strike a contrast with Jim's predicament, as the poignant scene of parental bed tucking is quite the opposite of Jim's striking aloneness, even within the cherished American dorm. However, given Spielberg's understanding of the image, it plays as neither nostalgic memory of things lost nor as ironic counterpoint. Rather, Jim on the right-hand side of the screen is the embodiment of what the parents in the painting are secretly concerned about: losing their children to a world at war. This reading is reinforced by the image's subsequent appearance in the film when Mrs. Victor solemnly and quietly pulls it out of Jim's suitcase upon his return to the British dorm and tacks it next to his bed, again reinforcing Jim's isolation and lack of true family, even among others. The last time we see the painting is in close-up as Jim packs it in his suitcase upon hearing that the Japanese are forcing the prisoners to evacuate the camp and march to a different location. It is essential that we realize the painting is inside the suitcase because Jim will soon throw the case in the bay, where it won't be seen again until the film's final image when it is linked to the coffins from the opening shot.

The presence of *Freedom From Fear* in the film is intricately linked to Jim and his parents, as it is first evoked by a tableau early in the film of John and Mary Graham (Rupert Frazer and Emily Richard) tucking him in at night. Film scholar Lester D. Friedman has recognized and explored the distinct differences between Rockwell's painting and Spielberg's cinematic replica of it, noting that the similarities between the parents in the Rockwell painting and the Grahams are largely superficial, with the former being dressed "more plainly" and "matronly" while the latter are characterized by "fancy" clothing and sexual voluptuousness.[19] Similarly, Friedman notes that Rockwell's painting uses light in the corners to express a sense of hope, whereas Spielberg's composition favors darkness, shadows, and a shuttered window. However, Friedman's reading of Rockwell's painting takes it largely at face value, seeing it as a depiction of "children safely sleeping, tucked warmly beneath their covers and protected from harm by their parents,"[20] which then puts the painting in ironic counterpoint to the depiction of Jim's parents, who despite going through the symbolic parental motions of tucking him into bed, in the end "utterly fail to protect him."[21] However, if one views Rockwell's painting through Spielberg's perspective, in which it is not so much a portrait of parental protection as it is a solemn evocation of the fleeting nature of safety despite the parents' best intentions, then the painting takes on a richer and more evocative role in the film that is not so much ironic counterpoint as it is thematically summative. There is no true freedom from fear because threats and danger are always present, even in the most seemingly benign and protected of circumstances—a narrative thread that links many of Spielberg's otherwise disparate films (a quiet beach community traumatized by a marauding shark in *Jaws*, families torn apart by a supernatural invasion in *Poltergeist*, an alien invasion in *War of the Worlds*, and Polish Jews forced from their homes by the Nazis in *Schindler's List*).

At this point we have to consider the nature of Jim's parents, as their depiction in the film is important for understanding its closing moments, when the family is reunited at the end of the war. While Spielberg saw in Rockwell's painting "a solidly happy family, a family unit," the Grahams do not fit that description at all. Mary Graham, Jim's mother, is first shown sitting impassively behind a stately piano at their home while gazing at the framed photos that sit atop the piano, none of which show her and Jim together (all of them are of Jim alone, except one photo that shows Jim looking down at a kite while his father stands over him with his hand on his hip, looking more authoritarian and patriarchal than warm and loving). In a sense, this is an idealized mother image—she is beautiful and refined and elegant—but her interactions with Jim mark her as distant and even somewhat cold, making

---

[19] Lester D. Friedman, *Citizen Spielberg* (Urbana: University of Illinois Press, 2006), 203–4.
[20] Friedman, *Citizen Spielberg*, 204.
[21] Ibid., 203–4.

FIGURE 4.5 No freedom from fear. *The presence of Norman Rockwell's painting* Freedom From Fear *is intricately linked to Jim and his parents, as it is first evoked by a tableau early in the film of John and Mary Graham (Rupert Frazer and Emily Richard) tucking him in at night. (Digital Frame Enlargment)*

her tendency to wear white seem more icy than angelic. In the scene that includes the shot replicating the composition in Freedom From Fear, she inadvertently awakens Jim by sitting on his bed and lighting a cigarette, the flame of which illuminates the model planes hanging from the ceiling in a manner that visually evokes the bomb blasts that are to come. Her reason for being there is vague; she is not there to tuck him in, as he has already been asleep for some time, enough time to have been dreaming. When Jim tries to engage her with discussion about his dreams and the nature of God, she dismisses his questions without much thought and tells him to go to sleep. Outside of that scene and her screaming at Jim to sit down while they are evacuating Shanghai, Mary has no on-screen interaction with her son.

John Graham, Jim's father, is similarly remote and emotionally distanced. As Mary is first seen behind the piano, a symbol of wealth and privilege, John is introduced practicing his golf swing in the backyard, using silver dollars as golf tees and chipping the balls over the crystal blue swimming pool. Jim also tries to engage his father in conversation, in this case about the impending war between China and Japan and their privilege as Europeans, and just as Mary did, John quickly scuttles him away so he can continue practicing his golf swing. He also displays anger and annoyance with Jim, in this case his appalled response to his son's declaration that he wants to join the Japanese Air Force. "For God's sake, Jamie!" he says with undisguised disgust as he chips the ball into the swimming pool, a line of dialogue that Mary will repeat verbatim when she loses patience with Jim's excited fascination with the violence around them while they are attempting to evacuate Shanghai. Thus, both Jim's mother and father don't particularly understand him or seem to want to expend the time and energy to do so. They are more concerned with keeping up appearances as wealthy European elite living in the exotic East and passing the parenting duties to their harried Chinese nanny. Their general lack of interest in Jim, which further isolates him even within his rarefied world of privilege, is later reflected and deepened by Mr. and Mrs. Victor, his adoptive parents in the internment camp, who dismiss his ideas and interests, as well (instead of being scandalized by his fascination with Japanese aviators, they are disgusted by his carefully separating and counting the weevils in his porridge).

The depiction of parental aloofness and emotional vacancy, which is quite the opposite of the scene depicted in Rockwell's painting, inflects the film's final images of Jim reunited with his parents, which some critics have used as evidence of Spielberg's resorting to sentimentality at the end of an otherwise harrowing film, reaching to find a maudlin conclusion in which the sanctity of home and family are reinforced in order to counterbalance and even sweep away the horrors of the previous two and a half hours. This is the conclusion that scholar Fred See reaches in writing that "the mother's embrace and the promise of home and a tranquil spirit which it implies oversimplify what we know of Ballard's narrative, and what we have been shown of Jim's experience over the last three years. Spielberg's film ends with the vision of a lost boy returned to the sentimental plentitude of home."[22] The problem with this reading is that there has been no "sentimental plentitude" to begin with. For Jim, home is a place of creature comforts and the illusion of physical safety, but at no point in the film is it depicted as a place of emotional security and familial love and connection. Rather, Jim is rarely seen with his parents inside the home (at one point he peers around the corner and watches his father burning papers in the fireplace), and never in any kind of loving embrace outside the replication of the *Freedom From Fear* tableau, which Friedman has already demonstrated to be a much darker and less secure depiction of a child's bedtime routine. In fact, one could argue that Jim's fascination with flying and war is his escape from an unsatisfying home life in which he has no siblings and parents who seem to be, at best, barely interested in him. His reunion with them at the end of the film is characterized by tentative movements and an initial lack of recognition that contrast sharply with the vocal joys of the parents and children reuniting

---

[22] Fred See, "Steven Spielberg and the Holiness of War," *Arizona Quarterly* 60, no. 3 (2004): 119.

around them: John walks right past Jim, who is standing silently and hollow-eyed, and when Mary recognizes and approaches him, Jim touches her lips, face, and hair like she is something alien before falling into her arms. It is a reunion that holds little promise. When Jim closes his eyes in his mother's embrace, it does not signal relief so much as it suggests his last bastion of self-sufficiency leaving him, his body and soul completely exhausted from his three-year ordeal, but with no promise of fulfillment in the years to come. That Spielberg follows this shot (which is often mistakenly referred to as the last shot in the film) with Jim's floating suitcase, now a coffin for his childhood exuberance and imagination, further solidifies the idea that Jim, while alive, is nevertheless lost and done for.

War Horse: Humanity through an animal's eyes

Based on the 1982 children's novel by Michael Morpurgo and the subsequent 2007 stage play by Nick Stafford, *War Horse* is an ambitious anthological portrait of both the devastation of warfare and the potential for human decency as seen through the eyes of the titular animal, a thoroughbred horse named Joey. It is, like *Empire of the Sun*, a film that is very much indebted to Spielberg's cinematic forebears, including David Lean, although it also draws thematically and aesthetically from films as varied as John Ford's *The Searchers* (1956), Stanley Kubrick's *Paths of Glory* (1957), Andrei Tarkovsky's *Ivan's Childhood* (1962), and Robert Bresson's *Au hasard Balthazar* (1966). It is, fittingly, an often contradictory film that puts into sharp relief both romantic aspirations toward human decency and a dour vision of war at its ugliest.

Unlike *Empire of the Sun*'s complex use of a spoiled, myopic child as the protagonist, *War Horse*, which is set against the backdrop of World War I, is often unabashedly romantic in the way it uses Joey as a mythical, almost supernatural embodiment of loyalty, nobility, determination, and strength (he is described more than once in the film as a "remarkable horse," and late in the film a character calls him a "miracle horse"). Yet, Joey is not just a simplistic vessel into which we can pour universal values and easy sentiment, as he is also at times stubborn, willful, disruptive, and fearful. While Joey has his moments of greatness, he also has moments of weakness and fright. To wit, the film's most powerful and moving sequence does not depict Joey racing bravely into battle or saving the life of a beloved owner as one might expect of an ostensibly uplifting "animal film," but rather shows him running terrified through the muddy "no man's land" of a battlefield in northern France, lit against the black night sky by hellish red flares as he tears across a barren wasteland devastated by war, over and through the trenches, eventually becoming horrifically ensnared in coil after coil of barbed wire. Joey is abject terror personified, and his flight into the barbed wire is as wrenching and painful a sequence as Spielberg has ever produced, and this from the filmmaker who has dealt cinematically with the Holocaust, the Middle Passage, and the invasion of Normandy.

Like *Empire of the Sun*, *War Horse* does not begin in battle. Rather, it opens in the English countryside, which is depicted with lyrical aerial shots moving slowly over the verdant moors bathed in the ethereal morning light of the rising sun. The tone is of storybook tranquility and almost impossible beauty and splendor, which Spielberg will return to at the end of the film, thus providing bookends of visual beauty that stand in stark contrast to the brutality and violence that take place during much of the film's middle section. The imagery is aesthetically idealized in its cinematic treatment, which establishes from the outset the film's dialectic between the beauty of nature and the horrors of violence that humanity unleashes within it, a theme that was similarly struck by Terence Malick in *The Thin Red Line* (1998). In Malick's film, the central image is a strategic hill on Guadalcanal which the American soldiers are trying to take from the Japanese. When the Americans first advance on the hill, it is covered with a lush and beautifully swaying carpet of long grass; by the time it has finally been taken, the hill has been reduced to a burnt-out wasteland of charred pits, corpses, and mortar shells. Spielberg achieves a similar effect by bookending *War Horse* with scenes of heightened natural beauty, while the central portions of the film move slowly but surely toward the complete devastation of nature by the machines of war, which Spielberg depicts as counterpoint to the natural grace and beauty of Joey and the film's other horses. Thus, some of the film's starkest violence unfolds against the backdrop of beautiful, natural locations: a massacre of British soldiers by German machine guns in a fairy tale forest; the execution of deserting German soldiers beneath a picturesque old windmill; and, most strikingly, the extended depiction of trench warfare that has reduced the French countryside to a scorched wasteland of mud, blood, barbed wire, and shattered, twisted tree trunks that take on an expressionistic power similar to the otherworldly landscapes of Tarkovsky's *Ivan's Childhood*, which, like *Empire of the Sun*, is the story of an adolescent boy whose childhood is subsumed by war. The destruction of the physical landscape is echoed in the film's depiction of how war destroys those who engage in it by forcing them into unnatural behavior, which is encapsulated in an exchange of dialogue between a German soldier and British soldier. "Running away is all they have," the German soldier says, referring to Joey's panicked flight through "no man's land" in the heat of battle, to which the British soldier replies, "Yeah, and we taught them the opposite. To run into the fray."

"LOST AND DONE FOR"

The opening half hour of *War Horse* is far removed from the horrors of warfare, although war eventually intrudes just as it did into Jim's rarefied life in Shanghai. However, Spielberg keeps all suggestions of war and violence at bay during the film's opening third, which gives *War Horse* a much different tone than *Empire of the Sun*, where the war machine was startlingly present from the very beginning. Whereas *Empire of the Sun* opens with images of death that foreshadow the forthcoming destruction of Jim's innocence and his illusions of safety, *War Horse* literally begins with life via the birth of Joey in an open field, which is witnessed with intense fascination and longing by a neighboring teenage farm boy named Albert Narracott (Jeremy Irvine), who will eventually become Joey's owner and trainer. After the title card (which looks much like that of *Empire of the Sun*, with the title emblazoned from behind with the light of a rising sun), Albert watches as Joey and his mother gallop about the fields—a symbolically idealized family that is far different from Albert's own.

Albert's father, Ted (Peter Mullan), is a financially strapped tenant farmer and veteran of the Boer War who drinks too much and often acts foolishly as a result, and his mother, Rose (Emily Watson), is a long-suffering woman of little humor who must frequently bear the burden of her husband's imprudent and rash decisions. However, unlike the Graham family in *Empire of the Sun*, there is a sense of warmth and connection in the Narracott family, despite their poverty, interpersonal struggles, and later humiliation at the hands of Lyons (David Thewlis), the cruel landlord who owns the farm they work.

The depiction of Joey and his mother as an idealized familial unit is central to *War Horse*'s recurrent themes of fear and loss. While the film's opening sequences focus heavily on pastoral imagery, distilled class conflict that associates wealth with cruelty and avarice, and comic touches including an aggressive goose and a slapstick moment in which Albert attempts to show off to a local girl by jumping Joey over a wall and ends up getting thrown instead, they are tinged with the persistent threat of loss. Joey's idealized life with his mother is cut short when he is forcibly taken from her and sold at auction in the village (Spielberg poignantly foreshadows their separation by framing Joey and his mother through the wooden slats of a gate, which visually isolates them from each other). The Narracotts face the loss of their farm (which for them means life) after Ted foolishly outbids Lyons for Joey, thus placing them in a financial hole from which they have little chance of digging out.

More importantly, though, the Narracotts' entire family dynamic is shaped by what Ted has lost as a result of his involvement in the Boer War some years earlier, which presages the film's physical depictions of warfare. As Rose explains to Albert, Ted's alcoholism and the social and personal problems it causes are not so much a moral failing as they are an outgrowth of his experiences on the battlefield. "He *drinks*, Mum!" Albert charges, to which Rose replies, "Well, so might you if you'd been where he's been, seen what he's seen." Where Ted has been and what he has seen are shrouded in mystery, as he refuses to talk about it because, in Rose's words, "He can't. There aren't words for some things." Whatever Ted did during the war, it resulted in commendations and awards, as Rose shows Albert his father's campaign pennant (he was a sergeant in the 7th Battalion of the Imperial Yeomanry); the Queen's South Africa Medal, which was given to every man who fought in the Boer War; and the Distinguished Conduct Medal, which he was awarded after being wounded and saving the lives of several other soldiers in the Transvaal. Rather than being proudly displayed in their home, Rose keeps these mementos of Ted's wartime experience hidden in the barn because Ted threw them all away as soon as he returned home. Far from being badges of honor, they are painful reminders of the horrors of war, the memory of which Ted is clearly unable to escape despite his heavy drinking. "He refuses to be proud of killing, I suppose," Rose ruminates.

Thus, before the film has shown us a single image of combat, it has already called into question any simplified notions of heroism and bravery—all the "macho, gung-ho stuff" that fed Spielberg's imagination as a child and was so central to Jim's illusory notions of the grandeur of warfare in *Empire of the Sun*. The fact that Ted's campaign pennant reappears throughout the film, going wherever Joey goes after Albert ties it to his harness, turns it into a kind of talisman that binds father and son together after Albert's own experiences on the battlefield, which in various ways reflect his father's unspoken

FIGURE 4.6 "There aren't words for some things." *Rose (Emily Watson) shows her son Albert (Jeremy Irvine) his father's wartime commendations, which she keeps hidden in the barn because they are painful reminders to him of his horrific experiences during the Boer War. (Digital Frame Enlargement)*

experiences. Both Ted and Albert save their fellow soldiers on the battlefield, and while Ted is wounded in the leg, Albert is temporarily blinded by mustard gas. Thus, while the ending of *War Horse* does not explicitly suggest as much, there is the lingering concern that Albert may be as damaged by his wartime experiences as his father was, which casts a pall over the film's painterly final images.

The film's narrative structure is built around Joey constantly changing owners, as he is either forcibly taken or sold or his owner is killed, which provides a framework of intersecting vignettes that individually and collectively depict the complexities of humanity in the shadow of war. Joey first comes into Albert's possession when his father bids for the horse at an auction primarily to assert himself in front of the other villagers by keeping him away from Lyons and his spoiled teenage son. Thus, Joey comes into the Narracott family through an imprudent, impulsive act that could potentially spell financial doom for them (being a thoroughbred, Joey is not a working horse and is not physically equipped to pull a plow). Desperate for money, Ted later sells Joey to the British army when they arrive in town to buy horses and sign up eligible men for service after the outbreak of World War I. Albert, who is too young to enlist at this point, is distraught over losing Joey, whom he has trained and with whom he has forged a strong bond, but Captain Nicholls (Tom Hiddleston), the British officer who purchases him, assures the boy that he will take excellent care of the horse and bring him back at the end of the war.

Joey's service with the British army ends in a battlefield slaughter, after which he changes hands to the German army. He and another horse named Topthorn are taken when two German brothers, Günther (David Kross) and Michael (Leonard Carow), desert the army and wind up at a farm in northern France owned by an older man (Niels Arestrup) and his adolescent granddaughter, Emilie (Celine Buckens), who hide the horses from German soldiers ransacking the farm for provisions. They cannot hide them forever, though, and when the protective grandfather finally consents to allow Emilie to ride Joey, they run across the German army again and Joey and Topthorn are forced back into the ranks of other war horses where, according to the German captain, "they will pull artillery until they die, or until the war is over."

This is perhaps the most grueling part of the film for Joey, as he is harnessed to heavy cannons and forced to pull them up muddy hills; the only decency that is shown to him come from Heigelman, the German private who is responsible for the care of the horses. "It's a pity they found you," he says, recognizing Joey's beauty and how it will be destroyed by the demands of the war machine (he even gives Joey a name, for which the captain chides him: "You should never give a name to anything you are certain to lose"). While

FIGURE 4.7 Humanism in the inhumanity of war. *As British soldier Colin (Tony Kebbell) and German soldier Peter (Hinnerk Schönemann) work together to free Joey from the barbed wire in which he has become ensnared, they break through their own prejudices and recognize the other man as a fellow human being, rather than simply an opposing soldier in uniform. (Digital Frame Enlargement)*

Topthorn is eventually killed by the labor he is forced to endure, Joey survives and escapes from the German army during a battle and becomes ensnared in barbed wire in the middle of no man's land, where he is eventually freed by the combined efforts of Colin (Toby Kebbell), a British soldier, and Peter (Hinnerk Schönemann), a German soldier. Colin takes Joey back with him after winning a coin toss, where he is eventually reunited with Albert, who has joined the British army and come of age amid the harrowing violence of war.

Just as Jim's various encounters with other prisoners of war throughout *Empire of the Sun* provide a portrait of humanity under extreme duress, so does *War Horse*'s anthological structure, whose narrative focus shifts from owner to owner, some of whom are humane and some of whom are cruel. Like Robert Bresson's *Au hasard Balthazar* (1966), which it echoes both structurally and thematically, Spielberg's film uses Joey and his constant movement among owners as a means of reflecting on the differing faces of humanity, both good and bad (Bresson's film featured a donkey as the central character). While Spielberg's formulation of the classical Hollywood style has little in common with the austere aesthetic favored by Bresson, *War Horse* is similarly powerful in its symbolic use of a "beast of burden" to evoke the pains and joys of the human experience. The fact that the empathy and decency embodied by most of the characters—Albert, Captain Nicholls, Gunter, Emilie, Heigelman, and Colin—far outweighs the militaristic cruelty of the German captain who thinks little of working the animals to death or the casual egotism of Lyons, who sees Joey as yet another object to enhance his stature, suggests that Spielberg is working in a more optimistic vein, drawing sustained attention to how people can maintain their humanity in even the worst of conditions.

Yet, at the same time, there is an underlying darkness to *War Horse* that is inherent in almost any story that is told against the backdrop of war, in which humanity literally turns against itself on a global scale. "The war is taking everything from everyone," the German captain tells Emilie and her grandfather as he takes Joey away after having already ransacked their farm for food and provisions—a microcosm of war's collateral damage.

Spielberg is particularly adept at making us feel the enormity of humankind's war machines and their destructive capacity. From the surprise revelation of a bank of German machine guns that quickly and brutally ends a British charge, to the thunderous emergence of a massive iron tank, to the use of sickly yellow mustard gas in the trenches, the film chronicles with unrelenting clarity the devastating mechanics of war, which seem all the more cruel and unnatural when set against the natural beauty and grace of Joey and the other horses harnessed to them. Thus, while an earlier sequence detailing Albert and Joey's grim determination to plow a field against all odds and expectations seems at first like a sentimental narrative ploy to elevate Joey to mythic status, it becomes clear that Joey's work in front of the plow foreshadows his future of being shackled to instruments of war. His work for Albert and the Narracott family has a genuine nobility to it, even as it physically degrades and wounds him (Spielberg draws attention to the bloody sores on his body after the field is plowed); his work for the military, on the other hand, particularly the German army, becomes a symbolic desecration, a horrible misuse from which he barely survives. "War horse," a soldier calls him late in the film. "What a strange beast you've become."

This is but one of the many oppositions that help structure the film's conflicted depiction of humanity and inhumanity: the pastoral beauty of the moorlands in Dartmoor vs. the devastated alien landscape of trench warfare in northern France; the beauty and physical grace of Joey and the other horses vs. the clanking ugliness of humanity's instruments of war; the kindness and decency of Captain Nicholls vs. the wanton cruelty of the German captain; the idealized family as seen in the relationship between Joey and his mother vs. the fractured family as seen in the Narracotts and their internal tensions and struggles with poverty. These oppositions allow Spielberg to comment on the darker impulses of humankind and its violence, but also to provide opportunities to explore the potential for human decency. This is most evident in the sequence in which Colin, the British soldier, and Peter, the German soldier, both risk their lives to enter no man's land between the opposing trenches in order to cut Joey free from the barbed wire in which he has become ensnared. Colin is the first to venture forth, against the orders of his commanding officer, but Peter soon joins him. Their interactions are initially wary—understandably so given that their positions in warring armies dictate that, in any other situation, they would be trying to kill each other. Yet, as the scene progresses and they work together to cut the horse free, they discover just enough about the other to break through their own prejudices to recognize the other man as a fellow human being, rather than simply an opposing soldier in uniform. The sequence is harrowing in its own right, especially given the agony of Joey's situation and the initial fear that their exchange might break down into violence, but Spielberg also makes it gently comical, finding a sense of humanism in the inhumanity of war that Jean Renoir, director of the anti-war humanist masterpiece *Grand Illusion* (*La grande illusion*, 1937), might appreciate.

This sense of reassurance in the potential for human connection across the trenches is counterbalanced by a clear-eyed view of the horrors of humankind's self-destruction. Spielberg, working in collaboration with cinematographer Janusz Kaminski, had already fully established his command of the language of cinema to convey the enormity of historical violence in *Schindler's List*, *Amistad*, *Saving Private Ryan*, and *Munich*, all of which rely on graphic verisimilitude to convey the awfulness of the physical destruction of the human body, whether by bullets, chains, or bombs. In each of those films he employed a different cinematic vernacular that connected with the overall aesthetic approach of the film. Thus, in *Schindler's List* he used black-and-white filmstock and primarily handheld cameras to produce a documentary-like aesthetic that captured the look and feel of wartime newsreels, while in the much celebrated Normandy invasion sequence in *Saving Private Ryan* he deployed a complex array of stylistic devices to "produce an imaginary of historicity and verisimilitude."[23] These included various in-camera and post-production processes to diffuse and desaturate the color, and the use of a 45-degree camera shutter to reduce motion blur and create a sharper, jerkier, more anxious image. Central to all of those films is an unwavering willingness to view the graphic destruction of the human body, which resulted in all four films being rated R by the Motion Picture Association of America's rating system.[24]

---

[23] Sue Tait, "Visualising Technologies and the Ethics and Aesthetics of Screening Death," *Science as Culture* 18, no. 3 (2009): 341. In this essay, Tait does an excellent job of discussing the numerous aesthetic devices that Spielberg and Kaminski deployed to generate the unique visual impact of *Saving Private Ryan*.

[24] All of Spielberg's other films have been rated either PG or PG–13, although several of those films, including *Jaws*, *Raiders of the Lost Ark*, and *Indiana Jones and the Temple of Doom*, pushed the envelope in terms of acceptable levels of graphic violence in a PG-rated film, with the latter leading

However, because *War Horse* was aimed at general audiences with a non-restrictive PG–13 rating, Spielberg had to develop a different approach to the horrors of war that would convey the enormity of the violence without always putting explicit bloodshed directly on screen. Rather than emphasize the gory details of bloody bullet holes and dismembered limbs as he did with such resounding aesthetic force in *Saving Private Ryan*, Spielberg instead uses abstract and poetic means of depicting the horrors of violence. For example, his depiction of the charge through no man's land between the British and German trenches (which Stanley Kubrick memorably depicted in *Paths of Glory*, a film Spielberg greatly admires) is therefore brutal without being graphic, relying primarily on the expressionistic devastation of the landscape to stand in for the details of corporeal mutilation. Even more instructive is the scene when Joey is first taken into battle when the British cavalry charges a German camp they think is unprepared and unprotected. The German soldiers flee into a nearby forest where they have set up a bank of machine guns that are quickly used to mow down the charging British soldiers and horses. Spielberg cuts from direct shots of the firing barrels to high-angle shots of riderless horses sprinting into the forest, thus suggesting the violence of the men being shot down rather than depicting it explicitly with blood squibs and falling bodies. He also emphasizes the emotional horrors of the violence via Captain Nicholls, whose realization of his and his soldiers' imminent doom is one of the most poignant moments in the film. Tom Hiddleston, the actor who portrayed Nicholls, noted that Spielberg directed him to "de-age" himself in the close-up in which he first sees the machine guns and recognizes what is about to happen: "[Spielberg] said, 'Give me your war face, and the camera is going to move across, and as you feel it come up in front of you, I want you to de-age yourself by 20 years. So, you're 29, and then when you see those killing machines, you're 9 years old. I want to see the child in you.'"[25] Thus, contrary to the typical charges that Spielberg deploys the aura of childhood sentimentally, here he uses it evocatively (and somewhat perversely) to further humanize Nicholls' impending death by symbolically killing him as a child.

And, while death is omnipresent throughout *War Horse*, so is the hope of life, and the film ends with a family reunion that is both strikingly similar and dissimilar to the ending of *Empire of the Sun*. In the film's penultimate sequence, Albert is fully reunited with Joey after the horse is auctioned by the military following the close of the war. Although his fellow soldiers and officers

---

directly to the MPAA's decision to create the PG–13 rating in the summer of 1984. See James Kendrick, *Hollywood Bloodshed: Violence in 1980s American Cinema* (Carbondale: Southern Illinois University Press, 2009), 170–203.
[25] "A Filmmaking Journey," *War Horse*, directed by Steven Spielberg (2011, Burbank, CA: Buena Vista Home Entertainment, 2012), Blu-Ray.

FIGURE 4.8 "What a strange beast you've become." *In the final shot of* War Horse, *Joey stands almost motionless, framed in profile as he looks out at the empty fields, suggesting not a moment of triumph or catharsis, but rather a moment of reflection on all that has been lost before this moment. (Digital Frame Enlargment)*

pool their money to help him buy the horse back, he is outbid at the last minute by the French grandfather from earlier in the film, who bids three times more than Albert to secure the horse for his granddaughter, for whom Joey "was everything." However, when he recognizes that Albert is Joey's true owner, he hands the horse over to him along with Ted's campaign pennant. When asked about his granddaughter's whereabouts, the grandfather repeats a variation on the line said to him earlier by the German captain: "The war has taken everything from everyone." This line of dialogue casts a bittersweet pall over the scene, as the final reuniting of Albert and Joey, replete with swelling music and a tracking shot into a close-up of them looking at each other, is shadowed by the off-screen death of Emilie, which, given the grandfather's dialogue, we can only imagine was a violent one. It is doubly painful given that Emilie's vignette in the film was framed by heartbreak: not only had she lost her parents, but she rechristened Joey "François" after a boy who "broke [her] heart" the previous year. We last see her on-screen as the image fades to black from her weeping in the arms of her grandfather after Joey is forcibly taken from them by the Germans. The fade-to-black, it turns out, was not just a transitional device, but a foreshadowing of her death and the fact that we, like her grandfather, will never see her again.

The final scene in the film returns the story to the Narracott farm as Albert rides Joey home against a sky turned intensely orange by the setting sun (the cinematography suggests the look of three-strip Technicolor with its artificially intensified hues), which is both a striking variation on the film's opening morning-sun aerial shots of the landscape and a visual echo of the scene in John Ford's *The Searchers* (1956) when the Edwards farm is attacked by a group of Comanche warriors, which leads to the kidnapping of a little girl. The final scene in *War Horse* borrows the visual language of *The Searchers*, but inverts the importance of the moment: rather than a child disappearing from a farm, a child is returning. Yet, Albert is no longer a child, having been through the hell of war, and, as noted earlier, his reuniting with his father and returning to him the campaign pennant he threw away decades earlier reminds us that both men are veterans of battlefield violence and there is no reason to think that Albert may not suffer some of the same trauma as his father, whose limp is a constant physical reminder of his scarred psyche. The fact that the sky behind them is suddenly bifurcated between the orange glow of the setting sun near the horizon and the darkness of clouds above visually emphasizes the conflicted nature of the moment, as the family reunion carries with it the heaviness of the violence and loss that preceded it. Unlike the emotionally vacant reunion at the end of *Empire of the Sun*, there is genuine sentiment in the wordless embraces shared by Albert and his parents. It is a particularly powerful moment that demonstrates Spielberg's mastery of the fine art—ungraspable by filmmakers who trade exclusively in irony and cynicism—of infusing the bleakest of material with a sense of optimism that nevertheless refuses to blot out the tragedies and losses that came before.

It is telling, then, that the film's very final image is not of the Narracotts, but of Joey, standing alone and apart from the tearful reunion. The final moment of the film alternates between two shots slowly tracking out from the Narracotts' embrace and two shots slowly tracking in on Joey's face, framed, like the Narracotts, against the intense twilight sky divided between light and dark. As the image cuts from the Narracotts to Joey, the music shifts from full orchestration to a lone horn, which imparts a sense of solemnity to the shot as Joey stands almost motionless, framed in profile as he looks out at the empty fields that surround them.

While it is impossible to "read" any kind of emotion into Joey's look, the framing of the shot, the shift in music, and the overall tone of the scene suggests not a moment of triumph or catharsis, but rather a moment of reflection on all that has been lost before this moment. Albert and Joey, like Jim in *Empire of the Sun*, have both survived their ordeals during wartime and been reunited with their family, but it is impossible to shake the idea that the damage has been done and they will never be the same again. Fittingly, as the image of Joey fades to black, the end credits do not immediately start. Rather, the film's title fades in once again, reminding us of what Joey, through no fault or cause of his own, has become. While not necessarily "lost and done for," as the ending of *Empire of the Sun* suggests, both horse and boy in *War Horse* have been irrevocably altered—made into "strange beasts"—and will carry with them the burden of their memories forever.

5

"For the World's More Full of Weeping Than You Can Understand"
Humanity and Inhumanity in *A.I. Artificial Intelligence*

Throughout *A.I. Artificial Intelligence*, the film's tragic protagonist David (Haley Joel Osment), a robot child who has been programed to love a human "mommy" and consequently desires to become a "real boy" so that she will love him back, insists that he is singular and unique—"one of a kind." David's intense need to see himself as unique is central to the identity crisis he endures, which is only appropriate given that *A.I.* is a unique film with its own identity crisis stemming from the fact that it was an unexpected and, for many, virtually unthinkable collaboration between Steven Spielberg and Stanley Kubrick, directors of decidedly different temperaments, aesthetics, and worldviews who had nevertheless maintained a close friendship and working relationship since Kubrick first confided in Spielberg about his work on the film in 1984. Thus, the film is divided both diegetically—Should we view David as fundamentally human (orga) based on his very human emotions or fundamentally mechanical (mecha) because of the nature of his physical constitution?—and artistically—Is it a Spielberg film or a Kubrick film or a hybrid of sorts? In both senses, the film's dualities are irresolvable.

A.I., which takes place in a recognizable near-future of environmental catastrophe in which the polar ice caps have melted and flooded all the continental coasts, unfolds in three distinct acts. In the first act, David, a prototype mecha child, is given to a young couple, Henry and Monica Swinton

(Sam Robards and Frances O'Connor), whose only son, Martin (Jake Thomas), has been cryogenically frozen while awaiting a cure for his unnamed fatal disease. While Monica at first rejects David as an inferior replacement for her flesh-and-blood son, angry at Henry for even suggesting the idea, she slowly comes to appreciate David's presence and eventually decides to activate his programming to love—a process known as "imprinting." However, soon after David is imprinted on her, Martin is cured, and through a series of accidents and misunderstandings, particularly an incident in which Martin convinces David to cut off a lock of Monica's hair while she sleeps, and an accident at Martin's birthday party in which David pulls him into the pool, the family comes to see David as dangerous. Monica is required to take him back to Cybertronics, the robotics company that designed and built him, for destruction, but at the last minute she can't bear to do it, and instead deserts him in the forest to survive on his own.

The second act begins with David, alone and distraught, setting out to win back Monica's love, a mission that is fueled by his belief in the story of Pinocchio, who through the magic of the Blue Fairy was changed from a puppet into a real boy. David is accompanied by Teddy, a mecha teddy bear given to him by Monica, and Gigolo Joe (Jude Law), a "love mecha" with whom he is captured and almost destroyed at a Flesh Fair, a raucous public spectacle in which rogue mechas are destroyed for public entertainment. David and Gigolo Joe eventually make their way to New York City, which is now mostly underwater, where David comes face to face with Dr. Allen Hobby (William Hurt), the scientist who designed him. By chance he discovers a Pinocchio-themed exhibit at Coney Island, which has long since been flooded beneath the ocean, and spends the next two millennia beneath the waters wishing over and over again in front of a Blue Fairy statue to be transformed into a real boy.

The third act begins 2,000 years later during a new ice age, with David being dug out of the now-frozen ocean by SuperMechas, highly evolved mechanical beings that have inherited the earth from the human race, which has died out for unknown reasons. With their advanced technologies, the SuperMechas are able to recreate the Swintons' household and temporarily resurrect Monica so that David can spend a single day with her before she disappears forever. In the film's final moments, David lies in bed with Monica as she sleeps, and closing his eyes he goes "to that place where dreams are born," which may or may not imply his death.

Released at the height of the summer blockbuster season in 2001, ironically the year in which Kubrick's austere science fiction masterpiece *2001: A Space Odyssey* (1968) is set, *A.I.* was the first science fiction film Spielberg had made since *E.T. The Extra-Terrestrial* (1982) and the first film for which he was the sole credited screenwriter since *Close Encounters of the Third Kind* (1977). And, while critical and popular opinion was sharply divided over the film, there was one thing that most viewers seemed to agree on: it was *different*. *Newsweek* critic David Ansen described it as "a rich, strange, problematical movie full of wild tonal shifts and bravura moviemaking,"[1] while *Chicago Reader* critic Jonathan Rosenbaum argued that "it defamiliarizes Spielberg, makes him strange."[2] Although *A.I.* bore obvious elements of Spielbergian aesthetics and thematic preoccupations, it felt off, not quite right, or at least not at all what people were expecting. The quickest explanation for this was also the most obvious: *A.I.* was not just a Spielberg film, but was rather born out of his collaboration with Kubrick, who passed away unexpectedly in the spring of 1999, just before the release of what would become his final film, *Eyes Wide Shut*. Kubrick's exacting, methodical, and often cruelly ironic films would seem to be the polar opposite of Spielberg's cinema of warmth, light, and reassurance, which is why it was so difficult for some to imagine the pair collaborating. David Ansen encapsulated the issue in asking, "Is it a Stanley Kubrick movie channeled through Steven Spielberg? Is it a Spielberg movie informed by the ghost of Kubrick? Is it a movie in which the sensibilities of two of the most powerful cinematic personalities of our times—who couldn't be more different—conduct a 140-minute duel for dominance?"[3]

Most viewers came to the conclusion that the different tone and feel of *A.I.* had to be the result of the collision of minds—Kubrick's cold rationality and cynicism and Spielberg's sentiment and mainstream appeal—fusing into something bizarre and uneven that is not quite one and not quite the other. Jonathan Rosenbaum, in a reassessment of the film a decade after its release, wrote, "Unlike many of my colleagues, I can't simply accept *A.I.* as either 'a film by Steven Spielberg' or 'a film by Stanley Kubrick.' I can only read it as a film deriving from the will and consciousness of both of them—one alive and one dead, and encompassing all the dialectical contradictions that this strange collaboration entails."[4] This view, at least in terms of the film's visuals, is supported by many of the people who worked on it. Producer Bonnie Curtis explained, "It's Steven's interpretation of what Stanley was trying to do. My joke is that it's Stevely Kuberg. It's a complete meld of both

---

[1] David Ansen, "Mr. Spielberg Strikes Again: The Director Goes Back to the Future with Kubrick at His Side." *Newsweek*, June 25, 2001, 84.
[2] Jonathan Rosenbaum, "The Best of Both Worlds: *A.I. Artificial Intelligence*," *Chicago Reader*, July 13, 2001, http://www.jonathanrosenbaum.com/?p=6306 (accessed September 15, 2013).
[3] Ansen, "Mr. Spielberg Strikes Again," 84.
[4] Jonathan Rosenbaum, "A Matter of Life and Death: *A.I.*," *Film Quarterly* 65, no. 3 (2012): 76.

of them. Every word, every thing you see has both of them in it."[5] Similarly, cinematographer Janusz Kaminski noted in an interview in 2002 that "he and Spielberg tried to maintain Kubrick's original vision for the story." He said they "[paid] a certain homage to Stanley" by "[shooting] the film very clean and stark, with no camera moves. Stanley's films are known for their simplicity and cleanness of the frame. That's what I tried to do."[6]

Even if we concede that *A.I.* is fundamentally a collaboration between Spielberg and Kubrick—a Stevely Kuberg film—it still provides significant insight into the fundamentally conflicted nature of so much of Spielberg's cinema. After all, writing and directing the final product entailed channeling through his own sensibilities several decades of creative energies invested by Kubrick and his collaborators; thus, it is undeniable that Spielberg left his inimitable stamp on *A.I.* More than that, it is arguably his most revealing and summative work, and not necessarily because of Kubrick's influence. Kubrick clearly recognized the resonance of the material with Spielberg's cinematic proclivities, which is why he confided with him about the project in the first place and why he asked him to direct it in the mid-1990s even though he had been working on it for more than ten years.[7] Kubrick's reasoning was twofold. First, having recognized that his original plan to use an animatronic puppet to play David was simply unfeasible, he knew that Spielberg's speed of production would be more amenable to a film featuring a child actor than his lengthy production schedules, during which time the child could conceivably age in a way that would create continuity errors. More importantly, though, he saw that Spielberg would be better attuned to the film's intense emotional currents and Oedipal anxieties. As executive producer Jan Harlan put it, "Stanley's version was too black and cynical for an expensive film that had to appeal to a broad family audience. Steven had the ability to lighten the tone without changing the substance."[8]

While Spielberg might have arguably "lightened the tone," *A.I.* remains a resolutely dark and even despairing film, one that held little appeal to "a broad family audience" and ultimately failed to satisfy both those looking for comfortable Spielbergian warmth and humanity and those looking for cold, Kubrickian irony in the vein of *A Clockwork Orange* (1971) or *Full Metal Jacket*

---

[5] Rachel Abramowitz, "Regarding Stanley: Steven Spielberg Felt the Aura of Stanley Kubrick as He Brought an Idea of the Late Director's to the Screen," *Los Angeles Times*, May 6, 2001, http://articles.latimes.com/2001/may/06/entertainment/ca-59783 (accessed September 15, 2013).
[6] Chris Gennusa, "Kaminski Fuses Kubrick, Spielberg." *Daily Variety*, January 15, 2002, A6.
[7] Steven Spielberg, "Foreword," *A.I. Artificial Intelligence—From Stanley Kubrick to Steven Spielberg: The Vision Behind the Film*, ed. Jan Harlan and Jane M. Struthers (London: Thames & Hudson, 2009), 7. See also Abramowitz, "Regarding Stanley."
[8] Jan Harlan, "Afterword: The Two Masters," *A.I. Artificial Intelligence—From Stanley Kubrick to Steven Spielberg: The Vision Behind the Film*, 148.

(1987).⁹ *A.I.* draws almost equally from the wells typically associated with its two cinematic minds: at times both emotional and intellectual, it is warm and humorous in some passages, cold and exacting in others. But, above all, it is a work of great courage and imagination that challenges the audience by questioning our basic assumptions about what it means to be human and the nature of love. As Kubrick originally intended, *A.I.* is a deeply philosophical film that uses the ages-old structure of the fairy tale, albeit to raise far more questions than it answers. Contrary to the traditional cultural work of the fairy tale to instruct and inform burgeoning minds, *A.I.* tackles enormous issues and leaves us at the end in a cloud of ambiguity. Scholar Stephen M. Glaister has since called it "the most explicitly philosophical mainstream film since *2001*,"¹⁰ and it is thus unsurprising that in a compilation of philosophical essays on Spielberg's films, *A.I.* is the only one that is the focus of two separate chapters.¹¹

While many critics, scholars, and philosophers have rightly recognized the moral and aesthetic complexities of *A.I.* and the tragic ramifications of its themes about humanity and cruelty, it has rarely been put in direct dialogue with the darker elements of Spielberg's previous films. Instead, the film is often understood and discussed as an aberration from the director's typical work, the explanation for which usually hinges on his collaboration with Kubrick. In his *Newsweek* review, David Ansen asserts that "It's like nothing else Spielberg has done," and suggests that the film's effectiveness stems from the "tug-of-war between the darkness of the fable and Spielberg's need for warmth," while philosopher Timothy Dunn notes, "It is considerably darker than most Spielberg films, reflecting, in part, the somewhat misanthropic influence of the late Stanley Kubrick."¹²

---

⁹ By Spielberg's box office standards, *A.I.* was a disappointment during its initial theatrical release, grossing only $78 million against a production budget in the range of $90 to $100 million. His previous film, *Saving Private Ryan*, an R-rated war film, had grossed $228 million domestically, and his follow-up film, *Minority Report* (2002), another science-fiction story whose look and themes felt Kubrickian, albeit one buoyed by the star power of Tom Cruise, grossed $132 million.
¹⁰ Stephen M. Glaister, "Saving AI: Artificial Intelligence: Philosophical Aspects of Spielberg's Neglected Robo-Epic," *Bright Lights Film Journal* 48 (2005), http://brightlightsfilm.com/48/ai.php (accessed September 15, 2013).
¹¹ Timothy Dunn, "*A.I. Artificial Intelligence* and the Tragic Sense of Life" and V. Alan White, "*A.I. Artificial Intelligence*: Artistic Indulgence or Advanced Inquiry?," in *Steven Spielberg and Philosophy: We're Gonna Need a Bigger Book*, ed. Dean A. Kowalski. Both philosophers regard the film as a profound philosophical work. Dunn calls it "Spielberg's most philosophically ambitious film" and "a profound meditation on the human condition" (82), while White argues that, "*A.I.* has not yet been adequately appreciated for its own thematic overtures about humanity and intelligence, and ... future reassessments might well launch the film into the starry firmament of *2001*" (210).
¹² Dunn, "*A.I.: Artificial Intelligence* and the Tragic Sense of Life," 82.

In this, the final chapter in a book exploring the darker aspects of Spielberg's cinema, I argue that *A.I.* is not an aberration at all, but rather a synthesis of Spielberg's previous themes, a summative work that makes explicit the darker undertones and thematic conflicts that shaded so many of his previous films. It is hardly the only one of Spielberg's films to feel conflicted, and it is not necessarily even the most conflicted of his works—just his most *obviously* conflicted. *A.I.* wears its thematic, visual, and emotional turmoil on its sleeve, which is why many viewers and critics had such a hard time knowing what to do with it. Viewed in terms of the darker elements of Spielberg's cinema that often get ignored, downplayed, or explained away, *A.I.* comes into much sharper focus as his summative film, one that engages virtually all of the major themes in his previous works. In the broadest sense, all of these themes involve the tension between humanity and inhumanity, which is present in the film's depiction of the cruelty and prejudices of human nature, familial fragmentation, and scientific hubris. *A.I.* also provides what is Spielberg's most challenging and contradictory ending, one that is simultaneously a fairy-tale celebration of wish fulfillment and a dark rumination on the extent to which self-delusion can mask the impossibility of fulfilling our deepest desires.

"He's so real, but he's not": Humanity and mecha identity

As in *E.T.* and *Empire of the Sun* (1987), the protagonist of *A.I.* is a child who is emotionally and/or physically abandoned and alone in a world whose threats convey both literally and metaphorically the difficult and often traumatic nature of childhood. However, unlike Elliott and Jim, David's identity and our identification with him are complicated by the fact that he is not physically human. A mecha child specifically designed and engineered to fill the needs of would-be parents who yearn for children but cannot have them because of government regulations on child bearing, David is not, in the strictly human sense, "real," something of which he is reminded repeatedly by various human characters. "He's so real, but he's not," Monica says when she first sees him, essentially summarizing David's identity crisis, while Henry assures her that inside he is "like all the rest—a hundred miles of fiber," a line that resonates in terms of both David's physical construction ("a hundred miles of fiber") and, more importantly, the conflict between his desire to be unique and the fact that he is an engineered mecha "like all the rest."

So real, but not—David is the film's central duality, which creates a fundamental conflict in how to view and identify with him. As a human? As a machine? As somehow both? And, of course, this duality is infinitely complicated by the fact that he is designed to look and programed to act like a child, which engages all of the sympathies and feelings we reserve for children because of their vulnerabilities and need for protection and nurturance. Although he is a mechanical being, David has been programed to experience human emotion, specifically love and its attendant emotional attachments, as fully as any biological human being, which makes him, for all intents and purposes, human in his emotional responses, behaviors, and beliefs—his "inner world of metaphor, of intuition, of self-motivated reasoning, of dreams," as Dr. Hobby puts it.

Thus, we must ask whether David's love (and hope and anger and despair) is any different simply because it has been hard-wired into his system. Why, the film asks, is human emotion different from mechanical emotion just because it springs from chemicals and brainwaves rather than wiring and microprocessors? This question—At what point, if ever, does a human technological creation become essentially human?—was, for Kubrick, a lifelong obsession. While most of his films were wary of machines and their connection with dehumanization, the most affecting character in *2001* is HAL, an onboard computer who, despite his malicious actions (including the murder of several astronauts), is the only character to generate audience sympathy when he dies, quietly saying those haunting words, "I can feel it. I'm afraid." In *A.I.*, David says something very similar, and it is an equally haunting moment. If he can feel, if he can be afraid, if he can love, who is to say that he is not human? Or, in better terms, who is to say that his experience is less than the human experience? In an essay on the film, philosopher Timothy Dunn chose to understand David as a person primarily because he feels human emotions and because he is regarded by the characters in the film closest to him as a person.[13]

Crucially, David sees himself as a person, which creates for him much cognitive dissonance whenever he is reminded that he is not, in fact, truly human. When a worker at the Flesh Fair who fears that he might be a human boy accidentally caught up with the rogue mechas examines him with a handheld X-ray device and declares that he's a machine, David replies simply, "I'm a boy." When the man's daughter asks if he's a "toy boy," he responds with his name: "My name is David," a refrain that he will repeat over and over again when he is dragged out to the center ring to be destroyed. For David, his name is his identity, part of the proof that he is

---

[13] Dunn, "*A.I. Artificial Intelligence* and the Tragic Sense of Life."

special and unique. When Gigolo Joe tells him that humans hate mechas, he responds angrily, "My mommy doesn't hate me because I'm special and unique. Because there has never been anyone like me before, ever. Mommy loves Martin because he is real, and when I am real Mommy's going to read to me and tuck me in my bed and sing to me and listen to what I have to say and she will cuddle with me and tell me every day, a hundred times a day, that she loves me!" This is the first point in the film that David displays anything that resembles anger or aggression, which suggests that he is becoming more consumed with his desire to be made real and that, when his identity is threatened, he responds, like many people both good and bad, violently.

This violence is most overt when he finds himself confronted with another David mecha at Cybertronics at the end of the film's second act. Until then, David had assured himself that he is unique, which is why seeing his exact likeness at the place where he thought "they make you real" is so utterly shocking to him. His name, the symbol of his unique identity, is revealed to be little more than a corporate logo, branded on hundreds of similar mechas who will serve the same purpose he did for other childless couples. "I'm David," the other mecha child says brightly, to which David replies, "No you're not. I'm David." The other mecha has no problem with them both being named David because the name is not part of his identity, which is a uniquely human trait. Thus, David is sent into a rage, screaming over and over "I'm David! I'm David!" in a voice that is alternately terrifying and pathetic as he grabs a lamp and smashes at the other David mecha with such fury that he decapitates him, sending his head flying across the room where it lands at the feet of Gigolo Joe, who is so disturbed and frightened by the outburst that he turns and leaves.

David's rage is shocking to us because he had, through his arduous journey, become a distinctly sympathetic character. Yet, in the film's early sequences after David is introduced to the Swinton home, Spielberg strategically alienates us from him by emphasizing his uncanny qualities—the unsettling middle ground he occupies between the humanlike and the obviously mechanical—thus aligning us emotionally and experientially with Monica, who is clearly disturbed by his presence. This is a daring and potentially dangerous conceit because it distances us from, and makes it initially difficult to identify with, the character who will become the film's protagonist and emotional core. However, the initially uncanny nature of David is crucial for emphasizing the effect that imprinting has on him, moving him from the awkwardly humanlike to being arguably human.

Spielberg employs a number of visual strategies to render David uncanny, beginning with the shot that introduces David simultaneously to

FIGURE 5.1 "I'm David! I'm David!" *When David (Haley Joel Osment), who has become completely consumed with his desire to be made real, is confronted at Cybertronics with another David mecha, his sudden crisis of identity sends him into a shockingly violent rage in which he attacks and decapitates the other mecha. (Digital Frame Enlargement)*

the viewer and to Monica. We first see David as the doors to the elevator in the center of the Swintons' circular home open to reveal him in an extremely out-of-focus long shot that radically distorts his head and body, making him strangely spindly and alien. David's movements are odd and somewhat unsure, and Spielberg pans down as he walks forward to frame him from the legs down as he tentatively steps down to a lower landing in the living room, taps his foot, and then steps back up, tapping once again. Oddly enough, David's entrance is marked by an apparent continuity error in spatial relations that disorients the viewing experience almost subconsciously, which suggests that it was perhaps intentional. When David steps out of the elevator, the establishing shot prior to the door opening shows Monica standing several feet in front of and to the left of the doors and above the step that leads to the lower level in the room. When David walks out of the elevator, he walks directly forward and presumably past Monica without paying her any attention. In the following shot, when he turns around to face Monica and Henry, his proximity to the back wall of the room makes it clear that he is now standing much further into the room than he actually walked, which makes him seem even more alien. The eeriness of this spatial error is underscored by the following shot of Monica in close-up looking both shocked and disgusted, and then Spielberg's slow tracking

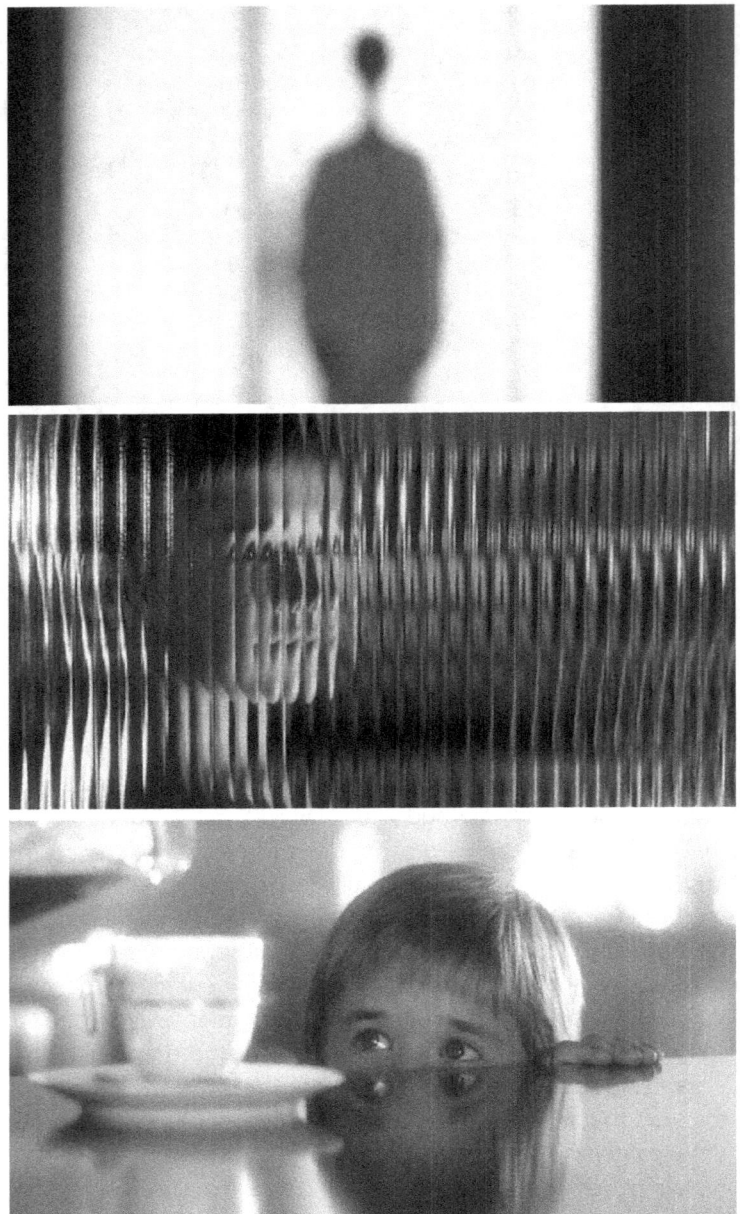

FIGURE 5.2 A machine approximating a child. *After David is introduced to the Swinton home, Spielberg strategically alienates us from him by employing a number of visual strategies to render David uncanny, particularly the use of reflections and refractions to constantly distort his face and body. (Digital Frame Enlargements)*

shot into David's artificially smiling, empty face. At this point, his behaviors and actions feel primarily mechanical and obviously programmed—a machine trying to approximate a child, rather than a child that happens to be a machine.

Despite her initial reluctance, Monica decides to keep David, at least for a while, and in the scenes that follow Spielberg continues to emphasize his otherworldly, odd qualities. Some of this is behavioral, including his penchant for suddenly appearing without noise (when Monica fluffs a sheet while making the bed, he is suddenly revealed as the sheet floats down, making him seem almost ghost-like and reinforcing the earlier continuity error that makes him appear to move without moving); his tendency to stare intently at Monica while she goes about her daily chores; and his awkward attempts to mimic human behavior. We see this most clearly at the dinner table scene, where he mimes eating and drinking (he needs neither) so as to be a part of the family gathering. David's being simultaneously part of and not part of the Swinton family table is reminiscent of the sense of alienation that Elliott felt in the dinner scene in *E.T.*, and it also plays as an uncomfortable mirror to the poignant scene in *Jaws* (1975) when Chief Brody's youngest son quietly mimics his father's exhausted movements. In *Jaws*, the scene is a brief, but moving depiction of a young child's fascination with and desire to emulate his father; in *A.I.*, it is something quite different, as David is simply mimicking, not feeling, at this point. Spielberg also enhances David's uncanniness with his visual choices, which utilize various reflections and refractions to constantly distort David's face. We see this in the silver mobile that hangs over his bed, in the multiplied images of his face as he looks back at Monica through the vertically beveled glass in his bedroom door, and in the upside-down reflection on the kitchen counter as he watches Monica make her coffee, which gives him the appearance of having a continuous face that doubles back on itself with two sets of eyes, but no nose or mouth.

Eventually Monica decides to activate the programming in David that allows him to love. This procedure, which is known as "imprinting," is irreversible, and if Monica were ever to decide she did not want David any more, he would have to be destroyed. David's response to being imprinted is immediate, as his face and eyes visibly soften, and he refers to Monica for the first time as "Mommy" when asking her about the string of words she reads to him as part of the procedure. The intensely backlit shot in which he slides off the chair in which he is seated and into Monica's arms is one of the most touching in all of Spielberg's films, although it carries with it an underlying sense of unease, as David's love, intense and unrelenting, is doomed to being unreciprocated.

"I'm sorry I didn't tell you about the world": Humanity's destructiveness, cruelty, and prejudice

Throughout *A.I.*, Spielberg depicts some of the darkest elements of human nature as enacted by both adults and children. As critic Tim Kreider put it in an essay in *Film Quarterly* published a year after the film's release, *A.I.* is "a film about human brutality, callousness, and greed ... one of the most unsentimental visions of mankind since—well, since Stanley Kubrick died." Taking place in a "closed and desolate worldview," he argues that *A.I.* is about "the death of humanity itself."[14]

In charting David's quest to become human, the film suggests that jealousy, anger, and violence, rather than dreams and hopes, are the fundamental elements of human nature, a philosophical stance that resonates particularly with Kubrick's *A Clockwork Orange*, which suggests that the loss of the capacity for violence is the loss of humanity itself, and *The Shining* (1980), which uses the tenets of the horror genre to depict the circular, never-ending nature of human violence. *A.I.* is nothing if not a film of violence, although much of it is emotional and psychological, rather than physical. It is telling that Spielberg chose to use "The Stolen Child," a nineteenth-century poem by William Butler Yeats, in several key moments of the film. Its refrain—"Come away, O human child! / To the waters and the wild / With a faery, hand in hand. / For the world's more full of weeping than you can understand"—encapsulates both the film's fairy tale qualities[15] and the desolate view of humanity it proffers, especially as viewed through the eyes of a child seeking love and finding only fear, resentment, jealousy, and rejection. In the end, David's journey to become a "real boy" is really an innocent's journey into a world full of weeping, none of which he ever understands.

Scientific hubris and the tragedy of the human condition

A.I. begins by establishing the world of a temporally undetermined, but immediately recognizable future in which scientific achievement and human

---

[14] Tim Kreider, "Review: *A.I. Artificial Intelligence*," *Film Quarterly* 56, no. 2 (Winter 2002): 34.

[15] In Yeats's poem, first published in the *Irish Monthly* in December 1886, a fairy tries to lure a child away from his home, an idea that derives from Irish folklore, particularly the myth of fairies known as changelings, who kidnap children and replace them. The kidnapped children then become immortal, living forever in a perpetual state of childhood with others in the same predicament. David, caught in a "freeze-frame" of perfect childhood, suggests how painful immortal childhood might be, especially when it means being separated from home and the love and security it offers. The irony is that, in Yeats's poem, the fairy tries to beguile the child away with promises of escape from a world that contains more weeping than he can understand, while David is intent on being part of that world because love and pain cannot exist without each other.

industry have begun to take a serious toll on the planet in the form of extensive and destructive climate change. Thus, the film begins with the implication that human-created technological progress has sowed the seeds of what will eventually be its own self-destruction. An off-screen narrator (Ben Kingsley) informs us over portentous images of crashing gray waves, "Those were the years after the icecaps had melted because of the greenhouse gases. Oceans had risen to drown so many cities along all the shorelines of the world ... forever lost." The simplicity and directness of the narration immediately brings to mind the idiom of the fairy tale, while also self-consciously framing the story as a story, a crucial narrative device given the prominence of stories within the film, particularly Carlo Collodi's 1883 children's novel *Pinocchio*. Temporally the narration places the future of the film's diegetic world in the narrator's past, as the story is being told at an unidentified point even further in the future (we learn at the end of the film that the narrator is, in fact, one of the SuperMechas 2,000 years in the future, when human beings have become extinct).

The narrator also informs us of the general state of humankind, which has been detrimentally affected by the environmental damage: the climate has become chaotic, millions of people have been displaced, and millions more have starved to death in poorer countries while "a high degree of prosperity" remains in the wealthier parts of the world due to "legal sanctions" that "strictly license pregnancies." Thus, not only do the inequalities of power and monetary wealth in today's world persist into the future, they have become even more pronounced, and the only way to maintain control is top-down authority in which one of the basic rights of humankind—the ability to reproduce—is curtailed and managed. This atmosphere of dwindling resources, competition, and growing despair has given rise to robots with artificial intelligence. As the narrator puts it, "this is why robots, who are never hungry and do not consume resources beyond those of their first manufacture, were so essential an economic link in the chainmail of society."

The narration's broad focus on humankind's destructive nature is focused in the opening scene on one cause of that destructiveness: scientific hubris. Although not one of the most prominent themes throughout Spielberg's cinema, scientific hubris is present in films both before and after *A.I.* We see it to some extent in *Jaws*, where the marine biologist Matt Hooper (Richard Dreyfuss) pits sophisticated scientific technology in the form of a supposedly shark-proof cage against the film's marauding great white only to discover that this particular force of nature is much stronger than steel bars, and also in *Poltergeist* (1982), where a trio of paranormal researchers equipped with high-tech sensors and cameras find their efforts to understand the ghostly intruders to be futile and are eventually driven from the home. Outside of *A.I.*, the danger of scientific hubris is presented most explicitly in *Jurassic Park*, in which genetic engineers successfully bring dinosaurs back from extinction by extracting their DNA from fossilized mosquitoes and then breeding them in labs, and later in *Minority Report* (2002), where a future United States has eliminated crime by creating an elaborate, technologically sophisticated Precrime Unit that uses a trio of "precogs" (people with the ability to see the future) to arrest and imprison people *before* they commit crimes.

In *Jurassic Park*, scientific hubris is expressly intertwined with the profit motive, as the lure of bringing dinosaurs back to life leads directly to an elaborate theme park and dinosaur zoo constructed on a private island. Thus, the film's central ideological critique concerns science becoming yet another tool of capitalist enterprise, which when wielded with a lack of humility and responsibility culminates in utter disaster, in this case the dinosaurs breaking free of their electrified paddocks and running amok. Dr. Ian Malcolm (Jeff Goldblum), a mathematician and ardent subscriber to chaos theory who is one of several characters brought to the park to assess its stability before it opens to the public, captures the fundamental essence of scientific hubris in criticizing John Hammond (Richard Attenborough), the billionaire creator of the park. Deeply disturbed by the talk of entrance fees and merchandising potential, he says,

> Don't you see the danger, John, inherent in what you're doing here? Genetic power is the most awesome force the planet has ever seen, but you wield it like a kid that's found his dad's gun. If I may, I'll tell you the problem with the scientific power that you're using here: it didn't require any discipline to attain it. You know, you read what others had done and you took the next step. You didn't earn the knowledge for yourselves, so you don't take any responsibility for it. You stood on the shoulders of geniuses to accomplish something as fast as you could, and before you even knew what you had, you patented it, and packaged it, and slapped it on a plastic lunchbox, and now you're selling it. You want to sell it.

When Hammond insists that Malcolm isn't giving the park's creators their due credit and that the scientists working for him have done things no one has ever done before, Malcolm delivers his most pointed critique: "Yeah, but your scientists were so preoccupied with whether or not they *could*, they didn't stop to think if they *should*." Dr. Malcolm's statement hangs heavy over *A.I.*, as Dr. Hobby, the robotic engineer at Cybertronics who creates David, is startlingly unreflective about the potential consequences of constructing a mecha child with the capacity to love and feel human emotion, not just mimic them. His is the very essence of being so wrapped up in the question of *could*, that he never ponders whether he *should*.

After the initial narration, the film opens inside a wood-paneled meeting room at Cybertronics Corporation where Dr. Hobby is first proposing the idea of David to a roomful of scientists and engineers. As an ominous roll of thunder moves across the soundtrack, he says, "To create an artificial being has been the dream of man since the birth of science," unconsciously alluding to the eternal desire of humankind to play God—a troubling sentiment at the heart of numerous science fiction stories from Mary Shelley's *Frankenstein* (1818) onward.[16] While proposing that they build a robot who can love, Dr. Hobby ironically demonstrates the fundamentally cruel attitude of humanity toward the mechas they have already created. He does this in both his speech, as he refers to mechas as "sensory toy[s]" and notes that they "[serve] the human race in all the multiplicity of daily life," which brings to mind nothing less than slavery, and also in his actions, as he callously uses a female mecha named Sheila (Sabrina Grdevich) for demonstrative purposes, first stabbing her in the hand with a pen and then asking her to undress for no apparent reason other than to exhibit how he is in control of her every action. His behavior also recalls Spielberg's subsequent film, *Minority Report*, in which the precogs, three genetically mutated humans who can see the future, are essentially enslaved by the Washington, DC, Precrime Unit. The precogs are not willing participants, as they are held in a special room known as "The Temple," where they are filled with dopamine and endorphins to maintain a perfect state of semi-consciousness while floating in a pool of "photon milk." John Anderton (Tom Cruise), the film's protagonist, is quite candid in saying, "It's better if you don't think of them as human," which is precisely the approach that human beings take toward David throughout *A.I.*, despite his clear signs of humanity.

Dr. Hobby is hardly alone in his attitude toward mechas, as no one in the audience seems at all disturbed by his words or actions, and they even laugh when he tries to stab Sheila's hand again and she recoils it, thus demonstrating her "pain memory response." Only one woman in the room dares to question the moral issue of creating a robot who can love: "If a robot could genuinely love a person," she asks, "what responsibility does that person hold toward that mecha in return?" Dr. Hobby's answer to this confounding moral quandary is no answer at all: "In the beginning, didn't God create Adam to love Him?" Instead, it simply reaffirms his God complex and uses it to justify his hubris in creating David.

Dr. Hobby and the others in the room have no qualms about separating the apparent surface humanity of mechas from their internal technology, which

---

[16] Philosopher Timothy Dunn explicitly refers to Dr. Hobby as "a kind of Dr. Frankenstein" due to his having "little understanding of the implications of his own technological marvels." See Dunn, "*A.I.: Artificial Intelligence* and the Tragic Sense of Life," 89.

is physically demonstrated when he pushes a button in the roof of Sheila's mouth, causing her face to slide open from the middle, revealing the robotic technology beneath. Yet, the creation of David is something entirely different. As Dr. Hobby puts it, he will be "a mecha of a qualitatively different order … a robot who can love … A mecha with a mind, with neuronal feedback … love will be the key by which they acquire a kind of subconscious never before achieved." This is the first, but not the last, moment in the film in which Dr. Hobby's language suggests an unconscious slippage between the human and the humanlike, as he refers to the proposed child mecha with the personal *who*, rather than the impersonal *that*. Later in the film, he asks if David is still "alive," yet another indicator that he is subconsciously blurring orga and mecha even as he continues to overtly treat David as a machine, albeit a more elaborate and fascinating one than Sheila. The crowd at the Flesh Fair also blurs the line between orga and mecha, as they ultimately reject the destruction of David because he acts too human, particularly by begging not to be burned and killed. "Mechas don't plead for their lives," one woman yells, unaware that her choice of words suggests that mechas are not just machines, but rather beings that have a life to lose, and are therefore, in some sense, "alive."

We see this blurring between orga and mecha most clearly near the end of the second act when David "comes home" to Cybertronics, fully believing that he will find the Blue Fairy there, but is instead faced only with Dr. Hobby, who, despite knowing about David's journey and how much he has suffered emotionally in his futile quest to become a real boy, can see him only as a successful "experiment." Dr. Hobby's inability to recognize and deal with David's humanity is all the more troubling given than he was responsible for programming David to love in the first place and even modeled David physically after his own deceased child, which suggests that, like David, he is tragically chasing something unattainable. Despite his soft demeanor and gentle, fatherly tone in speaking to David, his speech to him is absolutely chilling in the way it simultaneously recognizes David's emotional journey and vulnerability, yet refuses to take any responsibility for the attendant suffering and pain:

> Until you were born, robots didn't dream, robots didn't desire unless we told them what to want. David, do you have any idea what a success story you've become? You found a fairy tale and inspired by love, fueled by desire, you set out on a journey to make her real. And, most remarkable of all, no one taught you how. We actually lost you for a while. But, when you were found again, we didn't make our presence known because our test was a simple one. Where would your self-motivated reasoning take you?

To the logical conclusion ... that Blue Fairy is part of the great human flaw to wish for things that don't exist, or the greatest single human gift—the ability to chase down our dreams. And that is something no machine has ever done until you.

This brief, impassioned speech is extraordinarily revealing about both Dr. Hobby's own limitations and the nature of David as both orga and mecha. In seeing David's "desire" and "love" as part of a technological experiment that has met with great success, Dr. Hobby fundamentally denies David's humanity, rendering him little more than a component of a research project—in other words, an object. Yet, once again he mixes cold, objective terms like "robot" and "machine" with rhetorical nods to David's humanity in the form of calling him by name and referring to him having been "born." Most importantly, he notes that David's ability to "wish for things that don't exist" is "part of the great human flaw ... or the greatest single human gift." Either way, David has demonstrated that he is capable of partaking in a fundamental aspect of humanity, which makes him arguably human, a point that was confirmed earlier when Gigolo Joe tells him, "Only orga believe what cannot be seen or measured. It's that oddness that separates our species."

The cruelest irony is that Dr. Hobby's intention to build the most human-like mecha ever has been a success, yet he has lost whatever humanity he still had in the process, which is seen in his inability to recognize that he

FIGURE 5.3 "Until you were born, robots didn't dream." *In seeing David's "desire" and "love" as part of a technological experiment that has met with great success, Dr. Hobby (William Hurt) fundamentally denies David's humanity. (Digital Frame Enlargement)*

now shares it with David. David is, in a sense, the thing for which Dr. Hobby wishes that does not exist: a mechanical being with human emotions that is still fundamentally not human, which frees him of any moral responsibility toward it. And, although Dr. Hobby appears benign on the surface—a balding, middle-aged man with a soft face and voice and a name that sounds like a character on a children's television program—he is a kind of monster, albeit one who doesn't recognize his own monstrousness. When he tells David, "We want to thank you and tell you what's in store for you next," his words have an unintended, yet intensely disturbing connotation given all that David has already been through. What more will he be forced to endure in the name of science? That question is answered in the next scene when David's sense of uniqueness is finally destroyed as he wanders through Dr. Hobby's office and finds himself in the meeting room where his creation was first proposed, which is now filled with dozens of David mechas, some encased in boxes ready for shipping and others hanging from the ceiling like corpses on meat hooks.

David's tragedy, then, is that he is exactly what Dr. Hobby intended him to be: "a perfect child caught in a freeze-frame, always loving, never ill, never changing." However, Dr. Hobby is either incapable of or unwilling to recognize the inherent cruelty of such a creation because it traps the mecha in an inescapable fixation with the parent on whom he is imprinted. The question is not just what if the parent rejects him, but also of what happens when the parent grows old and dies while the mecha remains in "a freeze-frame, always loving." The implication is that love, at some point, will invariably turn to unmitigated pain that can only be absolved by death, which is why philosopher Timothy Dunn connects the film with what he calls "the tragic sense of life": "what makes the human condition tragic is that the things that we desire most, that give our lives meaning (such as the desire for love), are bound ultimately to be destroyed; that what we value most will soon be lost; and that all our striving and progress will be wiped out forever."[17] Filmmaker David Cronenberg, in discussing the tragic components of his science fiction-horror hybrid *The Fly* (1986), noted as much, albeit in the context of romantic, rather than filial love: "Every love story must end tragically. One of the lovers dies, or both of them die together."[18] *A.I.* ends on exactly that note, although it is curiously unclear as to whether one or both die in the final scene (which will be discussed at length later in this chapter).

To compound the tragic status forced on him by the scientific hubris of his creators, David becomes aware of this reality. One of the very first things

---

[17] Dunn, "*A.I. Artificial Intelligence* and the Tragic Sense of Life," 87.
[18] Chris Rodley, ed., *Cronenberg on Cronenberg* (New York: Faber & Faber, 1997), 125.

we hear him say after Monica has imprinted him is a quiet, fearful question: "Mommy, will you die?" When she replies that yes, someday she will die, but not to worry because it won't happen for at least 50 years, David replies in a sad whisper, "I'll be alone," thus fully confirming his recognition of the tragic consequences of his love for Monica, specifically that it is fated to conflict with the fact that she is temporally bound while he is not. When he says, "I love you, Mommy. I hope you never die. Never," it is the first time we hear him express a wish or desire or hope. This is followed by a close-up of Monica's reflection in the mirror, where the flash of guilty concern in her eyes indicates her realizing the position she's put David in by imprinting him. She suddenly feels morally conflicted, knowing that he will last infinitely longer than she will and that his intense love will never—can never—change. It is at this point that she bequeaths Teddy, who was once Martin's toy, to David, perhaps to assure him that he will have some kind of companionship after she is gone and therefore assuage some of her own guilt.

David's love is touching in its completeness, but it is also disturbing because it did not develop organically through shared interactions and resultant emotional connection. Rather, like the obsession with the image of Devil's Tower implanted in Roy Neary's mind in *Close Encounters of the Third Kind*, David's love is essentially forced on him, first by the programming installed by Cybertronics and then by Monica, who chooses to activate that programming to fulfill her own emotional needs. Thus, David is, through no fault of his own, the ultimate expression of human selfishness. A robot programed to love—to feel all the wonderful, horrible complexities of human emotion—he nevertheless has no promise of reciprocation. As Gigolo Joe tries to tell him late in the film, "She loves what you do for her, as my customers love what it is I do for them. But she does not love you, David. She cannot love you." And, even more cruelly, even if Gigolo Joe were to be proved wrong and his love were reciprocated, it would be trapped within the limited time frame of the human lifespan, while he would conceivably persist for eons afterwards, trapped in an abiding love for someone who has died and incapable of loving anyone else. That he becomes so despondent by the end of the film that he allows himself to fall off the top of the Cybertronics building in a suicidal gesture is sadly understandable.

Tim Kreider notes that "It's important to understand here that David's life of thralldom, and his awful disillusionment, doesn't necessarily reflect some tragic, inevitable part of the human condition; his condition has been deliberately manufactured, programmed into him to make him a better product."[19] Instead, the tragic aspect of the human condition, as depicted in *A.I.*, is that

---

[19] Kreider, "Review: *A.I. Artificial Intelligence*," 36.

cruelty and selfishness are inevitable and that they cause pain, suffering, and eventual destruction. Kreider suggests that the film's true image of the human condition is the one in which David, after the incident in which he falls into the pool with Martin, is left at the bottom after Martin has been pulled to safety: "[he] floats alone, his face blank, arms open and empty. This is the condition to which his 'love' condemns him: eternal faith in a fickle, absent mother, his arms expectantly outstretched even after he's been abandoned. It is, in this film, the human condition."[20]

Fragmenting families and the cruelties of childhood

Threats to and the disintegration of the American family form one of the strongest and most persistent themes throughout Spielberg's films, having been present since his earliest works: the tension in the marriage between David Mann and his wife in *Duel* (1971) as revealed in his stressed, argumentative phone call to her from the roadside diner;[21] the desperate, pathetic attempt by Lou Jean to rescue her young son from government services by breaking her estranged husband out of prison and kidnapping the child in *The Sugarland Express* (1974); Roy Neary's lack of commitment to his family and barely repressed resentment toward his children in *Close Encounters of the Third Kind*; the divorced family and absentee father in *E.T.*; and the role of incest and domestic violence in *The Color Purple* (1985). And, even in the early films in which the family is seemingly strong, it is still put under immense pressure and threat from which it might not entirely recover: the marauding shark in *Jaws* that leaves a woman childless, almost kills one of Martin Brody's sons, and then threatens to leave his family fatherless by devouring him; and the ghostly invasion in *Poltergeist*, which leaves the previously contented Freeling family battered, homeless, and despondent by the film's final frames.

As the opening narration in *A.I.* makes clear, the very idea of the family is in danger given that chaotic weather caused by climate change and lack of resources has already resulted in the deaths of millions in poorer countries, while the wealthier nations have persisted only because of restrictions on

---

[20] Kreider, "Review: *A.I. Artificial Intelligence*," 35.
[21] This was one of four scenes added to the television version of *Duel* to make it feature length for a theatrical release in Europe in 1972. Spielberg eventually regretted shooting the scene and adding it to the film because he concurred with original writer Richard Matheson's assessment that it was "so soap-opera-ish and unnecessary." However, while it does disrupt the flow of the film, it still contributes the first strand in a consistent thread of marital discord throughout Spielberg's films. See Joseph McBride, *Steven Spielberg: A Biography* (Jackson: University Press of Mississippi, 2010), 201.

child-bearing. Thus, the very idea of the family is under threat and in danger on a global scale.

On a more intimate level, *A.I.* is a depiction of a marriage under stress, to the point that it is about to crack. Henry and Monica have clearly become emotionally separate under the duress of Martin's cryogenic condition. They rarely talk when alone, which is evidenced by their tense faces during their silent drive to the hospital and Monica's walking briskly ahead of Henry once they arrive, as if he were merely her driver, rather than her husband. The scene establishes the emotionally exhausting nature of their predicament, as Martin's cryogenic status robs them of the freedom to mourn their son even as he is, for all intents and purposes, lost to them, but it also serves to demonstrate how Henry and Monica deal with this emotional trauma in completely opposite fashion. While Monica attempts to maintain a close parental connection with Martin's frozen, unresponsive body by playing him classical music and reading to him from *Robin Hood*, Henry engages Martin's doctor with a medical journal article he read about "virus locators, synthetic hunter killers," the discussion of which clearly disturbs Monica: "I can still hear you," she says sharply without looking up, conveying that she literally does not want to hear her husband or partake in his means of coping with the situation. Instead, she has drawn deep into herself, locking him and others out, which has their doctor deeply concerned: "Henry, your son may be beyond our science," he says, "but it's your wife who can still be reached." Yet, everything about her demeanor suggests that Monica is beyond reach, which explains why Henry would risk bringing David home and the fear he feels in presenting him to Monica: "I love you, don't kill me," he whispers in her ear before opening the elevator doors to reveal David. And, when Monica responds with vitriol at the idea of a mecha child—"I can't accept this!" she yells. "There is no substitute for your own child!"—he is clearly desperate to placate her, pleading twice, "I'll do whatever you want!"

The tension between them is later manifested in the uncomfortable silence punctuated by the awkward sounds of eating at the dinner table after David has been introduced into their home. The dinner scene is particularly telling in that it is a portrait of material comfort—beautifully prepared food, elegantly appointed table and settings, everything sparkling clean and arranged as if it were being shot for a culinary magazine layout—yet there is no sense of interpersonal connection between husband and wife. They literally have nothing to say to each other, and their emotional distance is reflected in the way Spielberg contrasts the elegance of the material appointments with the general darkness of the mise-en-scène, which recalls the similarly uncomfortable dinner scene in *E.T.* that revealed the various tensions in Elliott's fragmented family.

The stress in their marriage is relieved when Martin comes home from the cryogenic facility after his unexpected cure. A later dinner scene, which Spielberg films in much warmer, lighter tones, finds Henry and Monica smiling, laughing, and happily chatting—ironically, but not inconsequentially, about a couple friend of theirs who is going through a divorce—although their banter is broken by an increasingly intense and emotionally fraught competition between Martin and David that signals a new set of issues for the family and David's place in it. Even before Martin returns, Henry and Monica clearly disagree on David's place in their lives, as Monica warms to him after he has been imprinted, referring to him as "a child" in a way that suggests she has internalized the idea of David's humanity, while Henry professes bitterly that he still finds him "creepy."

These tensions are foreshadowed in the scene when David is first brought to the Swinton home. As he looks at a series of framed photographs, we see David's face partially reflected against the empty space in a family portrait of Henry, Monica, and Martin, which visually suggests the transient nature of his presence in the family, simply filling space until their flesh-and-blood son—their *real* child—can be returned. The subsequent tracking shot as David looks at each framed photograph ends with Martin's portrait, over which David's face is eerily superimposed via his reflection, which provides a visual foreshadowing of the two children vying for the same coveted space in the family. While David looks at the photographs, Spielberg cuts away and shows us Monica and Henry watching him from behind a corner in a shot that is distinctly reminiscent of the shot in *Empire of the Sun* in which Jim watches from behind a corner his father burning papers in his office. Although the roles of watcher and watched are reversed between parent and child in the two films, the effect is still the same in conveying a disconnect between family members, who must watch each other from a distance in fascination and mystery.

With Martin's return, the film shifts its focus from the tensions between Henry and Monica to a studied depiction of the casual cruelties of childhood, as David, now imprinted and full of human emotion, becomes the central point of identification even as he is steadily marginalized from his adopted family. Spielberg's previous films had painted childhood as complex, lonely, and often painful. Even in "Kick the Can," his much maligned contribution to the omnibus film *Twilight Zone: The Movie* (1983) about a magical talisman in the form of a tin can that returns a group of elderly retirees to childhood, the ultimate message is that, as appealing as it seems in theory, the idea of reliving childhood is not a desirable reality. "I'm cold, where are we going to sleep, who's going to take care of us?" 80-year-old Mrs. Dempsey, now a wide-eyed eight-year-old, asks, while others lament the idea of enduring

FIGURE 5.4 Empty spaces. *David's partial reflection against the empty space in a family portrait of Henry, Monica, and Martin visually suggests the transient nature of his presence in the family, simply filling space until their flesh-and-blood son— their* real *child—can be returned. (Digital Frame Enlargement)*

school and losing loved ones all over again. Pain and trauma during childhood are constants in Spielberg's films, which we see in the fantastical horrors endured by the children in *Poltergeist* and *War of the Worlds* and the haunting description of the precogs' experience as children in *Minority Report*: "when these little children closed their eyes at night, they dreamt only of murder, over and over, one after the other." His films are sprinkled with honest portrayals of the meanness with which kids treat other kids, often in throwaway moments such as the students making fun of each other at the bus stop in *E.T.* Childhood is not a place of safety in Spielberg's films, but rather a place of danger, both physically and emotionally.

Martin, however, is a different kind of child character, one who embodies in almost every manner the worst tendencies of childhood, especially the childhood of upper-class privilege: Not just someone who takes his place in the world for granted, as Jim does at the beginning of *Empire of the Sun*, he is conniving, manipulative, and at times openly mean and vindictive. He is in many ways David's doppelgänger, one of the film's many instances of doubling, and he represents a kind of base humanity to which David's desire "to be a real boy" threatens to devolve. Spielberg visually emphasizes the connection between David and Martin with a series of doubled images: first, David's previously mentioned reflection on the glass of a framed portrait of Martin, smiling sweetly and innocently, and later the visual connection between David frozen at the bottom of the ocean near the end of the film and Martin frozen in his cryogenic chamber at the beginning. Most troubling, though, is the manner in which David and Martin begin to blur in their jealousy and subsequent desire to "destroy" their double. Martin effectively destroys David's place in the Swinton home by manipulating David into behavior that is seen as dangerous, particularly by convincing him to sneak into Monica and Henry's bedroom and snip off a lock of her hair, while David literally destroys his double when he comes face to face with another David mecha at the Cybertronic headquarters. David's violence is angry and overt, truly frightening, in fact, while Martin's is more subtle, malicious, and calculated, although they both emphasize the deep connection between love, jealousy, and violence. In both cases, the double they destroy attempts to befriend them (the other David mecha saying to David "Let's be friends" recalls David happily giving Martin a birthday present at his party) and the destruction is predicated entirely on the perceived threat the other poses to Monica's attention. "You can't have her," David tells the other David, his voice steadily rising. "She's mine! And I'm the only one!"

Martin's more subtle sense of cruelty and emotional violence is established in the very first scene after he returns home, as he picks up Teddy by the ear, ignoring the bear's clear discomfort and protestation: "Martin, *no*." This casual cruelty and disregard for others is followed by the first of Martin's many attempts to cause friction and competition with David, whom he views as a plaything, a "supertoy" like Teddy. His initial interactions with David are all forms of instigation. He tries to convince him to break a toy amphibicopter ("These things do look better in pieces, you know," he says slyly when David responds to his request with, "I better not") and compels him to compete for Teddy's affection by placing the bear on the floor and having them both call to him simultaneously, which causes Teddy serious distress. When Teddy solves the problem by running after Monica when she enters the room, she asks absent-mindedly as she carries him out of the door, "Are they torturing you, Teddy?"—a question that has more resonance than she realizes.

Martin's treatment of David throughout the film amounts to a growing escalation of psychological and emotional torture, as he manipulates David's feelings and desires to satisfy his own sense of competition and jealousy, neither of which David feels at this point. All of his initial statements to David are either commands—"You call him, too," "Stand up"—or questions—"What good stuff can you do?"—that demonstrate no recognition of David's humanity. He values him only for his ability to "do stuff" and resents his presence in the house. While Martin's resentment is understandable, as he has come home to find a new sibling sharing his space and his mother's affections, the extent to which Spielberg goes in depicting his cruelty toward David crosses from childhood immaturity into caustic humanity at its worst. We see this with particular clarity when Martin tricks David into cutting Monica's hair by promising him to tell her that he loves him. "And then she'll love you, too," he says, demonstrating his clear understanding of David's deepest desire and emotional need and how that can be used against him.

Later in the film, Martin instigates a competition at the dinner table by opening his mouth to show David the remnants of chewed-up spinach on his tongue. In another situation this would amount to nothing more than a childish instance of being gross for its own sake, but here the action carries the ugly charge of Martin distinguishing himself from David by demonstrating his human capacity to chew and swallow food. Earlier Martin had told David, "I'm *real*," thus suggesting that David is not, which is why his dinner table demonstration that "I can eat and you can't" instigates David into his first moment of misbehavior as he starts shoveling spinach into his own mouth, ignoring Teddy's dire warning, "You will break," which indeed he does. Thus, Martin is the first to bring out the ugly side of human emotion that is unlocked with David's imprinting, leading him to disobey Monica for the first time and engage in behavior that is potentially self-damaging. David is effectively becoming more human by giving in to the lesser human impulses that define Martin.

The most overt and knowingly cruel thing Martin does to David is suggest that Monica read *Pinocchio* to them. When he hands the book to her, smiling with a sly, even sadistic smirk, he says, "David's going to *love* it." Monica immediately recognizes the potentially uncomfortable implications of reading a story about a wooden puppet who longs to be a real boy to a robot who has the same desire, but she reads it to them anyway, which suggests that she is already pulling away from David in favor of her biological son.

The reading of *Pinocchio* is a central plot point in that it introduces the idea of the Blue Fairy and instills in David the fantastical belief in magic that he will spend the second half of the film pursuing in his quest to become a real boy and win back Monica's love. But, it also provides a parallel commentary to the manner in which mecha are treated by orga in the world of *A.I.*, which in turn offers a metaphorical parallel for the historical manner in which people have treated others whom they viewed as inferior, weak, or somehow less than truly human. We see Monica reading *Pinocchio* to Martin and David, first while they are floating in a boat in the middle of a sun-dappled, picturesque pond, and later in Martin's bed at night. In the first shot, Monica is reading a particularly violent passage in which the showman who has taken possession of Pinocchio orders his minions to bring the puppet to him so that he can break him up to use as firewood for his roast, while in the second shot she reads the passage in which Pinocchio, having labored intensely making baskets, falls asleep, dreams of the Blue Fairy, and learns that his past misdeeds have been forgiven and, because of his "good heart," he is rewarded by being magically transformed into a "real boy just like other boys." Crucially, David is sitting alone on the floor while Monica and Martin cuddle in the bed when he hears this passage and has his imagination fired with dreams of magical transformation. The irony, of course, is that for David to become a "real boy" would potentially make him like Martin—cruel, jealous, self-interested—which we see throughout the rest of the film as his quest to become human makes him more and more morally conflicted like the rest of humanity.

David's emerging complex of emotions is evident in the scene that follows the poolside party for Martin's birthday. At the party, David is surrounded by Martin's friends, whose childish fascination with the mecha boy is more perverse than innocent, thus providing additional evidence of the casually cruel nature of childhood. While one of them, after asking if David can pee, wants to look down David's swimsuit to see "what [he] *can't* pee with," the biggest boy in the group, Todd (Theo Greenly), seeks to demonstrate David's Damage Avoidance System (DAS) by stabbing a serving knife into his arm. David reacts to this assault, viewed so offhandedly by the boys around him, as anyone would—with pain, but also fear and panic, which causes him to grab onto Martin for protection. They both fall backward into the pool, which Henry and others misinterpret as David trying purposefully to hurt Martin and leads directly to David's expulsion from the family.

When Monica comes into David's room later that day, she finds him sitting at his desk drawing pictures. She picks up the pages and sees that he has been writing to her a series of unfinished, unpunctuated messages that convey a complex mixture of childhood emotion: love, jealousy, competition, insecurity:

DEAR MOMMY, HOW ARE YOU REALLY, DO YOU LOVE ME AS MUCH

DEAR MOMMY, TEDDY IS HELPING ME WRITE TO YOU I LOVE YOU AND TEDDY

DEAR MOMMY I LOVE YOU AND HENRY AND THE SUN IS SHINING

DEAR MOMMY GUESS HOW MUCH I LOVE YOU

DEAR MOMMY I'M REALLY YOUR SON AND I HATE TEDDY HE IS NOT REAL LIKE

DEAR MOMMY I'M YOUR LITTLE BOY AND SO IS MARTIN BUT NOT TEDDY[22]

As Monica reads each message, she begins to cry as she clearly recognizes how they show evidence of David's humanity in all its conflicted messiness. Yet, at this point the damage is done and she has already agreed with Henry to return David to Cybertronics for destruction.

The scene in which Monica makes the spontaneous decision not to return David to Cybertronics, but instead to leave him in the nearby forest is quite possibly the most emotionally primal, heart-rending scene in all of Spielberg's films, particularly because it plays as the most overt example of the recurring theme of parental abandonment that is woven through so much of his work. Just as Roy Neary leaves his children behind to fly into outer space with the aliens at the end of *Close Encounters of the Third Kind*, Elliott's unseen father is unavailable because he's with his new wife in Mexico in *E.T.*, Jim's mother fails to hold onto his hand during the evacuation of Shanghai in *Empire of the Sun*, and Indiana Jones's father is revealed to have paid him little attention as a child in *Indiana Jones and the Last Crusade* (1989), Monica is a failed parental figure, unable to maintain the responsibility she holds toward David after imprinting him. Her desertion of him is nakedly cruel in being fully intentional, yet it is complicated by the fact that it is also driven by her affection for David and unwillingness to allow him to be destroyed (at the birthday party scene, she explicitly tells Henry that she will not take him back because she knows what will happen to him if she does). Her desertion is, in a perverse but understandable way, her one action toward David that is driven by something that looks like love, even if that means leaving him to deal on his own with a world for which she failed to prepare him ("I'm sorry I didn't tell you about the world," she says tearfully just before driving away).

The desertion scene is the culmination of Monica's conflicted feelings about David, which to a large extent parallel the viewer's. Once she has imprinted him she treats him like a son, yet she is at various points troubled by the implications of what she has done to fulfill her own emotional needs. The guilty look in the mirror when David asks if she is going to die is the first, but we also see it after the spinach competition between David and Martin where she is holding David's hand while robotic engineers perform "surgery" on him to remove the spinach from his exposed mechanical innards. At

---

[22] These messages are taken almost word-for-word from Brian Aldiss's short story, one of the rare instances in the film in which the source text was used literally in the film. Ironically, Aldiss made notes on a copy of his story after first meeting with Kubrick, and he crossed out the messages and wrote, "If you were filming, you would throw this stuff out." See Harlan and Struthers, *A.I. Artificial Intelligence*.

one point she has to step away from him, as she is clearly disturbed by seeing his physical robotic nature exposed, leaving his hand dangling empty in the air (which foreshadows the shot of him at the bottom of the pool, outstretched hands floating empty above him). When Henry tries to comfort her, she pushes him away saying, "Shhhhh! I have to—, I have to—," but never finishes saying what she "has" to do. That statement is not completed until the desertion scene, when she repeats over and over again, "I have to go! I have to go!" Her temporary desertion of David on the operating table presages her full desertion of him in the forest, although the reasons for each are dramatically different. Nonetheless, they still feel the same for David.

When Monica first tells him that she must leave him there for reasons he won't understand, he asks when she's coming back, and she replies, "I'm not. You have to be here by yourself." At this point, David's face falls as he asks, "Alone?" The manner in which he delivers that line, with a mixture of confusion and growing fear, recalls psychologist Bruno Bettleheim's assertion in his psychoanalytic study of fairy tales, *The Uses of Enchantment*, that "There is no greater threat in life than that we will be deserted, left all alone. Psychoanalysis has named this—man's greatest fear—separation anxiety and the younger we are, the more excruciating is our anxiety when we feel deserted, for the young child actually perishes when not adequately protected and taken care of."[23] For David, the anxiety of being left alone is arguably even more excruciating because, being mecha, he will not perish physically, but rather emotionally, as he has no recourse but to love the mother who has deserted him with no opportunity to love anyone else (he can only be imprinted once by one person, which denies him the human capacity to transcend loss and grow to love others). The emotional tenor of the scene makes it nearly unbearable to watch, as David, full of fear and panic at the prospect of being deserted, runs after Monica, begging tearfully for her not to leave him, pleading with her and promising to become real for her. Compounding his pain, Monica is forced to deny his humanity in order to leave him, declaring, "*You're not real*!" as she physically disentangles herself from his arms. Yet, she recognizes how horrible her act of parental abandonment is and that, even if it offers David the chance to continue living physically, it is emotionally and psychologically devastating for him.

Spielberg visually connects the desertion scene with the imprinting scene by staging David and Monica in similar positions. When she imprints him, she has him sit in a chair while she kneels in front of him, and when she deserts him, at one point she falls to her knees in front of him clutching his arms while

---

[23] Bruno Bettleheim, *The Uses of Enchantment*, 145. Stanley Kubrick read this book and used it extensively when working on *A.I.* See Harlan and Struthers, *A.I. Artificial Intelligence*, 12–16.

trying to instruct him to stay away from people. Both of these shots are also intensely backlit with powerful blooms of sunlight, making them, with only a few exceptions, the only scenes in the film that prominently feature sunlight. The overt presence of the natural backlighting also recalls David's message "DEAR MOMMY I LOVE YOU AND HENRY AND THE SUN IS SHINING," which ironically associates sunlight, usually assumed n Spielberg's films to be a symbol of brightness and hope, with betrayal and desertion.

FIGURE 5.5 Primal scenes. *Spielberg visually connects Monica's imprinting David with her deserting him in the forest by staging them in similar positions and intensely backlighting them with powerful blooms of sunlight, which associates sunlight, usually assumed in Spielberg's films to be a symbol of brightness and hope, with betrayal and desertion. (Digital Frame Enlargements)*

The cruelty and prejudices of humanity

Monica's desertion of David is a conflicted act that saves his life while inflicting on him great emotional suffering, which reflects the film's overall conflicted view of humanity. We see this conflict inherent in Dr. Hobby's assertion to David that wishing for things that don't exist is either "the great human flaw" or "the greatest single human gift." We also see it late in the film when one of the SuperMechas confides in David: "David, I often felt a sort of envy of human beings, of that thing they called 'spirit.' Human beings created a million explanations of the meaning of life in art, in poetry, in mathematical formulas. Certainly human beings must be the key to the meaning of existence. But human beings no longer exist."

The SuperMechas see David as "the enduring memory of the human race. The most lasting proof of their genius," and yet, their "genius" in creating David derived from a selfish desire to fulfill their own emotional needs and resulted in his suffering. Even more to the point, throughout the film we do not see human genius outside of technological innovation, and as the opening narration makes clear, human technologies are the direct cause of planetary damage and are not enough to save humanity from eventual extinction. Instead of genius, we see jealousy and manipulation in Martin; fear and prejudice, especially as enacted at the Flesh Fair, but also in Henry's distrust of David; lust as embodied in Rouge City, a neon-lit, morally vacant urban playground that takes the mixture of sex and commerce to almost absurd new heights (many of the buildings are designed as objectified female bodies forever caught in submissive sexual poses); and short-sightedness, which has resulted in both the melting of the polar icecaps and the creation of a mecha who can love, but has no promise of being loved in return. While at first blush it seems that the SuperMecha's statement is a lapse into sentimentality, a means for the film to mourn the passing of humanity, all evidence in the film suggests that the line is meant to be understood with some irony, perhaps suggesting that one of the things humanity passed down to its robotic creations is that great flaw of wishing for things that don't exist.

Rather than genius, the intertwined barbs of prejudice, hatred, and fear are the dominant characteristics of humanity as depicted in *A.I.*, especially in the Flesh Fair sequence. Almost immediately after being deserted by Monica, David is captured and put on display at a Flesh Fair, a kind a futuristic combination of a rock concert, monster truck show, and public execution in which rogue mechas are corralled, brought before a jeering audience, and destroyed in any number of ghastly ways. The tag line for the Flesh Fair is "A Celebration of Life," which is darkly ironic given that its primary means of celebrating life is destruction—"the purg[ing] of artificiality," as graphic artist Chris Baker puts it.[24] The ringleader is Lord Johnson-Johnson (Brendan Gleeson), who views the Flesh Fair as a kind of performance art in which the grisly destruction of human-like robots is an assertion of human superiority, an illustration that, despite their outward appearance, mechas are not human. Publicly destroying mechas is an act of revelation, with the need to expose their technologies via elaborate modes of demolition, assuaging the audience's fear that they might someday be replaced by them (which, of course, they are).

The Flesh Fair sequence is particularly uneasy in the way it evokes the genocidal imagery from *Schindler's List* (1993) and the depictions of human slavery in *Amistad* (1997). The connection is made quite explicitly in a dialogue exchange between David and several other mechas who have been caught and are awaiting their destruction inside a cage. "What is happening?" David asks, to which another mecha, who is dressed in the tattered remnants of a security guard uniform, replies, "History repeats itself. It's the rite of blood and electricity." In other words, the destruction of mechas in the name of celebrating humanity is just another iteration of the same human impulse that drives genocide and slavery and justifies the most horrendous acts of violence via appeals to fear. Another mecha, this one a particularly outdated model whose body is like a enormous tin drum and whose face is a computer screen displaying the low-res visage of an angry man, bellows, "So, when the opportunities avail themselves, they pick away at us, cutting back our numbers so they can maintain numerical superiority." This particular sentiment is echoed later in the film by Gigolo Joe, who tells David, "They hate us, you know, the humans. They'll stop at nothing ... They made us too smart, too quick, and too many. We are suffering for the mistakes they made because when the end comes, all that will be left is us. That's why they hate us."

Although the mechas being demolished are mechanical creations, Spielberg stages their destruction in ways that are visually reminiscent of the destruction of the human body, which makes the violence enacted on them even more viscerally impactful. When the mechas are dismembered, for example, some of them spray various fluids from their torn limbs like blood. Also, in the shot in which David is brought up on stage, Spielberg shows us a close-up of the burned, corpse-like remnants of the security guard mecha being dragged away, looking very much like an emaciated, decaying concentration camp victim. Spielberg also foregrounds the idea that the mechas feel pain by having one of the older robots request that another turn off his "pain sensors" before he is dismembered. It also cannot be incidental that the first

---

[24] Harlan and Struthers, *A.I. Artificial Intelligence*, 63.

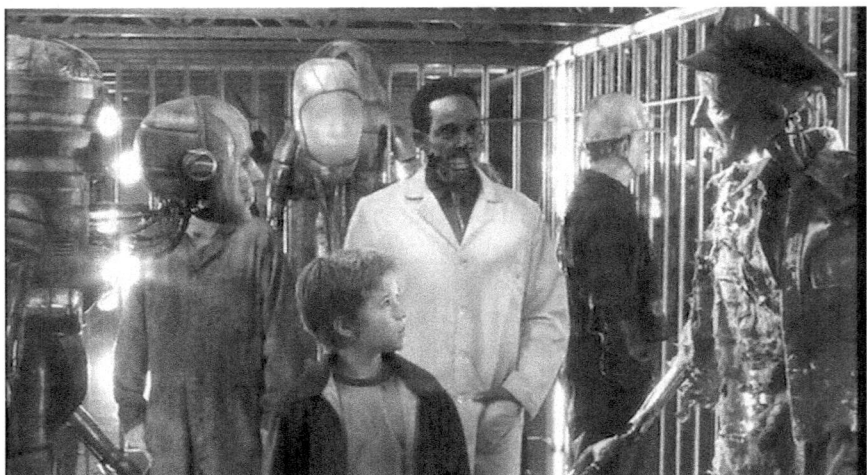

FIGURE 5.6 "The rite of blood and electricity." *The Flesh Fair sequence is particularly uneasy in the way its depiction of rogue mechas being destroyed for the delight of a jeering and fearful audience evokes the genocidal imagery from* Schindler's List *(1993) and the depictions of human slavery in* Amistad *(1997). (Digital Frame Enlargement)*

mecha destroyed has been designed to look like an African American (the voice is supplied by Chris Rock) and is shot out of a cannon through a burning hoop and then into a whirling propeller, which sends his flaming, decapitated head flying into the bars of the cage in which David and the other mechas are trapped, thus re-envisioning the manner in which American blacks were lynched throughout the late nineteenth and early twentieth centuries, oftentimes being burned alive during the process.

Some critics have taken issue with the Flesh Fair sequence, particularly in the way it associates the worst aspects of humanity, particularly bloodlust and reactionary fear, with the working class. In his largely positive reassessment of the film, critic Jonathan Rosenbaum highlights the Flesh Fair as an aspect of the film that he "intensely dislikes": "The brawling human crowd at the Flesh Fair is exclusively working-class—an irrational lynch mob howling for blood, with echoes of the Christian right—which implicitly absolves the middle class and the wealthy, particularly because this scene is meant to make the expulsion of David from the security and comfort of his suburban nest (which has so far dominated the film to the near exclusion of everything else) even harsher."[25] While Rosenbaum is generally accurate in describing the Flesh Fair crowd as "exclusively working class"—raucous bleachers full of denim, untucked flannel,

---

[25] Rosenbaum, "The Best of Both Worlds."

and trucker hats—their violence does *not* absolve the middle class and the wealthy at all. In fact, the "brawling human crowd at the Flesh Fair" is simply a more honest expression of the consistently cruel nature of human interaction with mechas throughout the film, from Dr. Hobby stabbing Sheila in the hand as part of a demonstration, to Todd stabbing David in the arm with a serving knife to see his damage avoidance programming in action. This is not entirely surprising since Spielberg has frequently made his protagonists working-class characters, including Roy Neary, a power company technician, in *Close Encounters*; Indiana Jones, an archaeologist whose working-class aesthetic is contrasted so sharply against his nemesis Belloq; Ray, a dock worker, in *War of the Worlds*; and Dr. Alan Grant in *Jurassic Park*, whose academic credentials as a paleontologist are less important than his identity as "a digger." In *A.I.*, the different social classes are blurred via their shared fear: Henry's irrational fear about David, the kind that makes it impossible for him to see David as anything other than dangerous, is exactly the same emotion that drives the crowds to cheer as mechas are dismembered, burned, and melted to satiate their need to feel safe and superior. Contrary to Rosenbaum's assertion, the "suburban nest" from which David is expelled is anything but secure and comfortable, as David is never allowed to fully fit in. Even after Monica imprints him and warms to him, Henry still treats him in a cool, objectified manner, and once Martin returns home, David is subjected to an escalating series of emotional manipulations. He is always to some degree on the outside looking in.[26]

Furthermore, the violence enacted by humans against mechas at the Flesh Fair is positioned within a continuum of humanity's violence against itself as seen in the bruises on the neck of Patricia (Paula Malcomson), a woman who has hired Gigolo Joe, and then Samantha, his subsequent client whose bleeding body he discovers on a hotel bed, murdered by her jealous husband for her infidelity. These two scenes open the film's second act, which begins with Patricia's off-screen voice saying, "I'm afraid." Thus, the Flesh Fair is only one variation of human violence, an admittedly crass, overtly sensationalistic variation, but just a variation nonetheless, and the fact that the film also prominently features domestic abuse and various forms of emotional torment affirms the idea that, at its core, humankind is violent and reactionary, protective of its own survival first and foremost.

This is a powerful theme in *A.I.*, and one that is found in a number of Spielberg's other films, most notably *War of the Worlds*, which updates

---

[26] Critic Andrew Sarris recognized this in his review of the film, as well, writing, "the domestic scenes are more harrowing than the subsequent mob scenes of enraged Orgas out to destroy the overly numerous Mechas." See Sarris, "A.I. = (2001 + E.T.)²," *New York Observer*, June 25, 2001, http://observer.com/2001/06/ai-2001-et-2 (accessed September 15, 2013).

H. G. Wells' Victorian-era Martian invasion epic by turning it into a startlingly effective depiction of how survival often comes at the cost of one's humanity. The film's protagonist, a single father named Ray (Tom Cruise), struggles throughout the film to keep his two children safe from the horrors of an alien invasion, yet he is constantly confronted with the violent actions of other people who are behaving just as he is—in the interest of self-preservation—but with a sometimes crueler (that is, more desperate) edge. The most disturbing sequence in the film doesn't involve aliens, but rather a mob of people who tear Ray, his son, and his daughter from the minivan in which they are driving. As Ray and his children stumble into a nearby diner, we see through the window behind them as strangers shoot each other to get control of the van. Later in the film, Ray finds himself in the horrible position of having to kill a fellow human being in order to keep his daughter safe, which forever associates him with the mob that almost cost him and his children their lives.

Thus, like *War of the Worlds*, *A.I.* sees humanity as desperate, violent, and fundamentally fixated on survival at all costs, which is why human beings take out their anxieties on the very mechas they have built to serve their needs and desires. The fact that David himself is so single-mindedly fixated on becoming a real boy and winning Monica's love aligns him with human nature, as does his increasingly jealous, violent, possessive nature, thus inverting Pinocchio's narrative arc, which went from selfish to loving.[27] Thus, part of David's tragedy is that, the closer he gets to becoming a "real boy," the more he takes on the worst characteristics of human nature, to the point that Tim Kreider argues that, like Moon-Watcher and HAL in *2001*, he "finally demonstrates his humanity by committing murder" when he decapitates and smashes the other David at Cybertronics.[28]

Dreams of death: The ultimate Spielberg ending

The initial critical response to *A.I.* was decidedly mixed for a number of reasons, one of the primary being the film's ending, which was frequently misunderstood during the film's theatrical release. A number of critics who appreciated aspects of the film still disparaged the ending because they saw it as the ultimate Spielbergian cop-out, a labored attempt to somehow graft a sentimental happy ending onto an otherwise dark and complicated film. Granted, the ending is deeply emotional, and it has drawn tears from numerous viewers who recognize its bittersweet qualities. Both

---

[27] See Harlan and Struthers, *A.I. Artificial Intelligence*, 66.
[28] Kreider, "Review: *A.I. Artificial Intelligence*," 36.

critic Jonathan Rosenbaum and film scholar James Naremore have openly admitted that the ending moves them to tears.[29] Some critics even blamed the ending on Spielberg, imagining that he must have tacked it on when he wrote the screenplay.[30] For *Newsweek* critic David Ansen, the ending "is where Spielberg's screenplay loses its grip, the film goes limp and you wonder whether the movie Kubrick envisioned and the one we're seeing have fatally parted ways."[31]

The ending for *A.I.* is certainly problematic, but not for the reasons that are often ascribed to it. Rather, it is problematic for precisely the reasons that are rarely attributed to Spielberg: it offers the viewer a scenario that is perfectly balanced in its ambiguity to support entirely contradictory readings. Contrary to the accusations that Spielberg always wants to reassure his audience, provide them with pat, happy conclusions that assuage them of any sense of trauma, and ensure that they leave the theater feeling secure and emotionally charged, the ending of *A.I.*, like the ending of *2001: A Space Odyssey*, leaves us with more questions than answers, challenging us to think beneath the immediate surface and ruminate on the film's various implications. As critic Andrew Sarris put it, "Its ending alone may invade your dreams, as it has mine ever since I saw it at a screening."[32] Heady and daring, laced with both genuine emotion and bitter irony, it is the ultimate contradictory Spielberg ending, one that simultaneously provides a "happily ever after" conclusion to its fairy tale journey and a brutal sucker punch to David's desire to be loved. In the ending we can see both David's fulfillment and a dark critique of the manner in which we blind ourselves to the larger reality in pursuit of our individual dreams.

Because David has spent the film's first two hours on a quest for something we know he can never find—the magical Blue Fairy from a nineteeth-century children's novel—his journey has become almost impossible to digest emotionally by the film's third act. For David, it is the search for his true essence, the fulfillment of his desire to have his intense love reciprocated, but we know that it is a hopeless, aimless endeavor that can only end in disappointment because there is no Blue Fairy, no magic that will transform him into a "real boy." Even as his behavior becomes more and

---

[29] Rosenbaum, "A Matter of Life and Death: *A.I.*"; James Naremore, "Love and Death in *A.I. Artificial Intelligence*," *Michigan Quarterly Review* 44, no. 2 (2005), http://hdl.handle.net/2027/spo.act2080.0044.210 (accessed September 15, 2013); James Naremore, *On Kubrick* (London: BFI Publishing, 2008).
[30] The fact that the film had been made under such a shroud of secrecy only enhanced the misunderstanding of the ending, and it was only in subsequent years that the revelation of the creative process revealed that it was very much Kubrick's ending as well as Spielberg's.
[31] Ansen, "Mr. Spielberg Strikes Again," 84.
[32] Sarris, "A.I. = $(2001 + E.T.)^2$."

more human throughout the film, there is no point at which his "miles of fiber" will become flesh and blood. No matter how human he behaves, there will always be someone with an X-ray gun to reveal the mechanics beneath, some kid wanting to test his Damage Avoidance System, some group of angry people wanting to destroy him in order to affirm their own need to feel superior and "real." There is a certain poignancy to David's faith in things that don't exist, which makes him that much more human. But, at the same time, it makes the film increasingly uneasy, as we constantly wait for a plot twist that will allow him to fulfill his journey.

Instead, David arrives back at the headquarters of Cybertronics where he meets his real "father," Dr. Hobby, who is only interested in his quest as evidence of his technological success in creating a robot who feels human emotions. More disturbingly, David is confronted with the fact that, rather than being unique, he is simply one of a new line of "David" and "Darlene" mechas. "I thought I was one of a kind," he says to Dr. Hobby, who replies, "You are the first of a kind." This realization throws David into such despair ("My brain is falling out," he says, staring blankly into space) that he allows himself to fall off the top of the building into the water below. His journey ended in failure, and knowing that he will never be loved the way he loves, he simply gives up and falls. However, at the bottom of the ocean he discovers the remains of Coney Island and a Pinocchio-themed exhibit that prominently features a statue of the Blue Fairy, and using a stolen police amphibicopter, he stays down there, wishing over and over again for her to make him a real boy. A cable snaps holding up the Coney Island ferris wheel, which falls over and lands partially on the amphibicopter. "We're in a cage," Teddy observes, not realizing in his assessment of their physical predicament that he is also describing metaphorically David's emotional entrapment in his love for Monica and his desire to be real for her.

After a long, slow crane out from the amphibicopter during which the narrator from the film's opening informs us that David stayed there, praying to the Blue Fairy statue day after day, the film jumps forward 2,000 years, when the Earth is once again covered in ice and the human race has become extinct. The planet is now populated by lithe SuperMechas, highly advanced robot descendants of the mechas created by Dr. Hobby and his ilk. Intent on learning the history of humanity, they excavate the ice and discover David and Teddy, frozen inside the stolen amphibicopter where he has been wishing to the Blue Fairy for two millennia. The SuperMechas, fascinated by David as a relic of human ingenuity but also moved by his fervent desire to be loved by his mother, take him to a detailed recreation of the Swintons' home constructed from his memories and resurrect Monica using a lock of her hair. However, their technology is limited to the extent that they can only resurrect her for 24 hours, after which time she will disappear forever. However, David is allowed to spend an entire day with her, freed from the presence of Henry and Martin. Though temporally limited to a single day, David's reuniting with Monica is the ultimate Oedipal dream fulfilled of a son having his mommy all to himself with no competition for her love and affection.

Or is it? Monica is resurrected, but is it really her? That is, she is brought back to life from an assemblage of the DNA contained in the strands of hair that Teddy has held on to for 2,000 years and the memories the SuperMechas are able to extract from David's mind, which means that she is a mixture of physical biological traits and David's highly subjective impressions of her. As David is a robot, it is conceivable that the data he would store about her in his "memories" would be objective in nature; however, that objectivity would have been clouded by his feelings of love and desire after being imprinted so that, in effect, the idea of her in his mind would be necessarily idealized. Thus, Monica becomes for David what he initially was for her: an idealized substitute for a missing loved one. David never gets to become a real boy, but he gets to live one day as if he were one, which further expands the film's emphasis on emotional experience. If David feels love, does that mean it is love? If he feels like a real boy, does that mean he is one?

The film's moments of pure bliss, what the narrator calls the "everlasting moment"—David calling Monica "mommy" for the first time, Monica telling David at the end of their day together that she loves him, that she has always loved him—are complicated by the fact that their emotional fulfillment derives from technological replication of something that has been lost. The question of whether the fundamental essence of love and affection and fulfillment is possible through such means is left open to interpretation. Monica certainly enjoys David's love and attention, but she has moments of guilt and eventually abandons him in favor of her biological son. David, on the other hand, is able to revel in all the focused attention and reciprocated love his programming caused him to so fervently desire, but it is necessarily limited, truncated by the SuperMechas' inability to bring Monica back for more than 24 hours. Thus, when the film ends with David tucking Monica in, climbing into bed with her, and holding her hand while closing his eyes, the image is necessarily ambiguous. His face suggests that he is in a state of pure bliss, looking genuinely happy for the first time since Monica drove him out to the forest for what he thought was a special day just for them, but is it delusional? That is, like the trip to the forest, is his 24 hours of bliss just an illusion masking a terrible fate? What happens when he wakes up the next morning and she has disappeared, and he is once again alone, the idea of which terrified him so much when she left him in the forest? Will the emotional pain of being functionally abandoned a second time be even worse?

Author Jane M. Struthers argues that the film's ending is indeed bleak, a final assertion of the futility of David's attempts to "chase down his dream": "David's journey is purposeful and successful, yet in actuality it is futile. The ending is as much an illusion as David's delusion of his own mother. His desire for affection and love has failed to be reciprocated, other than in his dreams, and instead his odyssey has exposed him to mankind's cruelty, greed, exploitation, and depravity. One cannot fail to notice that humankind has become extinct."[33] Tim Kreider sees a more complicated ending, two endings, in fact, that are "superimposed over one another but utterly dissonant in tone." On the one hand, the film's ending supplies "the childish dream of reunion we long for." On the other hand, though, the film's ending, set against the extinction of humanity, is utterly desolate, trapping David in an eternity of longing for a dead mother.[34]

The exact nature of David's final moments is unclear. The narrator tells us over a long crane shot that pulls out from the bed shared by David and Monica, "Should he shake her, she would never rouse. So David went to sleep, too. And for the first time in his life, he went to that place where dreams are born." Given that it was made clear early in the film that David is incapable of sleeping, it is possible that his "going to sleep" means death. Having completed his journey and felt Monica's love, he effectively has nothing left to live for, and simply shuts down. This, of course, is the easiest ending, even as it fulfills David Cronenberg's assertion that every love story must end in tragedy with one or both people dying. Yet, even then there is a dark, uneasy edge to it, as it suggests that David's intense need for love can find resolution only in an idealized 24-hour period, and that afterwards all that remains is to die and disappear like the object of his affection. The other option, that David does wake up the next morning to find Monica gone forever, is the most difficult and troubling, as it means that he will be once again left alone, his intense love for Monica still hardwired into his very being with absolutely no possibility of further reciprocation. For David, the memory of that one day will have to suffice and somehow justify all of his previous suffering and all of the suffering he now faces in a frozen world alone.

Kreider astutely connects *A.I.*'s ending with the ending of *Schindler's List*—"Just as the saving of the six hundred couldn't quite redeem the horror of the Holocaust in *Schindler's List*, this upbeat ending is so thin and meaningless that it can't obscure the larger tragedy"[35]—but it is more than

---

[33] Jane M. Struthers, "The Film: Part 3: The Discovery," in *A.I. Artificial Intelligence—From Stanley Kubrick to Steven Spielberg*, 124.
[34] Kreider, "Review: *A.I. Artificial Intelligence*," 37–9.
[35] Kreider, "Review: *A.I. Artificial Intelligence*," 37.

that. While the ending of *A.I.* is Spielberg's most overtly contradictory, it is in no way an aberration from the rest of his films. Rather, the explicit means by which *A.I.* forces us to deal with the multiple layers of its conclusion—the triumph and the heartbreak, the wish fulfillment and the willful myopia, individual happiness against a backdrop of decimation—draws our attention back to so many of his other films that featured endings of a similar nature. It reminds us of how Roy Neary's fateful rendezvous with benevolent aliens who take him up into the cosmos is a delusion forced on him by said aliens and requires that he desert his wife and children, leaving them and the rest of humanity back on Earth to an uncertain future. It reminds us of how, in *Raiders of the Lost Ark* (1981), Indiana Jones, despite successfully rescuing the Lost Ark of the Covenant from the Nazis, ultimately finds himself sidelined as "bureaucratic fools" of the U.S. government take control of the Ark and hide it away, turning the ending into a stunning critique of how the government and other power structures persist by hiding their most dangerous secrets. It reminds us of how Elliott's life-affirming relationship with the titular alien in *E.T.* is destined to be short-lived, and even though the film ends with him bathed in the light of E.T.'s spaceship as it flies off, he must then return to a broken family and absentee father. It reminds us of how survival in films as varied as *Poltergeist*, *Empire of the Sun*, *Saving Private Ryan*, and *War Horse* carries with it the underlying suggestion that the scars accumulated in the process of surviving have their own terrible price.

When viewed in the larger context of Spielberg's career, it becomes clear that the ending of *A.I.* is the ultimate Spielberg ending in the way it moves us emotionally, drawing tears in the eyes of many, while also drawing attention to the ways in which individual moments of bliss may temporarily, but never completely, usher away the darkness that surrounds them.

Works Cited

Abramowitz, Rachel. "Regarding Stanley: Steven Spielberg Felt the Aura of Stanley Kubrick as He Brought an Idea of the Late Director's to the Screen." *Los Angeles Times,* May 6, 2001. http://articles.latimes.com/2001/may/06/entertainment/ca-59783 (accessed September 15, 2013).
Alcott, Todd. "Spielberg: *1941* Part 1." *Todd Alcott: What Does the Protagonist Want?* http://toddalcott.livejournal.com/184028.html (accessed April 30, 2013).
Anders, John. "No Sneaks, No Squeaks at Preview." *Dallas Morning News,* October 26, 1979.
Andrews, Suzanna. "The Man Who Would Be Walt." *New York Times*, January 26, 1992.
Ansen, David. "Mr. Spielberg Strikes Again: The Director Goes Back to the Future with Kubrick at His Side." *Newsweek,* June 25, 2001.
Arnold, Gary. "The Blazing Cinematic Sensation Of 'Raiders of the Lost Ark.'" *Washington Post*, June 12, 1981.
—"Horror With the Spielberg Touch." *Washington Post,* June 4, 1982.
Aronstein, Susan. "'Not Exactly a Knight': Arthurian Narrative and Recuperative Politics in the Indiana Jones Trilogy." *Cinema Journal* 34, no. 4 (1995): 3–30.
Auty, Chris. "The Complete Spielberg?" *Sight & Sound,* Autumn 1982.
Ayers, Drew. "Bodies, Bullets, and Bad Guys: Elements of the Hardbody Film." *Film Criticism* 32, no. 3 (Spring 2008): 41–67.
Baird, Robert. "Animalizing *Jurassic Park*'s Dinosaurs: Blockbuster Schemata and Cross-Cultural Cognition in the Threat Scene." *Cinema Journal* 37, no. 4 (1998): 82–103.
Bakhtin, Mikhail. *Rabelais and His World.* Translated by Helene Iswolsky. Bloomington: Indiana University Press, 1984.
Barefoot, Guy. "Who Watched That Masked Man? Hollywood's Serial Audiences in the 1930s." *Historical Journal of Film, Radio, and Television* 31, no. 2 (2011): 167–90.
Baxter, John. *Steven Spielberg: The Unauthorized Biography.* New York: HarperCollins, 1998.
Berliner, Todd. *Hollywood Incoherent: Narration in Seventies Cinema.* Austin: University of Texas Press, 2010.
Biskind, Peter. "Blockbuster: The Last Crusade." In *Seeing Through Movies*, ed. Mark Crispin Miller, 112–49. New York: Pantheon, 1990.
Black, Ilsa J. "The Look Back in *E.T.*" *Cinema Journal* 31, no. 4 (1992): 25–41.
Bouzereau, Laurent. "The Making of *1941.*" *1941*, directed by Steven Spielberg (1979, Universal City, CA: Universal Home Video, 1996). Collector's Edition DVD.
Brahms, William B., and Sandra White-Grear with the Haddon Township Historical Society. *Haddon Township.* Charleston, SC: Arcadia Publishing, 2011.

Britton, Andrew. "Blissing Out: The Politics of Reganite Entertainment." *Movie*, Winter 1986.
Brode, Douglas. *The Films of Steven Spielberg*. New York: Citadel Press, 1995.
—*From Walt to Woodstock: How Disney Created the Counterculture*. Austin: University of Texas Press, 2004.
Brown, William. "It's a Shark Eat Shark World: Spielberg's Ambiguous Politics." *New Review of Film and Television Studies* 7, no. 1 (2009): 13–22.
Buckland, Warren. *Directed by Steven Spielberg: Poetics of the Contemporary Hollywood Blockbuster*. New York: Continuum, 2006.
Calabrese, Omar. *Neo-Baroque: A Sign of the Times*. Princeton, NJ: Princeton University Press, 1992.
Canby, Vincent. "'1941' and a Mirthless Future." *New York Times*, December 23, 1979.
—"Movie Review: *Raiders of the Lost Ark*." *New York Times*, June 12, 1981.
—"Exploring Inner and Outer Space With Steven Spielberg." *New York Times*, June 13, 1982.
—"Amid Gloom, Good Comedy Staged an Exhilarating Comeback." *New York Times,* December 26, 1982.
Cawelti, John G. *The Six-Gun Mystique*, 2nd edn. Bowling Green, OH: Bowling Green University Popular Press, 1984.
Champlin, Charles. "Spielberg's Pearl Harbor." *Los Angeles Times*, December 14, 1979.
Cherry, Brigid. *Horror*. London: Routledge, 2009.
Combs, Richard. "Primal Scream: An Interview With Steven Spielberg." In *Steven Spielberg Interviews*, Lester D. Friedman and Brent Notbohm (eds), 30–6. Jackson: University Press of Mississippi, 2000.
Comolli, Jean-Luc, and Jean Narboni. "Cinema/Ideology/Criticism." In *Film Theory and Criticism: Introductory Readings*, 5th edn, Leo Braudy and Marshall Cohen (eds), 752–9. New York: Oxford University Press, 1999.
Cook, David A. *Lost Illusions: American Cinema in the Shadow of Watergate and Vietnam, 1970–1979* (History of the American Cinema, Vol. 9). Berkeley: University of California Press, 2000.
Dickson, Greg. "The *Pleasantville* Effect: Nostalgia and the Visual Framing of (White) Suburbia." *Western Journal of Communication* 70, no. 3 (2006): 212–33.
Donovan, Barna William. *Conspiracy Films: A Tour of Dark Places in the American Conscious*. Jefferson, NC: McFarland, 2011.
Dorough, Jason. "The 100 Greatest Fictional Characters of All Time." *Fandomania*. August 31, 2009. http://fandomania.com/100-characters (accessed November 13, 2013).
Dunn, Timothy. "*A.I. Artificial Intelligence* and the Tragic Sense of Life." In *Steven Spielberg and Philosophy: We're Gonna Need a Bigger Book*, ed. Dean A. Kowalski, 82–94. Lexington: University Press of Kentucky, 2008.
Ebert, Roger, and Gene Siskel. *The Future of the Movies: Interviews With Martin Scorsese, Steven Spielberg, and George Lucas*. Kansas City, MO: Andrews and McMeel, 1991.
Entertainment Law Reporter. "MGM Is Ordered to Pay $15,000 to the Directors Guild of America and to Director Tobe Hooper for Violating Guild Credit Size

Requirements in Trailer Advertising for 'Poltergeist.'" *Entertainment Law Reporter*, August 1, 1982.

Erickson, Glenn, and Mary Ellen Trainor. *The Making of 1941*. New York: Ballantine Books, 1980.

Farber, Stephen. "Nuts!" *New West*, January 14, 1980.

"A Filmmaking Journey." *War Horse*, directed by Steven Spielberg (2011, Burbank, CA: Buena Vista Home Entertainment, 2012), Blu-Ray.

Fishman, Robert. *Bourgeois Utopias: The Rise and Fall of Suburbia*. New York: Basic Books, 1987.

Friedman, Lester D. *Citizen Spielberg*. Champaign: University of Illinois Press, 2006.

Friedman, Lester D., and Brent Notbohm (eds). *Steven Spielberg: Interviews*. Jackson: University Press of Mississippi, 2000.

Gennusa, Chris. "Kaminski Fuses Kubrick, Spielberg." *Daily Variety*, January 15, 2002.

Gilbey, Ryan. *It Don't Worry Me: Nashville, Jaws, Star Wars, and Beyond*. London: Faber and Faber, 2003.

Glaister, Stephen M. "Saving *AI: Artificial Intelligence:* Philosophical Aspects of Spielberg's Neglected Robo-Epic." *Bright Lights Film Journal* 48 (2005). http://brightlightsfilm.com/48/ai.php (accessed November 13, 2013).

Gordon, Andrew M. "*Close Encounters:* The Gospel According to Spielberg." *Literature/Film Quarterly* 8, no. 3 (1980): 313–18.

—"Steven Spielberg's *Empire of the Sun*: A Boy's Dream of War." *Literature/Film Quarterly* 19, no. 4 (1991): 210–21.

—*Empire of Dreams: The Science Fiction and Fantasy Films of Steven Spielberg*. Lanham, MD: Roman & Littlefield, 2008.

Hall, Mark A. "Romancing the Stones: Archaeology in Popular Cinema." *European Journal of Archaeology* 7, no. 2 (2004): 159–76.

Hall, Stuart: "The Problem of Ideology: Marxism Without Guarantees." In *Stuart Hall: Critical Dialogues in Cultural Studies*, David Morley and Kuan-Hsing Chen (eds), 25–46. London: Routledge, 1996.

Harlan, Jan. "Afterword: The Two Masters." *A.I. Artificial Intelligence—From Stanley Kubrick to Steven Spielberg: The Vision Behind the Film*, edited by Jan Harlan and Jane M. Struthers. London: Thames & Hudson, 2009.

Harlan, Jan, and Jane M. Struthers (eds). *A.I. Artificial Intelligence—From Stanley Kubrick to Steven Spielberg: The Vision Behind the Film*. New York: Thames & Hudson, 2009.

Harty, Chris. "Into the Breach: *Saving Private Ryan*." *Saving Private Ryan*, directed by Steven Spielberg (1998, Burbank, CA: DreamWorks Home Entertainment, 1999). DVD.

Hayden, Dolores. *Building Suburbia: Green Fields and Urban Growth, 1820–2000*. New York: Random House, 2004.

Hibbs, Thomas. *Arts of Darkness: American Noir and the Quest for Redemption*. Dallas, TX: Spence Publishing, 2008.

Hoberman, J. "Laugh, Cry, Believe: Spielbergization and Its Discontents." *Virginia Quarterly Review* 83, no. 1 (2007): 119–35.

Hodenfield, Chris. "*1941*: Bombs Away!" In *Steven Spielberg: Interviews*, Lester D. Friedman and Brent Notbohm (eds), 70–83. Jackson: University Press of Mississippi, 2000.

WORKS CITED

Isenberg, Michael T. "World War I Film Comedies and American Society: The Concern With Authoritarianism." *Film & History* 5, no. 3 (1975): 7–21.

Jacobs, Lewis. *The Emergence of Film Art*. New York: Hopkinson and Blake, 1969.

Jeffords, Susan. *Hard Bodies: Hollywood Masculinity in the Reagan Era*. New Brunswick, NJ: Rutgers University Press, 1994.

Kael, Pauline. "Trash, Art, and the Movies." *Harper's*, February 1969.

—"The Current Cinema: The Greening of the Solar System." *The New Yorker*, November 28, 1977.

—"The Current Cinema: Dizzy, Dizzy, Dizzy." *The New Yorker*, November 10, 1980.

—"The Current Cinema: The Pure and the Impure." *The New Yorker*, June 14, 1982.

Kauffmann, Stanley. "Epiphany." *New Republic*, December 10, 1977.

Kendrick, James. Review of *War of the Worlds* (2005). *The QNetwork*. http://www.qnetwork.com/index.php?page=review&id=1485 (accessed April 30, 2013).

—*Hollywood Bloodshed: Violence in 1980s American Cinema*. Carbondale: Southern Illinois University Press, 2009.

Kinder, Marsha. "The Return of the Outlaw Couple." *Film Quarterly* 27, no. 4 (1974): 2–10.

Kolker, Robert. *A Cinema of Loneliness*, 4th edn. New York: Oxford University Press, 2011.

Kowalski, Dean A. "Introduction." In *Steven Spielberg and Philosophy: We're Gonna Need a Bigger Book*, ed. Dean A. Kowalski, 1–6. Lexington: University Press of Kentucky, 2008.

—(ed.). *Steven Spielberg and Philosophy: We're Gonna Need a Bigger Book*. Lexington: University Press of Kentucky, 2008.

Kreider, Tim. "*A.I.: Artificial Intelligence*." *Film Quarterly* 56, no. 2 (2002): 32–9.

Lawrence, Lynn S. "War as a Holding Environment: An Analysis of *Empire of the Sun*." *Psychoanalytic Review* 78, no. 2 (1991): 301–7.

Le Gall, Michel, and Charles Taliaferro. "The Recovery of Childhood and the Search for the Absent Father." In *Steven Spielberg and Philosophy: We're Gonna Need a Bigger Book*, ed. Dean A. Kowalski, 38–49. Lexington: University Press of Kentucky, 2008.

Macdonald, Dwight. *On Movies*. Englewood Cliffs, NJ: Da Capo, 1969.

"Making *Close Encounters*." *Close Encounters of the Third Kind*, directed by Steven Spielberg (1977, Santa Monica, CA: The Voyager Company, 1990). Laserdisc.

Maser, Wayne. "The Long Voyage Home: Steven Spielberg's Film, *Schindler's List*." *Harper's Bazaar*, February 1994.

Maslin, Janet. "How Old Movie Serial Inspired Lucas and Spielberg." *New York Times*, June 7, 1981.

McBride, Joseph. "A Reputation: Steven Spielberg and the Eyes of the World." *New Review of Film and Television Studies* 7, no. 1 (2009): 1–11.

— *Steven Spielberg: A Biography*. 2nd edn. Jackson: University Press of Mississippi, 2010.

Meacham, Jon. "Caught in the Line of Fire." *Newsweek*, July 13, 1998.

Mecklenburg, Virginia M. *Telling Stories: Norman Rockwell From the Collections of George Lucas and Steven Spielberg*. Abrams, NY: Smithsonian Art Museum, 2010.

Morris, Nigel. *The Cinema of Steven Spielberg: Empire of Light*. London: Wallflower Press, 2007.

Muzzio, Douglas, and Thomas Halper. "Pleasantville?: The Suburb and Its Representation in American Movies." *Urban Affairs Review* 37, no. 4 (2002): 543–74.

Naremore, James. "Love and Death in *A.I. Artificial Intelligence*." *Michigan Quarterly Review* 44, no. 2 (2005). http://hdl.handle.net/2027/spo.act2080.0044.210 (accessed September 15, 2013).

— *On Kubrick*. London: BFI Publishing, 2008.

Neale, Steve. "Masculinity as Spectacle: Reflections on Men and Mainstream Cinema." *Screen* 24, no. 6 (1983): 2–17.

Neustadter, Roger. "Phone Home: From Childhood Amnesia to the Catcher in Sci-Fi—The Transformation of Childhood in Contemporary Science Fiction Films." *Youth and Society* 20, no. 3 (1989): 227–40.

New York Times. "Child Abductions a Rising Concern: With 150,000 Incidents Each Year, Units Are Forming to Aid Victims' Families." *New York Times*, December 5, 1982.

Paul, William. "The Rise and Fall of Animal Comedy." *Velvet Light Trap* 26 (1990): 73–86.

Pirie, Dave. "A Prodigy Zooms In: A Child Cineaste Who Now Makes Movies and Money With Equal Facility." In *Time Out Interviews 1968–1998*, ed. Frank Broughton, 104–6. London: Penguin Books, 1998.

Pollock, Dale. "*Poltergeist*: Whose Film Is It Anyway?" *Los Angeles Times*, May 24, 1982.

Rafael, Frederic. *Eyes Wide Open: A Memoir of Stanley Kubrick*. New York: Ballantine Books, 1999.

Rockwell, Norman. *My Adventures as an Illustrator*. Garden City, NY: Doubleday, 1960.

Rodley, Chris (ed.). *Cronenberg on Cronenberg*. New York: Faber & Faber, 1997.

Rosenbaum, Jonathan. *Movies as Politics*. Berkeley: University of California Press, 1997.

— "The Best of Both Worlds: *A.I. Artificial Intelligence*." *Chicago Reader*, July 13, 2001. http://www.jonathanrosenbaum.com/?p=6306 (accessed September 15, 2013).

— "A Matter of Life and Death: *A.I.*" *Film Quarterly* 65, no. 3 (2012): 74–8.

Roth, Lane. "Raiders of the Lost Archetype: The Quest and the Shadow." In *The Films of Steven Spielberg: Critical Essays*, ed. Charles L. P. Silet, 59–67. Lanham, MD: Scarecrow Press, 2002.

Royal, Susan. "Steven Spielberg in His Adventures on Earth." In *Steven Spielberg Interviews*, Lester D. Friedman and Brent Notbohm (eds), 84–106. Jackson: University Press of Mississippi, 2000.

Samuelson, David W. "Introducing the LOUMA Crane." *American Cinematographer*, December 1979.

Sanello, Frank. *Spielberg: The Man, the Movies, the Mythology*. Dallas, TX: Taylor Publishing, 1996.

Sarris, Andrew. "A.I. = (2001 + E.T.)²." *New York Observer*, June 25, 2001. http://observer.com/2001/06/ai-2001-et-2 (accessed September 15, 2013).
Savran, David. "The Sadomasochist in the Closet: White Masculinity and the Culture of Victimization." *Differences* 8, no. 2 (1996): 127–52.
Schiff, Steven. "Seriously Spielberg." In *Steven Spielberg: Interviews*, edited by Lester D. Friedman and Brent Notbohm, 170–92. Jackson: University of Mississippi Press, 2000.
Schrader, Paul. "Canon Fodder." *Film Comment*, September–October 2006.
Scott, A. O. "Film Review: Do Androids Long for Mom?" *New York Times*, June 29, 2001.
See, Fred. "Steven Spielberg and the Holiness of War." *Arizona Quarterly* 60, no. 3 (2004): 109–41.
Sheehan, Henry. "The Peter Panning of Steven Spielberg: Part 1." *Film Comment* (May–June, 1992). http://henrysheehan.com/essays/stuv/spielberg-1.html (accessed November 14, 2013).
—"The Peter Panning of Steven Spielberg: Part 2." *Film Comment* (July–August, 1992). http://henrysheehan.com/essays/stuv/spielberg-2.html (accessed November 14, 2013).
Shohat, Ella, and Robert Stam. *Unthinking Eurocentrism: Multiculturalism and the Media*. London: Routledge, 1994.
Siegel, Lee. "Why Does Hollywood Hate the Suburbs?" *Wall Street Journal*, December 27, 2008. http://online.wsj.com/article/SB123033369595836301.html (accessed March 25, 2012).
Silet, Charles L. P. (ed.). *The Films of Steven Spielberg: Critical Essays*. Lanham, MD: Scarecrow Press, 2002.
Simon, John. *Reverse Angle: A Decade of American Films*. New York: Clarkson N. Potter, 1982.
Sobchack, Vivian. "Genre Film: Myth, Ritual, and Sociodrama." In *Film/Culture: Explorations of Cinema in Its Social Context*, ed. Sari Thomas, 147–65. Metuchen, NJ: Scarecrow Press, 1982.
Spielberg, Steven. "Foreword." *A.I. Artificial Intelligence—From Stanley Kubrick to Steven Spielberg: The Vision Behind the Film*, Jan Harlan and Jane M. Struthers (eds). London: Thames & Hudson, 2009.
Spielberg at Sixty. University of Lincoln. http://www.lincoln.ac.uk/media/spielbergatsixty (accessed June 20, 2011).
Sragow, Michael. "A Conversation With Steven Spielberg." In *Steven Spielberg: Interviews*, Lester D. Friedman and Brent Notbohm (eds), 107–19. Jackson: University Press of Mississippi, 2000.
Stevens Jr., George. *Conversations at the American Film Institute with the Great Moviemakers: The Next Generation*. New York: Alfred A. Knopf, 2012.
Stiller, Lewis, "Suo Gân and *Empire of the Sun*." *Literature/Film Quarterly* 24, no. 1 (1996): 344–7.
Struthers, Jane M. "The Film: Part 3: The Discovery." In *A.I. Artificial Intelligence—From Stanley Kubrick to Steven Spielberg: The Vision Behind the Film*, Jan Harlan and Jane M. Struthers (eds). London: Thames & Hudson, 2009.
Tait, Sue. "Visualising Technologies and the Ethics and Aesthetics of Screening Death." *Science as Culture* 18, no. 3 (2009): 333–53.

Thomson, David. *America in the Dark: Hollywood and the Gift of Unreality*. New York: William Morrow, 1977.
Time magazine. "Up From the Potato Fields." *Time*, July 3, 1950.
—"Gaining on the Cities." *Time*, September 6, 1976.
—"*Animal House* Goes to War: Steven Spielberg Makes *1941* a 'Stupidly Outrageous' Film." *Time*, April 16, 1979.
Variety. "Spielberg Ducks Politics." *Variety*, September 12, 1973.
Walker, Brent. *Mack Sennett's Fun Factory*. Jefferson, NC: McFarland, 2009.
Wasser, Frederick. *Steven Spielberg's America*. London: Pclity Press, 2010.
White, V. Alan. "*A.I. Artificial Intelligence*: Artistic Indulgence or Advanced Inquiry?" In *Steven Spielberg and Philosophy: We're Gonna Need a Bigger Book*, ed. Dean A. Kowalski, 210–26. Lexington: University Press of Kentucky, 2008.
Williams, Tony. "Close Encounters of the Authoritarian Kind." *Wide Angle* 4, no. 5 (1983): 23–9.
Wloszczyna, Susan. "Spielberg, Reel to Real Brutality of War 'Needed Telling.'" *USA Today*, July 20, 1998.
Wood, Robin. "The Incoherent Text: Narrative in the '70s." *Movie* 27–8 (1980/1981).
—*Hollywood From Vietnam to Reagan*. New York: Columba University Press, 1986.
—"Ideology, Genre, Auteur." In *Film Genre Reader II*, ed. Barry Keith Grant, 59–73. Austin: University of Texas Press, 1995.
Zimmerman, Patricia. "Soldiers of Fortune: Lucas, Spielberg, Indiana Jones, and *Raiders of the Lost Ark*." *Wide Angle* 6, no. 2 (1984): 34–9.

Index

A.I. Artificial Intelligence 15, 25, 30, 171–209
   ending 204
   reception 204
abandonment 197, 207
Abyss, The 52
Academy Awards 85, 142
action films 117, 119
adventure films 121
aesthetics 11, 12, 164, 166, 167, 171, 175
alienation 16
All That Heaven Allows 14
Allen, Woody 76
allusionism 87
Altman, Robert 76, 82–4, 108
Always 62
ambiguity 205
Amblin' 7
American Film Institute 103
American Graffiti 90, 108
Amistad 3, 8, 11, 143, 166, 201
animal comedy 89–90, 91, 92, 93, 97, 99
Animal House 71, 75, 89, 90, 93, 95, 99
antiheros 114–15
anxiety 15
Apocalypse Now 75
Aristophanes 90
Aristotle 11
art cinema 14, 17
   European 1
Arthurian legends 133
Au hasard Balthazar 159, 164
auterism 18

Avondale 28

backlighting 199
Bambi 6
Bantam Press 102
beauty 11, 160, 165
Beowulf 114
Berger, Bennett 28
Bettelheim, Bruno 198
Bicycle Thieves 13
Black Stallion, The 36
Black, Ilsa J. 3–4
black-and-white 166
Blackhawk: Fearless Champion of Freedom 106
Blow Out 10, 133
Bob & Carol & Ted & Alice 27
body 115–16, 165, 166, 200, 201
Body Heat 108
Bogart, Humphrey 102
Bresson, Robert 159, 164
Britton, Andrew 2–3
Bullit 85
Buñuel, Luis 78

Caddyshack 95
Cahiers du cinéma 18
Cameron, James 52
Capra, Frank 2, 6, 21
caricatures 95
Cassavetes, John 76
Catch Me If You Can 30, 71, 123
Catch-22 75
censorship 12
Changing Face of the Suburbs, The 28
Chaucer, Geoffrey 90

child abduction 64
childhood 190–9
childhood experiences 24
childhood trauma 56–7
childhood victimization 64
childishness 55
children 106
China 102
Chinatown 10, 108
choreography 85, 86
CIA 128
cinematography 85, 111
Cinerama Dome, Los Angeles 70
Citizen Kane 13, 135
climate change 183
Clockwork Orange, A 174–5, 182
Close Encounters of the Third Kind 3, 23–68, 69, 74, 85, 104–5, 108, 144, 173, 189, 190, 197, 203
   Special Edition of 1980 47
clowns 37
Collodi, Carlo 183
colonialism 123
color 166
Color Purple, The 8, 11, 142, 143, 190
Columbia Pictures 36, 70, 73, 105
combat films 97
comedy 11, 20, 27, 70, 71, 75, 80, 84–6
   animal 89–90, 91, 92, 93, 97, 99
   New Comedy 90
   Old Comedy 90
   romantic 90
   slapstick 86, 87, 99
Coming Home 75
Commando Cody: Sky Marshal of the Universe 106
Comolli, Jean-Luc 19–20
conspiracy theory films 133
consumer products 102
Continental Divide 108
continuity 179
Conversation, The 133
Coppola, Francis Ford 26, 76, 133
Crack in the Picture Window, The 27
crisis 15
critics *see* film critics

Cronenberg, David 188
cruelty 8, 165, 190–9, 204
Cubism 12
Curtiz, Michael 2
cynicism 169

Dalí, Salvador 7
Dark Horse Comics 102
Day the Earth Stood Still, The 52
De Palma, Brian 26, 133
Death Wish 119
Deer Hunter, The 75
DeMille, Cecil B. 2
despair 16
Destino 7
dialogue 88
Dirty Harry 119
Disney, Walt 2, 6, 9, 10, 47, 55, 59, 80, 95, 119
"Disneyfication" 7
divorce rate 50
Dr. Strangelove 11, 87
Don Winslow of the Coast Guard 106
Double Indemnity 108
Dreyer, Carl Theodor 13
Duel 30–3, 34, 87, 190
Dumbo 80, 95, 98
Duncan, Hugh Dalziel 75

E.T. 1–2, 3, 4, 7, 8, 9, 21, 23–68, 111, 133, 144, 172, 176, 181, 191, 193, 197, 209
Earth vs. the Flying Saucers 52
Eastwood, Clint 108
Edwards, Blake 89
Eisenstein, Sergei 7
Empire of the Sun 3, 11, 25, 75, 121, 139–59, 160–2, 164, 167, 169, 176, 192, 193, 197, 209
Empire Strikes Back, The 108
endings 65–8, 207–9
environment 183
Escape to Nowhere 141, 145
escapism 103, 104
evil 10, 33, 63
Evil Dead, The 58
exceptionalism 130
expressionism 12, 51, 167

INDEX

German 13, 15
Eyes Wide Shut 173

fairy tales 175, 198
family breakdown 190
family life 50
Fantasia 6, 59
Father of the Bride 27
FBI 51
Fellini, Federico 13
feminism 136
film criticism 11, 17
film critics 18, 24, 54, 74, 103, 106, 123, 175, 202, 205
film noir 16
film scholars 18, 54, 105, 106, 107, 110, 115, 155–6, 175, 205
fine arts 12
Firelight 34–5, 52
First Blood 116
Flash Gordon Conquers the Universe 106
Fly, The 188
Ford, Harrison 36, 105, 111, 117
Ford, John 2, 13, 14, 36, 142, 159, 168
Fordham, Frieda 109
foreign policy 127–8
Fraker, William A. 84, 85
framing 123
Frankenstein 185
Free Cinema 13
Freedom From Fear 153–8
French New Wave 15
Freud, Sigmund 2, 78
Full Metal Jacket 174–5
Funhouse, The 39

Gale, Bob 73
gender 18
Generation X 133
genre theory 18
German expressionism 13, 15
Godard, Jean-Luc 78
Godfather, The 26
Goldsmith, Jerry 44, 59
Graduate, The 27
Grais, Michael 37
Grand Illusion 166

Great Northfield Minnesota Raid, The 108
Great Race, The 89
Greetings 26
Gremlins 58
grotesque 95–6
group dynamics 99
group psychology 97
Guy Named Joe, A 62

Hammer Films 114
"hardbody films" 115
Harlan, Jan 174
Hawks, Howard 2, 5, 108
Helzapoppin' 84
heroism 101–37, 145
Heston, Charlton 102
Hi, Mom! 26
Hibbs, Ben 153
Hitchcock, Alfred 6, 13, 21, 137, 143
Hollywood *see also* New Hollywood 3, 5, 8, 12, 25, 81, 82, 90
Holocaust 11, 160, 208
home video market 102
Hook 30
Hooper, Tobe 37–8, 39
horror 40, 42, 59–62, 67, 113, 182
horror stories 37
human condition 182–90
human nature 182
humor 70, 72, 120, 136

I Am a Fugitive From a Chain Gang 14
iconography 142
incest 190
incoherence 78–9, 84
Indiana Jones (character) 104–9
Indiana Jones and the Kingdom of the Crystal Skull see Indiana Jones series
Indiana Jones and the Last Crusade see Indiana Jones series
Indiana Jones and the Temple of Doom see Indiana Jones series
Indiana Jones series *see also Raiders of the Lost Ark* 101–37, 142, 197
appeal 129
commercial popularity 101–2

individuality 93, 97
intertextuality 87
intratextuality 87
Invaders from Mars 52
invasion fears 70, 88, 97
invasion movies 52
invasion narratives 51–65
irony 10, 71, 123, 135, 154, 156, 169, 174–5, 200
It's a Mad, Mad, Mad, Mad World 87
It's a Wonderful Life 21, 59
Italian neorealism 13, 15
Ivan's Childhood 159, 160

James Bond (character) 131
James Bond films 121
Jaws 5, 8, 30, 33, 34, 54, 64, 71, 74, 76, 85, 87, 94, 108, 110, 142, 145, 181, 183, 190
Jaws 2 36, 67
jingoisim 74, 107, 115
Johnny Got His Gun 75
Jungle Jim 103
Jurassic Park 8, 39, 102, 145, 184, 203

Kael, Pauline 1–2, 3, 7, 21, 24, 36, 39, 85
Kahn, Michael 70
Kaminski, Janusz 166
Kant, Immanuel 11
Kasdan, Lawrence 105, 108, 114, 117
Kaufman, Philip 105, 108
Keats, John 27
Kelly's Heroes 75
Kes 10
Keystone Studio 87
"Kick the Can" 192
"kitchen sink dramas" 13
Kramer, Stanley 87
Kubrick, Stanley 11, 87, 159, 167, 171, 174–5, 177, 182, 205
Kurosawa, Akira 95

Ladd, Alan 102
laissez-faire capitalism 128
Landis, John 71
Lean, David 142, 143, 159
lenses 83, 85

LeRoy, Mervyn 14
Levittown 27–8, 41, 44
Lincoln 11, 141
linguistics 2
Little Big Man 75
Long Goodbye, The 108
Louma crane 85
Lucas, George 15, 90, 104–5, 106, 108, 114, 127

M*A*S*H 75, 82, 90
Mabinogion 114
Malick, Terence 160
Man in the Gray Flannel Suit, The 27
Man with a Movie Camera 13
Marcuse, Herbert 78
marketing campaigns 103
Marshall, Frank 37
Marvel Comics 102
Marx, Karl 2
Mascot Pictures 105–6
masculinity 105, 117
materialism 136
Mathison, Melissa 36
Mean Streets 26
Medallion Theater, Dallas 69, 88
MGM 38
Middle Passage 160
Milius, John 71, 73, 82
Minority Report 30, 145, 184, 185, 193
Missing Children's Assistance Act 64
Mr. Blandings Builds His Dream House 27
Mitchum, Robert 112
Moral Majority 50, 128
"Morning in America" 127–37
Morpurgo, Michael 159
Motion Picture Association of America rating system 166–7
Mummy series 114
Munich 3, 4, 8, 11, 141, 143, 166
Murnau, F. W. 13
music 44, 58, 59, 66, 70, 83, 88, 109, 110, 119, 120, 135, 148, 168, 169
Mussorgsky, Modest 59
Mutual Film Corporation v. Industrial Commission of Ohio 12
mythology, European 114

Narboni, Jean 19–20
narrative 97
narrative incoherence 79–84
narrative perversity 76–9
Nashville 82, 84
National Center for Missing and Exploited Children 64
neorealism, Italian 13, 15
New American Cinema 14, 16
New Comedy 90
New Hollywood 107
New Right politics 129
New Wave, French 13
New Yorker, The 1, 24
Newsweek 140
Night of the Hunter 112
Night of the Living Dead 61
Night Skies 36
nightmares 24
nihilism 10, 16
1941 35, 69–100, 103, 141, 143
   budget 73–6
   critical reception 73–6
   narrative 76–9
   preview 69
Normandy invasion 160, 166
Norris, Chuck 115
nuclear family 66, 67

Old Comedy 90
On Golden Pond 101
optimism 10
Organization Man, The 27
Oscars *see* Academy Awards
Outlaw Josey Wales, The 108
Ozu, Yasujiro 13

Pakula, Alan J. 133
Panavision 85
Parallax View, The 133
Paramount Pictures 101
parody 87
Passion of Joan of Arc, The 13
pastiche 94
paternalistic values 130
Paths of Glory 159, 167
patriotism 100
Peckinpah, Sam 108

Peter Pan mythos 144
philosophers 121, 175, 177, 188
Pinocchio (film) 47, 55, 60
Pinocchio (novel) 183, 195, 204, 206
Pinocchio story 172
Plato 11
Polanski, Roman 108
polls 12, 103, 110
Poltergeist 8, 23–68, 135, 156, 183, 190, 193, 209
Porky's 95
Primary Colors 39
Protestant work ethic 18

race 18
racism 98, 142
Rafelson, Bob 76
Raiders of the Lost Ark see also *Indiana Jones* series 3, 4, 8, 35, 36, 103, 109–15, 119, 121, 124, 125, 126, 127, 129–30, 141, 143, 209
Rambo (character) 116
Rambo: First Blood Part II 116
Rambo III 116
Reagan, Ronald 127–8
   foreign policy 127–8
   New Right politics 129
realism 46, 84–6
Renoir, Jean 13, 166
Republic Pictures 106
Requiem for a Dream 10
Revolutionary Road 27
Rockwell, Norman 152–8
Rome, Open City 13
Roosevelt, Franklin D. 153
Rosemary's Baby 85
Rossellini, Roberto 13
Rules of the Game, The 13

Salem's Lot 39
satire 27, 90, 132, 136
Saturday Evening Post 153, 154
Saving Private Ryan 3, 4, 8, 9, 11, 71, 75, 139, 140, 141, 143, 145, 166, 167, 209
Sayles, John 36
Schindler's List 3, 4, 8, 11, 75, 123,

139, 141, 143, 156, 166, 201, 208
scholars *see* film scholars
Schubert, Franz 59
Schwartz, Barry 28
Schwarzenegger, Arnold 115
science fiction 40, 185
scientific hubris 182–90
Scorsese, Martin 25, 26, 76
Searchers, The 13, 14, 36, 159, 168–9
Secret of the Incas 102
self-awareness, reflexive 87–9
selfishness 189–90
self-sacrifice 145
Sennett, Mack 87
sentimentality 158, 204
separation anxiety 198
sex 14
sexual desire 91–4
Shadow of a Doubt 21
Shakespeare, William 90
Shelley, Mary 185
Shining, The 59, 182
Shot in the Dark, A 89
Sica, Vittorio de 13
Sight & Sound 12, 14
single parenthood 50, 57
Sirk, Douglas 14
Sisters 26
sitcoms 41
slapstick 86, 87, 99, 119
Slaughterhouse-Five 75
slavery 11
Snow White 6
social decay 16
socio-economic status 18
Soldier Blue 75
Song of the South 11
sound effects 40, 58, 70
Sound of Music, The 5
soundtracks 83, 148
Soviet montage 15
special effects 25, 35, 40, 58, 71, 84, 141
Stafford, Nick 159
Stallone, Sylvester 115
Star Wars 15, 104, 108, 110
Stepford Wives, The 27

"Stolen Child, The" 182
subject matter 10, 11
suburbia 26–7, 29–46, 51
Sugarland Express, The 4, 7, 20, 34, 64, 69, 76, 85, 190
Sunrise 13
supernatural 25, 40, 46, 61
surrealism 12, 87

Tarkovsky, Andrei 159, 160
Taxi Driver 10, 26
Technicolor 168
terrorism 11
Texas Chain Saw Massacre, The 10, 37
Thin Red Line, The 160
Third World 103, 107, 127, 128, 129, 130, 136
Time 28, 51
Time Out 30–1
To Kill a Mockingbird 103
Tokyo Story 13
Tracy, Spencer 62
trauma 65, 144, 191, 193
Treasure of the Sierra Madre, The 102
Truffaut, François 18, 56
20,000 Leagues Under the Sea 119–20
Twilight Zone: The Movie 33, 192
2001: A Space Odyssey 13, 172, 177, 204, 205

UFOs 34, 52
unconscious 78
Universal Pictures 36, 70, 73, 105, 114
Untouchables, The 95
Uses of Enchantment, The 198

Van Damme, Jean-Claude 115
Vertigo 13
Vertov, Dziga 12
victimhood 15
victimization, childhood 64
Victor, Mark 37
Village Voice, The 5
violence 6, 8, 14, 16, 47, 98, 111, 114, 115, 117, 118, 142, 145, 147, 148, 149, 152, 160, 165–6, 167, 178, 182, 190, 194, 201, 203

aesthetic 10
  gendered 11
violent crime 51
visual effects *see* special effects
Volsung Saga 114

Walking Tall 119
war 11, 165–6
war films 141
War Horse 11, 75, 139–42, 159–69, 209
  ending 163
  narrative structure 163–4
war machines 165
War of the Worlds 25, 52, 141, 156, 193, 203, 204
Warner Brothers 14
Wayne, John 14, 72, 88
"weekend America" 25–33, 46
Weissmuller, Johnny 102
Welles, Orson 6, 13, 135
Wells, H. G. 52, 204
westerns 20
What Did You Do in the War, Daddy? 89–90
Who's Having More Fun? 154

Who's That Knocking at My Door 26
Whyte, William H. 27
Wild Bunch, The 108
Wilder, Billy 108
Williams, John 83, 88, 108, 110, 119, 120, 135
Wilson, Sloan 27
Wise, Robert 52
wish fulfillment 25, 51, 66, 176, 209
Wizard of Oz, The 84
women's rights 128
work ethic, Protestant 18
Working-Class Suburbs 28
World War I 159
World War II 139–40
  cultural memory 139
Written on the Wind 14

Yates, Richard 27
Yeats, William Butler 182
You're a Big Boy Now 26
Young Indiana Jones Chronicles, The 102

Zemeckis, Robert 73

www.ingramcontent.com/pod-product-compliance
Lightning Source LLC
Chambersburg PA
CBHW062141300426
44115CB00012BA/2003